McFarland
Classics

Russ Meyer — The Life and Films

Russ Meyer—
The Life and Films

*A Biography and a Comprehensive,
Illustrated and Annotated
Filmography and Bibliography*

by

David K. Frasier

McFarland & Company, Inc., Publishers
Jefferson, North Carolina, and London

Front cover: Russ Meyer behind the camera
Back cover: A publicity still for *Common-Law Cabin*
(Eve Productions, 1967)
Frontispiece: Russ Meyer, circa 1988 (photographed by Paul Huf)

The present work is a reprint of the library bound edition of Russ Meyer—The Life and Films, *first published in 1990.* **McFarland Classics** *is an imprint of McFarland & Company, Inc., Publishers, Jefferson, North Carolina, who also published the original edition.*

British Library Cataloguing-in-Publication data are available

Library of Congress Cataloguing-in-Publication Data

Frasier, David K., 1951–
   Russ Meyer—the life and films : a biography and a
comprehensive, illustrated, and annotated filmography and
bibliography / by David K. Frasier.

     p.   cm.
    [Includes index.]
    Includes bibliographical references.
    ISBN 0-7864-0472-8 (paperback : 50# alkaline paper) ∞
    1. Meyer, Russ, 1922–   .   2. Erotic films—United States—
History and criticism.   3. Sex in motion pictures.   I. Title.
PN1998.3.M49F7   1997
791.43'023'092—dc20   89-43688
                                            CIP

Manufactured in the United States of America

McFarland & Company, Inc., Publishers
  Box 611, Jefferson, North Carolina 28640

To my dear wife
Mary
for all the reasons

ACKNOWLEDGMENTS

I wish to acknowledge and thank the following individuals and institutions for their kind and generous support:

Douglas K. Freeman (Associate Librarian, Indiana University) for his unfailing support of and belief in the validity of this project; Natalie Alfonso Hubers (I.U.) for tireless clerical support; Michael Cavanagh (Photographer, I.U. Art Museum) for his photographic assistance and friendship; Dr. Sam Stetson for his subject expertise, wisdom, and friendship; Kenneth Anger for his life in films, friendship, and kindness; Jeff Graf (Senior Reference Assistant, I.U.) and Dr. C. Patricia Riesenman (Associate Librarian, I.U.) for their fine translations of French and German materials; Rhonda Stone and Ron Luedemann (Interlibrary Loan Dept., I.U.) without whose dedication and professionalism this work could never have been compiled; Frederick Musto (Associate Librarian, I.U.) for his comments, friendship, and suggestions; Thomas Glastras (Associate Librarian Emeritus–retired) for bibliographic verification; Betty M. Jarboe (Librarian, I.U.) for her kindness and understanding; Diana Hanson and Marty Sorury (Microforms, I.U.) for their great help; Dr. Harry M. Geduld (Dept. of Comparative Literature and Film) for his scholarship and suggestions; William Cagle (Lilly Library, I.U.) for his honesty and support; Robert U. Goehlert (Associate Librarian–Subject Specialist, I.U.) for his professionalism and indexing tips; Murlin Croucher (Associate Librarian–Subject Specialist) for computer support; Tom Chase for his exhaustive research assistance; Andy Balterman (Reference Librarian, Cincinnati Public Library) for his interest and research help; Jack Widner for his research assistance in Great Britain; Jim Meier for his assistance; and Ray Soto and Sharon Fard (Reference Librarians, UCLA Theatre Arts Dept.) for their invaluable help, interest, and professionalism.

I would also like to acknowledge grants from both the Indiana University Librarians Association and the Office of Research and Graduate Development of Indiana University which helped defray the costs of on-site research in California. Also, a very special appreciation to Dr. Paul H. Gebhard (Professor Emeritus of Anthropology, I.U.) whose integrity and scholarship continue to serve as an inspiration to some and an indictment of others.

Lastly, I would like to thank the subject of this work, Russ Meyer, for his complete cooperation in and support of this project. Despite working on both film and print autobiographies, Mr. Meyer was never too busy to answer questions, provide materials, entertain, or to just listen. It is most gratifying for a researcher to have one's subject turn from an interest into a friend.

David K. Frasier
January 1990

TABLE OF CONTENTS

LIST OF ILLUSTRATIONS

xiii

A NOTE ON THE TEXT

This bibliography is a selected list of materials which have been published in various print sources on independent filmmaker Russ Meyer through May 1989. In his own 100 volume–plus archive, Meyer has collected considerably more information on his career than has been included in this present work. Every attempt has been made to verify all the various bibliographic elements in these items, but in many cases the nature of Meyer's career and the publications covering it have made it virtually impossible to do so. Unverified items have been omitted in order to provide the most accurate bibliographic access possible to the diverse range of material on this remarkable filmmaker. Even so, some citations contained in this volume lack complete bibliographic information, but have nevertheless been included because the date of the item has been verified. In many instances, some universities holding material (industry trade papers, newspapers, etc.) were unwilling to lend it or else when they did, failed to supply needed bibliographic data. Far too often, material on Meyer in various sources which happen to contain illustrative photographs has been simply torn out by persons who share the filmmaker's notions of feminine beauty. In any event, these incomplete citations have been included to apprise the serious researcher of their existence.

Please note that the numbered information following the source in journal/ magazine entries is the volume number, issue number, and page number(s). For example: Irving, Lee. "Interview: Kitten Natividad." *Adult Video News,* 1(35):36, 38, Feb. 1986. The "1(35):36, 38" refers to volume 1, number 35, pages 36 and 38. For the sake of brevity, certain recurring film titles like *Beyond the Valley of the Dolls* and *Beneath the Valley of the Ultravixens* have been abbreviated as *BVD* and *Beneath,* respectively. Other abbreviations and truncations are self-evident by their context.

An asterisk (*) has been placed next to the numbers of citations to denote works of particular merit or interest. Altogether, the materials so denoted constitute an indispensable core collection for the study and appreciation of Russ Meyer.

I. RUSS MEYER, AMERICAN *AUTEUR*

Russ Meyer ... *auteur?* When film scholars discuss American directors like Alfred Hitchcock, John Ford, Vincente Minelli and others elevated to the rank of *auteur,* the name of Russ Meyer is seldom mentioned. After all, what claim can a director alternately praised and damned as "King Leer," "the Walt Disney of Porn," "the Nudie King," and "the Chaucer of Sex" possibly make to that august title? Whatever directorial merits Meyer may possess, critical ambivalence has placed an asterisk beside his controversial name, for Meyer, whose career has spanned over thirty years and includes more than 23 films, has spent most of his creative life independently producing and directing in the critically "disreputable" genre of softcore sexploitation. To his diverse legion of fans, who run a cultural and intellectual gamut from the "Raincoat Brigade," that "one-armed" audience viewing solely with prurient interest, to cinéastes entranced by "Eisensteinian montage," Meyer has been apotheosized as an "American institution" (see entry **257**). And indeed, Meyer cult classics like *The Immoral Mr. Teas* (1959), *Lorna* (1964), *Faster, Pussycat! Kill! Kill!* (1966), *Vixen* (1968), *Beyond the Valley of the Dolls* (1970) and *Supervixens* (1975) are a virtual history of the development and maturation of the sexploitation film.

Equally vocal in their condemnation of Meyer are those critics who view his talent as lying primarily in "convincing large-breasted women to take their shirts off and jump around for his camera" so that "he can subsequently keep them in focus long enough to get enough film together to stitch into a movie" (see entry **992**). For them he is far from the icon of popular culture that many of his fans consider him, and they contend that his supercharged film fantasies featuring top-heavy women and the moronic men who pursue them more properly qualify Meyer to be *in* an American institution than to be one. The dubious genre in which Meyer works and the critical passions his films excite do not create a calm atmosphere for impartial assessment of his worth as a filmmaker, let alone consideration of *auteur* status.

To escape the perpetual and insolvable rounds of emotional debate over the merits of Russ Meyer's work, we need a working definition of the *auteur* concept. The British critic Alan Lovell provided it in a 1969 *Screen* article, where he writes, "By the 'auteur' principle I understand a descriptive method which seeks to establish, not whether a director is a great director, but what the basic structure of a director's work is. The assumption behind the principle is that any director creates his films on the basis of a central structure and that all his films can be seen as variations or developments of it." While the softcore sexploitation genre has by definition a certain internal structure (nudity and sex, most notably) which on the surface accounts for a good deal of the consistency in Meyer's cinema, Meyer expanded beyond the conventions of the genre to make a unique cinematic statement which satisfies Lovell's definition.

The internal consistency of Meyer's work is the result of the unusual and frank assimilation of his rich and varied experiences into the filmmaking process. His biography, a paean to the American Dream, echoes Horatio Alger's "sink or swim" philosophy of success in which the filmmaker has always believed. Born in Oakland, California, on March 21, 1922, to a registered nurse and an Oakland policeman, Meyer was raised almost solely by his devoted mother, Lydia, who began his career when she pawned an engagement ring to buy the 14-year-old youngster a $9.95 8mm Univex camera. At the outbreak of World War II Meyer joined the army. He was assigned to the 166th Signal Photographic Corps and spent most of the war filming the advances of General Omar Bradley's First Army and General George S. Patton's Third Army through France to Germany. It was during the war, which he called the "greatest experience" of his life, that the young soldier gloriously lost his virginity in a French brothel courtesy of Ernest Hemingway.

Discharged on December 13, 1945, the would-be cinematographer found the doors of Hollywood closed. The local chapter of the International Alliance of Theatrical Stage Employees refused to let him join the union, because all their jobs were being held for the returning prewar membership. In 1946, however, Meyer landed a job in San Francisco with Gene K. Walker Productions as an industrial filmmaker. Always eager to supplement his income, Meyer was approached in the early fifties by army buddy Don Ornitz, who suggested shooting cheesecake for pinups and the burgeoning men's magazine industry inspired by the success of *Playboy*. Prophetically, Ornitz convinced an initially reluctant, doubtful Meyer that "what you lack in experience, you'll make up for in enthusiasm."

An enthusiastic Meyer soon married the glamorous Eve Turner, his principal photographic subject and later his business partner in Eve Productions, and in the space of a few short years had photographed her and other beauties as *Playboy* centerfolds. Following their divorce in 1968 after 12 years of marriage, Meyer again demonstrated his penchant for beautiful women by wedding the "last starlet," Edy Williams, on June 27, 1970.

From the first, Meyer approached filmmaking as an intense, personal experience to which he applied the practical lessons of life he learned at home, in the military, and on the job as an industrial filmmaker and cheesecake photographer. The optimistic lessons of Horatio Alger, whom he avidly read as a youth, he believed. Success was possible if one applied the virtues of self-reliance, hard work, and perseverance. If you work you win. If you have pluck, you will have luck.

As a frontline combat photographer, Meyer trudged over Europe risking his life to capture the most eye-catching newsreel footage possible (some of which can be seen in the 1970 movie *Patton*). Trained to rely on himself and a few trusted friends for survival, Meyer brought this "bunker mentality" to his filmmaking. Fiercely independent, Meyer does it himself or allows a small cadre of talented friends to help with the production and editing. Trust, for Meyer, is gained or given only after he has been through a "war" with someone. His best friends continue to be army buddies or a few "industry" friends among whom he numbers first *Chicago Sun-Times* film critic Roger Ebert, with whom he cowrote the 1970 20th Century–Fox release, *Beyond the Valley of the Dolls*. Significantly, Meyer refers to the film as "Ebert's and my war."

Other parallels exist between Meyer's military and film career. Traditionally shot in deserts or forests to keep production costs down, the making of a Meyer film is remarkably like basic training. Meyer bivouacs his crew, often for six weeks or more. In remote settings the top kick sergeant maintains the discipline necessary to keep his film on budget. He expects each member of the small cast and crew to pitch in and perform jobs other than those for which he specifically hired them. The voluptuous actress called upon to look provocative for a 6 A.M. shoot can be found later in the day operating a sound boom and preparing dinner for her colleagues. Fifteen to twenty hour days are the rule rather than the exception. Meyer's love of the arduous and his drive to surmount obstacles through single-minded, hard work even extend to the simulated sex in his films. It strikes Meyer as somehow heroic and funny to have couples making love in uncomfortably incongruous settings like trees, swamps, and deserts, as if their passion were so great that they would suffer any pain or indignity to consummate it. Many of Meyer's most notable heroes like Clint Ramsey in *Supervixens* or Burt Boland in *Good Morning and Goodbye!* overcome tremendous obstacles ultimately to taste the carnal fruit won by their herculean efforts. Leave it to Meyer to add this new dimension to Alger's "pluck and luck" formula for personal success.

At the heart of any Meyer film are the outrageously bosomy women whose description demands broad superlatives. Meyer is quick to point out that his movies represent his "filmed fantasies" and that he makes them for "lust and profit." He is unabashedly candid in sharing his sexual interests and his preference for a particular type of female body with his audience. They have responded by making him a very rich man. While Meyer's "filmed fantasies" have shifted with the prevailing commercial winds, the relationship between the man, his women and his films has remained close.

Art and life have always imitated one another in Meyer's career. After marrying Eve Turner, a legal secretary when they met, he transformed her into one of the top pinup models of the fifties, Eve Meyer. In 1970 Meyer married sultry 20th Century–Fox contract player Edy Williams, whom he had directed in *Beyond the Valley of the Dolls*. Both wives were physically well-endowed, and Meyer molded each into a preeminent object of male sexual fantasy. If one accepts Meyer at face value when he states that he merely films his own fantasies, his marriages attempt to sustain the fantasy even after the cameras have stopped rolling.

The two marriages ended in divorce, and Meyer blames the nature of his work as the major factor. According to Meyer, his total involvement in his films does not permit him to turn off the fantasy. Most people divide their time neatly between their personal and work lives, but Meyer strives to be only what he does. This refusal to compromise between the two fuses the sexual and creative impulses that inform his life and animate his work. The evolution of Meyer's cinema illustrates how he was also able to integrate into his films the psychology of cheesecake photography and the techniques of wartime and industrial filmmaking.

Meyer's work, as Roger Ebert points out in his excellent article in *Film Comment*, "Russ Meyer: King of the Nudies" (see entry 47), can be divided into three periods, which illustrate his development as a filmmaker and shrewd reading of the commercial marketplace. A fourth period brings the critic's 1973 list up to date.

1. The "nudie-cuties" comedies—*The Immoral Mr. Teas* (1959) through *Heavenly Bodies!* (1963)
2. The "Drive-in Steinbeck" period of black-and-white, synch-sound Gothic-sadomasochistic melodramas—*Lorna* (1964) through *Faster, Pussycat! Kill! Kill!* (1966)
3. The color, synch-sound sexual dramas—*Common-Law Cabin* (1967) through *Cherry, Harry & Raquel* (1969)
4. The parody-satires—*Beyond the Valley of the Dolls* (1970) through *Beneath the Valley of the Ultravixens* (1979)

Five of Meyer's films fall outside these categories and are not truly representative of his work. *Europe in the Raw* (1963), although considered by Meyer a "nudie-cutie," is a 16mm color travelogue of the vice dens of Europe "secretly" filmed using a camera hidden in a briefcase. *Fanny Hill* (1964), a U.S./German coproduction, found an unhappy Meyer directing, or more accurately "refereeing," for producers Albert Zugsmith and Artur Brauner. In *Mondo Topless* (1966), Meyer produced a curious "documentary" on the swinging topless scene featuring a bevy of buxom beauties dancing to fast music and commenting on their bodies. With *The Seven Minutes* in 1971, Meyer attempted to adapt Irving Wallace's elephantine novel on censorship into a two hour movie that would serve as a platform from which to air his own views on the subject. The film failed, as did his next effort, *Blacksnake!* (1973), an R-rated historical drama filmed on location in Barbados.

To understand Meyer's evolution as the filmmaker who expanded the narrow genre of sexploitation until he transcended it to become "a genre unto himself," one ought to examine representative films from each period. The development of the major themes in his work charts the evolution of his signature cinematic style and clearly shows how successful Meyer was in integrating his personal experiences into his films.

With the release of *The Immoral Mr. Teas* in 1959 Meyer saw the first of his three critically acknowledged breakthrough films significantly change the look and content of the sexploitation genre. To the recognized roll of *Teas*, *Lorna*, and *Vixen*, Meyer adds *Beyond the Valley of the Dolls*, *Supervixens*, and *Beneath the Valley of the Ultravixens*. The three universally recognized breakthrough films transcended the genre itself and directly influenced mainstream cinema in the United States.

In the late fifties, the narrow subgenre of sexploitation had degenerated from films exploiting social ills like teen pregnancy, prostitution, and incest to badly made nudist-colony sagas shot in a pseudoscientific, pseudodocumentary style which extolled the healthy virtues of the open-air lifestyle. While such films featured nudity, they did so within the nonerotic context of saggy-bottomed, frolicsome sunworshippers engaged in perpetual games of volleyball, ping-pong, and croquet. When first approached in 1958 by Pete DeCenzie, owner of the El Rey Burlesque Theatre in Oakland, California, to write, direct, and photograph a similar film which would serve as the basis of the "burly" impresario's travelling road show, Meyer refused. Although he had earlier worked with DeCenzie filming legendary burlesque queen Tempest Storm and others performing their acts at the El Rey for the lost 1950 production *The French Peep Show,* Meyer had no desire to make a film in the nudist colony vein which failed to excite or interest him. While Meyer had no idea at the time that such a genre as sexploitation existed, he did know what *he* liked. Banking on his belief that a lot of other men shared his interests, he broke with tradition, laboriously scraped together $24,000 with DeCenzie and shot *The Immoral Mr. Teas* in five days.

Teas showed how seamlessly Meyer was able to make the transition from cheesecake "tittyboom" photography to motion pictures. In content and theme *Teas* is a literal translation of what he had been doing for *Playboy,* a movie version of the girlie magazine. Replacing flabby nudists with sexually alluring female models, many of whom he had previously shot for men's magazines like *Adam, Modern Man* and *Night and Day,* Meyer transcended the confines of nudist films by adding a simple, but coherent plot to the nudity. Unknowingly, Meyer and DeCenzie had created the first American "nudie" film and assured their place in cinema history.

The film's plot centers around one Mr. Teas, played by Meyer's army buddy Bill Teas, a bicycle deliveryman of false teeth who longs to return to the bosom of nature to escape the pressures of modern urban life. Complicating the conflict between the pastoral and the urban is Teas' uncontrollable ability to see naked any woman he meets. Mr. Teas goes to the dentist where an attractive dental assistant appears naked to him as does the buxom psychiatrist he visits to discuss his problem. As the film continues Mr. Teas has a variety of opportunities to peep at attractive nudes engaged in diurnal pursuits. That no physical contact occurs between Mr. Teas and any of the nudes is due in no small part to the omnipresent threat of obscenity prosecution and the devastating financial drain litigation would have meant for a young, "independent filmmaker" already eyeball-high in debt. More importantly, physical contact would have undermined the film's theme of self-conscious voyeurism and run contrary to Meyer's design to transfer the content and psychology of the girlie magazine to film.

Combining the understanding of the male psyche he gained from his years of photographing nudes with his own rich fantasy life, Meyer was able to create in Mr. Teas a character with which the average male reader of *Playboy* and its imitators could readily identify. In the film, Mr. Teas, the perpetually put upon Everyman, acts as a stand-in for the audience. His look-but-don't-touch voyeurism parallels the experience of his audience which can also never hope to meet, let alone attain, the fantasy women who excite their senses. The women in the film are all pinups come to life. They lack the emotional substance to make them real and are thereby immune to any form of relationship other than visual.

Technically, *Teas* is a 63-minute silent film with voice-over narration, a form Meyer continued to use throughout the first period of his career. Despite being shot in five days, mostly weekends, on a minuscule budget of $24,000, the film's superior production values presage the sense of technical perfectionism so often noted in Meyer's later work. The film's Eastmancolor is crisp and clear, with Meyer's workmanlike editing and his use of a narrator directly attributable to his postwar employment as a maker of industrial films. In 1979 with the release of *Beneath the Valley of the Ultravixens,* Meyer would pay generous homage to this formative period in his filmmaking career.

In this his first "true" effort (Meyer does not consider *The French Peep Show* to be "his"), Meyer, in addition to tapping into the common fantasy life of his audience, also brought humor into the genre. Both elements would continue to distinguish his work throughout his career. Unlike the nudist-colony or burlesque films of the day, *Teas* contains a measure of amusement absent in the traditionally dreary genre, although present in the humor of live burlesque. The character of Mr. Teas sporting a straw hat and riding a rickety bicycle is reminiscent of the baggy-pants burlesque house comic who introduces the strippers and performs skits with them. Humor also characterizes the film's narration. Filled with double-entendre and grandiloquent paeans to the joys of unspoiled nature, it reinforces the film's sense of the absurd.

Meyer, consciously or unconsciously, was able to allay the guilt feelings his audience may have been suffering at attending a skin film by simultaneously provoking laughter *and* lust. As Roger Ebert, Meyer's most perceptive chronicler, has written and repeated in his lectures, it was Meyer who first brought laughter into the usually solemn environs of the "skin" theatre.

Commercially, *Teas* was an unprecedented box office smash which ultimately grossed over $1.5 million on its $24,000 investment, a staggering profit ratio. Besides proving the commercial viability of such films and inspiring a "nudie-cuties" craze that resulted in over 150 inferior productions in three years (including, Meyer admits, five of his own), it also forced the Hollywood Establishment to recognize the phenomenon. Exhibiting an "integrity" which has become synonymous with its name, Hollywood publicly condemned the films and called for the prosecution of their makers, while waiting to see what leeway the courts would leave them to incorporate into their product many of the sexual and flesh displays featured in the sexploitation genre. David F. Friedman, pioneer sexploitation producer, accurately observes that the obscenity and censorship prosecutions involving sexploitation films have been almost solely responsible for expanding the boundaries of the sexual content that can be depicted in mainstream films.

Teas was busted in San Diego, California, and since that time Meyer has spent hundreds of thousands of dollars defending his work against obscenity prosecutions in states like Ohio, Florida, and Wisconsin. Often praised or damned, depending on one's perspective, for opening the floodgates of sexual permissiveness in American cinema, Meyer, by successfully integrating nudity into a structured plot in *The Immoral Mr. Teas,* marked a major advance in screen freedom and laid the foundation for increasingly bolder sexual statements in all genres of film.

By 1964, Meyer was in danger of becoming a casualty of the epidemic of epidermis he had unleashed with the commercial success of *The Immoral Mr. Teas.* He had already made five "nudie-cuties" *(Eve and the Handyman, Erotica, Wild Gals of the Naked West!, Europe in the Raw,* and *Heavenly Bodies!)* which helped sharpen his technical skills but did not stretch him creatively. The limited plot options offered by the genre also did little to sustain audience interest, so by 1964 the "nudie-cuties" cycle was dying, a result of the torrent of cheaply produced U.S. schlock and the stream of bolder, earthier Italian and French films like *And God Created Woman*, starring the French sensation Brigitte Bardot.

The foreign imports were targeted to play the "art houses" which had sprung up to cater to adult tastes. Meyer, long a fan of the sexual frankness of these films and ever attuned to the commercial prospects of a well-produced, homegrown entry into the prevailing market, released in 1964 *Lorna*, his second breakthrough film. From the first, Meyer saw *Lorna* as a violent action melodrama that realistically portrayed lovemaking as an integral part of the plot. Identified by many cinema historians as the first "roughie" because of its linkage of sex with violence, *Lorna* marked Meyer's first attempt at producing a film with serious subject matter — a young woman's unhappiness and frustration with her sexually inept husband.

Starring the voluptuous Lorna Maitland, who was touted at the time as "America's answer to foreign sexpots," *Lorna* successfully transplanted the turgid melodrama and sexually supercharged atmosphere of the European art film to the backwoods redneck river country of the American South. According to Meyer, whose one unfailing precept as a self-described "class pornographer" has been his belief that a scene must arouse him sexually before he knows it works, the first time Maitland stood naked in the film and "nothing went south," he heard a small voice in his head say, "BOX OFFICE!"

Lorna did more for Meyer than make him money. It introduced the cinematic themes he would expand, redefine, and ultimately parody in his more mature work. It is in *Lorna* that Meyer presents the central icons in his films — the unusually voluptuous, sexually insatiable woman who is desired by a square-jawed he-man of low intelligence who will go to the most absurd extremes to possess her. The action in the film is entirely motivated by lust, and Lorna's drive for the sexual fulfillment she cannot experience at home is ultimately realized in the arms of a fugitive from justice who rapes her.

Billed in the ads as "a woman . . . too much for one man," Lorna is the prototype for Meyer's cinematic view of women — large breasted, wasp-waisted, sexually aggressive — and, in a case of art imitating life, embodies Meyer's own physical and sexual preferences. Lorna's exaggerated physique serves as a metaphor for her unfulfilled sexual appetite, which is also "too much." Her physical overabundance simultaneously separates her from the "average" woman of "normal" sexual needs and declares her awesome carnal appetite. The attempt to sate this appetite, to fulfill this all-consuming need motivates the film's action.

The isolated, natural setting of *Lorna* in bayou-like river country is also a Meyer trademark, one which appears in most of his later films. The need to reduce production costs dictated shooting in remote areas, where preexisting structures could be used as sets. Remoteness also minimized the risk of prosecution for photographing nudity, but beyond economic or legal considerations, the isolated setting created a distinct element of fantasy, traceable to the influence on Meyer's creative life of cartoonist Al Capp's *L'il Abner*. In *Lorna* (and more dramatically in *Mudhoney*), as in *L'il Abner*, one is immediately struck by the incongruity of a stunningly sexual and physically awesome woman living in primitive, squalid conditions and relentlessly pursued by men neither her physical nor intellectual equal. Acknowledging his creative debt to Capp, Meyer admits to studying closely *L'il Abner* and later when writing or filming, simply enlarging the actresses' breasts.

The result of an isolated area populated by overblown characters is the creation of a distinct "fantasy microcosm" that mundane reality never seems to violate despite its overwhelming grittiness. In viewing Meyer's best work of this period, *Lorna, Mudhoney,* and *Faster, Pussycat! Kill! Kill!,* one never gets the impression that a larger world exists beyond this emotionally supercharged microcosm. The operatic, primal passions of Meyer's characters, like the physical endowments of the women, are *too* big, so big they overshadow the lesser emotions of reality.

Like reality, though, Meyer's supercharged fantasy microcosm is subject to a moral law of cause and effect. That law is as fully ritualized as his characters are recognizably stereotypical, and like the characters, so obviously overstated it offers fertile ground for parody. In 1964, however, films with sexual content had to prove to local authorities that they contained enough "socially redeeming" significance to exempt them from prosecution. To meet the requirements, but also to satisfy his inherent sense of personal morality, Meyer loaded *Lorna* with an overtly top-heavy theme of moral retribution and punishment. Biblical symbolism abounds. In its opening sequence a fire-and-brimstone prophet warns the audience to proceed at its own risk and pronounces impending doom upon the town's sinners. The young, sexually inept husband works at a salt mine with two scrofulous coworkers, the serpents in his redneck garden of Eden, who cast doubt on the faithfulness of his wife, Lorna. When Lorna is killed attempting to atone for the sin of adultery, the camera focuses upon a salt statue in female form.

The film's central theme is Lorna's need for atonement after her adulterous relationship with the fugitive who first rapes her, but is then invited back to the shack to pleasure her in consensual sex. To satisfy the omnipresent prosecutors as well as to maintain the structural integrity of his own cinematic microcosm, Meyer harshly punishes the sinners. By doing so, he fulfills the law of cause and effect that functions with such inevitability in his films. However, in true sexploitation fashion, Meyer first allows the sinners heartily to enjoy themselves for nine-tenths of the movie. Only then does he dispatch them with ice tongs and a switch-blade knife in the film's closing moments. In keeping with the biblical motif, their deaths are an Old Testament punishment for their sexual trespass against Lorna's innocent, but clumsy, husband—and Good triumphs over Evil.

The addition of a strong plot to a film realistically presenting exploitable sexual elements permitted *Lorna* to play more venues than *The Immoral Mr. Teas* and the other "nudie-cuties." Meyer had created a box office success that again spawned hundreds of inferior imitators. Unlike *Teas,* however, man and woman had touched in *Lorna.* Time and a relaxation of legal restrictions would further open the door for hardcore filmmakers willing to risk prosecution. With *Lorna,* his second breakthrough film, Meyer again demonstrated his uncanny ability to share his rich fantasy life with an audience while anticipating a new commercial direction for sexploitation films.

Two more films of this period, *Mudhoney* (1965) and *Faster, Pussycat! Kill!*

Kill! (1966), deserve special consideration. Both show the increasing sophistication of Meyer's themes and a continuing refinement of his creative and technical abilities. *Mudhoney,* considered by many to be Meyer's best film, is so strongly reminiscent of *Lorna* that it seems almost its "spiritual sequel." As in *Lorna, Mudhoney* unfolds in an isolated setting, this time in the Erskine Caldwell, tobacco-road country of Depression-era Missouri where "poor white trash" again are living and loving in squalor. It too features excellent black-and-white photography (Meyer could not afford 35mm color film) and solid editing. What distinguishes the film from *Lorna* is its depth of characterization.

In one of the rare such instances in Meyer's cinema, a male character, the alcoholic sadist "Sidney Brenshaw," is more memorable in *Mudhoney* than the anatomy of the actresses. Brenshaw's painful descent into the hell of alcoholic dementia, brilliantly realized by Hal Hopper, and its devasting effects on the lives of others is portrayed with careful attention to psychological detail that far surpassed anything attempted in the genre before or since. Its lukewarm box office reception Meyer attributes to an unsophisticated sexploitation audience more interested in flesh than Freud.

Mudhoney did feature two actresses configured in the Meyer mold. Lorna Maitland, the sexually unfulfilled wife in *Lorna,* plays Clara Belle, an open wanton. And in a remarkable bit of casting, German newcomer Rena Horten, who had previously appeared briefly in *Fanny Hill* (1964), appears in the difficult role of Eula, an innocent unknowingly corrupted by her unsavory environment. Choosing the buxom Horten for a role which required that in addition to being decorative she also act, underscored a Meyer commandment that strictly forbade the casting of a good actress over a great body. Meyer later violated this principle in *Blacksnake!* (1973), when a sudden illness struck the overendowed actress set for the lead and forced him hurriedly to recast talented, but frail, Anouska Hempel in the role. The film failed, and Meyer never again strayed from his own party line.

Instead of demanding acting ability, Meyer relies on his skill as an editor to create through quick cuts the impression of creditable performances from female casts recruited for their anatomy. In the case of Horten, her thick Teutonic accent would have been jarringly out of place in a tale set in the Midwestern sticks. Overdubbing was an option for Meyer, but it would prove prohibitively expensive for an independent production budgeted at around $60,000. Ever creative when a body like Horten's was at stake, Meyer neatly solved the problem by making her character a deaf-mute!

Faster, Pussycat! Kill! Kill! (1966), Meyer's eleventh effort and the end of his "film noir" period of black-and-white sadomasochistic sex-and-violence melodramas, is thematically one of his most important films. Today it ranks as a bona fide cult classic that is among Meyer's top video sellers. In the film before *Faster!*, the 1965 *Motorpsycho!*, Meyer had anticipated the wave of outlaw motorcycle gang pictures usually attributed to the American International Pictures release *The Wild Angels* (1966), by constructing a violent melodrama centered around the exploits of a rampaging trio of nomadic cycle riding misfits. In *Faster!*, Meyer reversed the gender of the gang from male to female and replaced their motorcycles with souped up sports cars in which they thundered across vast expanses of the desert Southwest looking for kicks. As in *Mudhoney,* the characterizations are particularly strong and Varla, played with bravado by the part–Cherokee, part–Japanese actress Tura Satana, is perhaps the strongest female role in the sexploitation genre, un-challenged until Erica Gavin's electrifying performance in *Vixen* (1968).

Varla is Meyer's boldest cinematic statement yet that women are sexually and intellectually superior to men. Their dominance is immediately established in the film's opening sequence where the go-go dancers, Varla and her two cohorts, hold a lustful male audience enthralled with their frenetic gyrations. Varla, though, quickly emerges as *the* "woman among women" who rules her gang with an iron fist encased in a jet black glove. One of them, Rosie, played by Meyer favorite Haji, is Varla's lover who plays slave to her demanding mistress. The other, Billie (Lori Williams), is a thrill seeker who repeatedly bows to Varla's will. The two follow Varla's lead as if she were a female Charles Manson and they her family.

Varla's dominance is further augmented by her lush physique and deadly skill as a karate master. She breaks the back of a man whom she had earlier cheated out of a victory in a challenge car race, and having murdered him, kidnaps his hysterical girlfriend for ransom. The essence of Varla is pure evil rather obviously emphasized by costuming her in the cinematic clichés of a low-cut, skintight black outfit, black gloves, and a small black cigar. Unlike the female leads in earlier Meyer films, who partake of physical pleasure out of unquenchable sexual need *(Lorna),* or childlike wonder *(Mudhoney),* Varla's interest in sex is purely prag-matic. Homosexually, she uses it to secure the compliant services of her loveslave Rosie; heterosexually it comes in handy to seduce Kirk (Paul Trinka) in order to gain information on a hidden family fortune.

Cinematically, the film is a Meyer tour-de-force. He again uses an off-camera narrator (John Furlong), this time to warn the viewer about a threatening new breed of woman who poses a physical threat to man. As the narrator speaks, a ver-tical, white, voice-synchronized optical sound track pulsates on the black screen. More tracks appear as the peroration nears an end. At its climax, Meyer quick cuts to fantastically angled closeups of the wildly shaking trio of go-go dancers, alter-nately intercutting the shots with tight closeups of the profusely sweating faces of the lust-crazed, bug-eyed men who shout them on. Meyer completes the scene by quick cutting to a laughing Varla behind the wheel of her Porsche, racing across the barren desert landscape with her gang struggling to keep up with her in their cars. Another much-discussed scene is the car murder of the Vegetable (Dennis Busch). Tight editing effectively generates and maintains a crisp tension as it alter-nates between three principal shots: the Vegetable's courageous, but doomed, at-tempt to prevent Varla's car from crushing him, the car's spinning back wheels and Varla's hate-distorted face.

Critical opinion of *Faster, Pussycat! Kill! Kill!*, as of most of his films, was sharply divided both upon its release and in reviews of later years. Baltimore-based filmmaker John Waters of *Pink Flamingos* and *Polyester* fame has unhesitatingly called it not only "the best movie ever made," but "possibly better than any film that will be made in the future" (see entry **28**). Negative reaction focused on the film's sadistic violence. Such criticism has plagued Meyer throughout his career, although he would learn to exploit it in advertising his films. In *Faster!*, Meyer cunningly exaggerates violence and sexual innuendo because it replaces and com-pensates for the nudity he chose not to include in the film.

Made for an estimated $45,000, *Faster!* was specifically targeted for the highly popular "passion pit" drive-in circuit of the day. Meyer took no chance on screen nudity that might bar the film from this lucrative market. However, even without nudity *Faster!* remains a classic sexploitation epic in the grand style with the sinister Varla triumphant for 82 of the film's 83 minutes. Only in the final seconds does she die, fit punishment for the evil she has done. Though Waters deliberately overstated the case, his assessment of *Faster, Pussycat! Kill! Kill!* might have been correct had he limited his claim to the sexploitation genre.

Meyer's work turned from black-and-white to color drama with the release of *Common-Law Cabin* in 1967. His cinematic vision crystallized. His creative output soared. Between 1967 and 1969 he produced five films: *Common-Law Cabin* (1967), *Good Morning and Goodbye!* (1967), *Finders Keepers, Lovers Weepers!* (1968), *Vixen* (1968), and *Cherry, Harry & Raquel* (1969). Each of these films from Meyer's third period are worthy of discussion, with his 1968 sexploitation masterpiece *Vixen* especially noteworthy as his third breakthrough film.

Common-Law Cabin and *Good Morning and Goodbye!*, both scripted by Meyer buddy John E. Moran, share the common theme of sexual tension between an older man and a sexually voracious younger woman. Both films contain snappy dialogue and barbed repartée, with the exchanges between Burt Boland and his errant wife Angel in *Good Morning and Goodbye!* often rising to the level of inspired bitching. To cut costs, Meyer sets the two films in isolated country which figures prominently in their respective plots. Most of the action in *Common-Law Cabin*, also known as *How Much Loving Does a Normal Couple Need?*, takes place in a remote resort on the banks of the Colorado River. Accessible only by boat, its isolation makes it attractive to the thief Barney Rickert who lays low there with his hostages to evade a police dragnet.

Always eager to expand the scope of his films and to "pad his hand" against possible ennui in his steadily growing regular audience, Meyer executed a casting ploy which he would later use to great effect in 1975 in his "comeback" film *Supervixens*. In a classic example of sexploitation overkill, Meyer cast in *Common-Law Cabin* three women with supposedly identical measurements of 44-24-34 (brunette Alaina Capri, blonde Babette Bardot, and Adele Rein), and then heavily advertised them as the "Big 6." While there is little nudity in the film, it is relentless in its visual and verbal titillation, with Alaina Capri attempting to seduce almost every male in sight and Ken Swofford, the dastardly Barney Rickert, alternately making the rounds of the "Big 6."

To this film, Meyer added a new element that he would use again in later films to solve plot or production problems. *Common-Law Cabin* ends with the classical convention of *deus ex machina* which Meyer gives a mystical twist that preserves the structural integrity of his wacky world of softcore morality. In the climactic scene in which the criminal Barney Rickert is knocked overboard during a desperate struggle with Coral (Adele Rein) and Laurence Talbot, III (Andrew Hagara), the unseen "spirit" of the drunken Cracker (Franklin Bolger) whom Rickert had earlier murdered steers the speeding boat in a wide arc, strikes the floating villain and kills him as a reward for his treachery.

In his next film, *Good Morning and Goodbye!*, which often played in tandem with *Common-Law Cabin* on the drive-in circuit, mysticism becomes a vital part of the plot. Burt Boland, played by Meyer stock veteran Stuart Lancaster, is a wealthy but impotent businessman who is unable to satisfy his younger and physically demanding wife Angel (Alaina Capri). In frustration she turns to construction foreman Stone (Patrick Wright), for servicing. Burt's carnal failure sets into motion a complex series of events that disrupts his home life and interferes with his other relationships. His world is in chaos until his sexual reclamation by the Catalyst (Haji), a mystical wood nymph. She kidnaps Burt and through an elaborate ritual in the forest which climaxes in sexual intercourse, revitalizes him. Manhood restored, Burt thrashes Stone with the timely aid of another disgruntled cuckold, makes passionate love to a delighted Angel, and restores order to his personal life as well as to Meyer's randy microcosm.

In no other film is Meyer's cinematic formula for health, happiness, and cosmic order so baldly stated. Burt, though a financially successful and respected member of the community, is a vilified failure at home because of his inability to satisfy his wife. Order is restored and domestic happiness ensues only *after* Burt's mystical sexual regeneration. In Meyer's cinema, "good" healthy sex is the operative moral imperative that ensures contentment and maintains cosmic order.

Technically, these two films show Meyer's continuing growth as a filmmaker. The Eastmancolor photography is crisp and clean, the editing polished. In the action sequences of *Good Morning and Goodbye!,* which feature Capri dancing and the pastoral nude, Carol Peters, capering through the woods, Meyer cuts the shots to accent the breasts in their most gravity defying perfection. As in *The Immoral Mr. Teas,* Meyer's women here are in essence fantasy images, pinups come to life, and his understanding of lighting, photography, and editing forms them into ideals of female anatomical perfection. Firmly believing that editing is the single most important contribution a director can make to a film, Meyer evolved an editing style that animated his pinups, and masked, as much as possible, the acting deficiencies of performers usually recruited from the top ranks of striptease. He had no choice. Nature seldom combines in a single individual the outrageous anatomical dimensions demanded by Russ Meyer with the acting ability demanded by the film industry.

In *Finders Keepers, Lovers Weepers!* (1968), Meyer added an extra dimension to his editing. As in past Meyer films, a female character is driven to infidelity by the neglect and philandering of her sexually inadequate husband. The lovemaking sequence involving aquatic adultery between illicit sexual partners Kelly (Anne Chapman) and Ray (Gordon Wescourt) remains faithful to Meyer's major themes — sex, humor and morality. To this he adds something new. As the sexual action between the two lovers in the swimming pool heats up to a point where ecstatic cries punctuate their pelvic thrustings, Meyer intercuts the scene with footage and sound effects of a stock car demolition derby. This editorial twist reduces the scene's sexual intensity and diminishes the risk of possible obscenity prosecution while simultaneously reinforcing the causal connection between sexual sin and redemptive punishment which serves as the moral foundation of Meyer's cinematic microcosm. The juxtaposition of illicit sex with destructive car crashes clearly warns us that adultery is dangerous, and by the film's end both sinners get their just deserts.

In *Cherry, Harry & Raquel,* his last independent production before signing with 20th Century–Fox to produce and direct *Beyond the Valley of the Dolls,* Meyer uses a similar intercutting, complete with a sonar ping, to dilute the sexual intensity of lesbian lovemaking.

The standout film of this period is *Vixen.* It represented for Meyer's career in 1968 what *Lorna* had in 1964, when he had successfully answered the artistic and commercial challenge posed by the decline of the "nudie-cuties" cycle by adding violence and gritty sexual melodrama to the stale, bare-breasted romps of the period. By the late sixties the prevailing commercial, cultural and social winds had shifted, and Meyer was for the second time in his career at a commercial and artistic crossroads. On the one hand, hardcore loops featuring gynecologic shots of penile penetration had already begun to play peep show stalls in adult bookstores in San Francisco, a harbinger of the triple-X theatrical features to come. On the other hand, Meyer faced the emerging boldness of mainstream films depicting sexual encounters between "name" stars. Steadfastly refusing to make hardcore, but unable on an independent's budget to hire "name" talent, if any would have consented to work for him, Meyer countered with *Vixen,* which he describes as his first and only serious attempt to make an erotic film.

Vixen presented Meyer with the opportunity to confront directly on his own terms the "brave new world" of screen eroticism that he had skirted with *Finders Keepers, Lovers Weepers!* and to speak out publicly against people he cannot abide: racists, draft dodgers, and Communists. By including the sociopolitical types in the screen treatment he and Anthony James Ryan jotted down during a long evening in a Hollywood laundromat, Meyer hoped to infuse his film with "redeeming social values" that he gambled would successfully protect it from the obscenity prosecutions that had dogged him throughout his career.

The film, shot in Eastmancolor, also held the promise of playing in class, first-run venues in large cities, as *Finders Keepers, Lovers Weepers!* had done in 1968 at Philadelphia's Randolph Theatre, where it replaced MGM's box office dud *The Shoes of the Fisherman.* While the Hollywood Establishment struggled to produce a product to meet the commercial threat posed by the "class" sexuality of foreign films like the Canadian-produced *The Fox,* that is, to arouse the moviegoing public's sexual interest, but not their moral indignation, Meyer quietly shot *Vixen* in Northern California for $72,000 on a six week schedule.

The film's success owes much to the striking sexual presence of Erica Gavin in the title role. Meyer, who considers the actress to possess a sensual quality that appealed equally to both men and women, readily acknowledged her contribution. As the physical embodiment of Meyer's fully realized idea of woman as a sexual predator, Gavin, with her lush physique and openly wanton face punctuated by heavily pencilled arching eyebrows, gave real substance to the character of Vixen and to her unashamed, unabashed, and unabated search for sensual pleasure.

Vixen, as the quintessential "Meyer woman," owes much to her predecessors in the Meyer cinema that she perfects. Like Lorna, Vixen is also "too much for one man." She couples with a woman, several men and even with her husband, but unlike previous Meyer heroines, she is not unhappy in her marriage. In fact, she deeply loves her husband and willingly risks her life to protect him from a gun-wielding Commie. Being the sexual animal she is (ads asked, "Is she woman or animal?"), her desire cannot be contained within the banks of gender. It overflows into a lesbian lovemaking session with the wife of a man whom she has previously seduced. Vixen's desire is undifferentiated and indiscriminate. She is single-minded in her determination to satisfy it, a quality she shares with Varla, the lesbian gangleader in *Faster, Pussycat! Kill! Kill!*

Vixen and Varla stand out as the most vivid female characters in Meyer's films, and he points to them with their clear superiority over men to refute the oft-repeated charge that he exploits and degrades women. Varla and Vixen show how Meyer continued to explore, expand, and redefine the myth of female sexual insatiability, aggression, and dominance that comprises the central theme of his work. Their most obvious similarities are physiques that are "too big" and appetites that remove them from the realm of the ordinary female. They are the mythic "superwoman," a role which Meyer reserves for all his "heroines." It is here, at the level of myth and symbol, that each larger-than-life character can best be understood.

Both Vixen and Varla are imposing sexual presences who use their bodies to pursue and satisfy their needs, but they differ in the object and intent of their quest. Varla calculatedly uses sex not for enjoyment or fulfillment, but to hold her gang in thrall and to manipulate them in order to satisfy a lust for money. Vixen, the feral, primal sexual being, is solely motivated by animal lust. She seeks nothing from her numerous partners but the good sex which fulfills her as a woman. In Varla's lesbian relationship with Rosie, it is dominance, not passion she seeks. Her heterosexual seduction of Kirk is for gain, not pleasure. The black-clad Varla stands as an open symbol of evil in Meyer's cinema, where honest, emotionally unfettered enjoyment of licit sex is essential to the orderly functioning of his highly moral microcosm. Lust motivates Vixen, like Varla, but hers is a natural passion for sexual joy. Vixen's lesbian relationship, an act usually punished or parodied in Meyer's films, is excused as beneficial to marriage, since Vixen was only seeking to give and to receive pleasure. Like a surrogate sex partner, Vixen offers her natural passion to heal. It is benevolent. Varla's "unnatural" passion is evil. It destroys, and is in turn destroyed.

Meyer's direction of the film's numerous sex scenes marks a radical departure from his previous methods and supports his assertion that *Vixen* was designed to be erotic. In pre–*Vixen* work, most of Meyer's women retain their pinup-like unattainability despite living and loving in the backwoods squalor of swamps and deserts where they are often brutally manhandled by villains and lovers. This illusion is sustained by the choices Meyer makes while shooting sex scenes and later constructing them in the editing room.

Before *Vixen,* Meyer maintained a level of titillation more by suggestion than by actual sexual contact, a technique which led many critics to conclude that his work was not erotic. When he did show contact, the female body was seldom obscured by a caressing hand or by lips pressed on lips. What the viewer most often saw was the female's orgasmic reaction to sex, seldom the sustained, although simulated, act. Tellingly, Meyer's rapid-fire editing with its heavy use of crosscutting and intercutting took the edge off the sex scenes by refusing to let them develop erotic tension.

With *Vixen,* Meyer shoots the film's sex, especially the lesbian encounter, in a straightforward, expository style which lets the action build without any intercutting. He does not, as he did in *Finders Keepers, Lovers Weepers!*, dissipate the scene's sexual tension. And in a rarity for a Meyer film, Vixen loses her pinup sheen. The viewer sees her sweat, and Meyer actually permits the caress of a breast. Again, Erica Gavin's astounding personal appeal and raw sexuality were major factors in the film's commercial and critical success. But the bold directorial choices Meyer made to escape a trap he had set for himself, the possibility of hardcore, make *Vixen* a landmark film in the history of sex in the cinema. Besides grossing in excess of $15 million worldwide on a $72,000 investment and provoking a national rash of costly and time-consuming prosecutions, *Vixen* brought Meyer to the attention of the ailing 20th Century–Fox which openly wondered if a self-professed "class pornographer" could help save the studio.

Meyer's period of parody and satire begins when he signed with 20th Century–Fox in 1969 to direct *Beyond the Valley of the Dolls*. It extends through his last independently produced feature, *Beneath the Valley of the Ultravixens* (1979). Ask Russ Meyer what he considers his "masterpiece"; he will unhesitatingly reply, *Beyond the Valley of the Dolls*, although many critics point to *Mudhoney* as his best work. For Meyer, *"BVD,"* as he affectionately calls it, represents a supreme achievement on many fronts.

The young combat photographer returning home after the war found the doors of Hollywood closed to him when the International Alliance of Theatrical Stage Employees refused him membership. With great satisfaction Meyer signed the contract to direct his first studio film 23 years after the movie establishment had told him no. For Meyer, who had made 17 independent films, bankrolling each out of the profits of its predecessor, the Mountain had come to Muhammad at last. The Fox contract acknowledged his past track record as a consistently successful filmmaker and gambled he could produce an immensely profitable film given the production facilities and staff of a major studio. With the stroke of a pen, the budget of a Meyer film skyrocketed from less than $80,000 to over $1 million, and a staff of 55 studio "Indians," eager to serve their "chief," replaced his traditional three-man crew.

One of the first and one of the best decisions Meyer made was to hire a young *Chicago Sun-Times* film critic to help him write the screenplay for a studio non-sequel to Jacqueline Susann's *Valley of the Dolls*, which had proven to be a big box office winner for Fox in 1967. Roger Ebert, who came to Meyer's attention when he praised a *Wall Street Journal* article on the filmmaker in a letter to the newspaper's editor (see entry **46**), took a leave of absence from his paper. He moved to Hollywood where he and Meyer cranked out the screenplay to *BVD* in six weeks of ten-hour days.

Ebert's greatest contribution to the film was undoubtedly his youth. He knew the jargon of the late sixties subculture. His nearly encyclopedic knowledge of cinematic clichés put a wacky sort of spin on a production about Hollywood's corruption of an all-girl rock band directed by a 45-year-old World War II combat veteran. While the film's style is pure Meyer, especially evident in a montage sequence presenting opposing views on the virtues and vices of Hollywood, the voice is very much Ebert's. His contribution to the film exhibits a flair for parody and satire that he would further develop in the screenplays for *Up!* (1976) and *Beneath the Valley of the Ultravixens* (1979).

Ebert's description of his experiences collaborating with Meyer and observing the filmmaker's direction of *BVD* reveals much about the director's style. While envisioning *BVD* as parody-satire, Meyer chose to direct the film "straight," at a "right angle" to the script which the actors were unaware was intended to be camp. Critics, who shared with the players uncertainty over what the film was meant to be, mercilessly panned the film as bad drama, unaware that what they had seen was a comic treatment of a turgid Hollywood soap opera.

Added to the early bad reviews was the X-rating *BVD* received from the Motion Picture Association of America (MPAA), in spite of Meyer's plea for a more palatable R-rating which would have ensured wider distribution for the film. A scant few weeks earlier 20th Century–Fox had released *Myra Breckenridge* under an MPAA X-rating, and another "Brand X" film so soon on its heels caused many critics to lament the decline of a once great studio to the level of pornography-peddler. Judith Crist spoke for many when she dubbed the studio "Twentieth Stenchery-Fox" (see entry **639**).

Twenty years after its release, it is difficult to understand the furor caused by *BVD* even considering the attitudes of the era. Some critics at the time commented on the film's restraint and noted Meyer's 1950's sense of Puritanism. While fleeting glimpses of bare breasts abound, the camera never "goes South" to the pubic region, and sex scenes are edited in such a quick cut fashion that erotic tension is never permitted to build. But the film does contain graphic acts of violence, especially in the orgy and murder sequence. Those, one suspects, were included to exploit the contemporary Sharon Tate massacre, and continue to be as unsettling today as they were in 1970. While perhaps in bad taste, the scenes of violence alone or in conjunction with the film's nudity fail to explain the nonnegotiable X-rating imposed on *BVD* by the MPAA.

A more plausible explanation, and one which Ebert continues to believe is that Meyer's involvement in the project automatically guaranteed its X-rating. Originally brought to the studio on the strength of the financial success of *Vixen*, Meyer was instructed by studio head Richard D. Zanuck to deliver an exploitable film as close to an X-rating as possible without making an "X," that is, a "hard R." Meyer submitted a print of *BVD* to the MPAA he felt had safely walked the razor's edge between "R" and "X." It had not. It could not. Newspaper and trade articles reporting almost weekly on the signing of "Nudie King" Meyer, combined with the highly publicized obscenity battle Meyer continued to wage in Cincinnati over the exhibition of *Vixen*, suggest no outcome other than the skull and crossbones "X" the MPAA awarded it.

Though critically panned early after its release, the film was "discovered" by some young critics, found a wide audience, and eventually grossed an estimated $10 million worldwide, easily qualifying it as a solid success for 20th Century–Fox. Meyer made one more film for Fox, *The Seven Minutes* (1971), based on Irving Wallace's novel dealing with the censorship of an allegedly obscene book, before falling victim to a studio shakeup that toppled president Richard D. Zanuck from power. *Beyond the Valley of the Dolls* remains the major achievement of his studio period, that brief three-year flirtation before he returned to independent production with the atypical R-rated exploitation film *Blacksnake!*

It is important to describe what the film *meant* to its collaborators, Ebert and

Meyer. *Beyond,* which Ebert calls a "camp sexploitation horror musical that ends with a quadruple ritual murder and a triple wedding" (see entry **593**), marked his first venture into the industry he had seen from the outside. For Meyer, the experience had a profound significance that extended beyond his three years at Fox. A major studio had asked *him* to make *his* type of film with *their* money. He had done so and delivered a solid financial hit which proved to him that he could compete with the major studios as an independent filmmaker (that he had done in his pre–*BVD* days) and he could also successfully work within the studio system. Meyer returned to independent production knowing that he had gone one for two in the majors, a good batting average for any filmmaker. Years later Meyer and Ebert looked back on this period and noted with the wisdom conferred by time that 20th Century–Fox had given them, the lunatics, the keys to the asylum.

With the release of *Supervixens* in 1975, Meyer felt like a busted-out gambler staking everything on one last roll of the dice. His two previous films, *The Seven Minutes* and *Blacksnake!,* while receiving the usual savage reviews, had also uncharacteristically failed to fill the theatres with his loyal fans. They expressed their disappointment with his talky courtroom drama and historical melodrama by staying away in droves. For a filmmaker who had always judged the success of a film primarily by the number of tickets it sold, Meyer realized that he was losing the faithful audience that he had carefully cultivated for 16 years.

Aggravating these career disappointments was the dissolution of his marriage to starlet Edy Williams, whom he had met and wed during the *BVD* experience, and the abandonment of his 1973 independent film *Foxy* in which she was set to star. Meyer's cancellation of this ambitious $400,000 budget film, ostensibly due to a Supreme Court ruling that empowered local communities to determine obscenity, sounded the death knell to their stormy three-and-a-half year marriage. A bitter divorce battle followed, and Williams was ultimately denied any profits from *Supervixens* in their divorce decree of November 5, 1975. All that remains of the failed *Foxy* project is an intriguing three-minute trailer tacked onto the end of *Blacksnake!* which features Williams waterskiing in the nude.

In this atmosphere of personal and professional frustration Meyer sought to recapture the box office punch he had last delivered in 1970 with the commercial success of *Beyond the Valley of the Dolls.* In many ways, this challenge brought out the best in Meyer. The "do or die" spirit of professional risk that animated *Supervixens,* returned. The front line combat photographer was not through. With characteristic energy and enthusiasm, Meyer launched into a period of personal and professional reevaluation. He painfully determined that his current predicament was the result of straying from the source of his success, his ability to put his own rich fantasy life on the screen for others to share and enjoy.

The Seven Minutes and *Blacksnake!* had noticeably lacked a sense of "personal vision" that had informed Meyer's earlier signature films like *Lorna, Good Morning and Goodbye!,* and *Vixen.* Perhaps he had tried to preserve too much of Irving Wallace's talky novel and offered too little of himself. The *Blacksnake!* world of historical drama was foreign to him, and its timing was bad, since the black exploitation picture genre's popularity had already waned by 1973. Now, in 1975, after two flops, a failed film project and a trying divorce, Meyer resolved to return to the formula of "big bosoms and square jaws" that had characterized his earlier successes, established his notoriety and made his career. The copy Meyer wrote to publicize his "comeback" film reveals the director's urgent desire to redeem his career and how, by 1975, he had integrated even personal travail into advertising fodder for this film:

"Russ Meyer comes bolting out of the burning Sonora desert, with the vengeance of a mad Visigoth lusting to regain his throne... Russ Meyer's *Supervixens* is the epitome of twenty years of gut-tearing film making, a rural 'Fellini,' geared for the young and old alike, the sophisticate and the blue collar... Never before has Meyer revealed so much of himself, or taken such umbrage with his personal life... scenes bulging with love, violence and unrelenting hate... each scene bearing his own indelible stamp... Russ Meyer's *Supervixens* wields the double-bladed axe of satire... cutting and hacking its way to the very bone of society..."

Leaving nothing to chance, Meyer exerted stricter control than usual over the mechanics of this production and added writing chores to his duties as producer, director, cameraman, editor, and even actor. The promotional copy he wrote and the prominence of his name above the title leave no doubt that Meyer is the real star of *Supervixens*. Like Hitchcock, another director whose name promised an audience a certain type of film, Meyer's name above the title of *Supervixens* assured his audience that he was back to the "big bosoms and square jaws" formula of his past. Meyer's appearance as a briefly glimpsed motel clerk, however, should not be construed as homage to the Master of Suspense's penchant for appearing in walk-on roles, but rather an attempt to keep production costs down.

Not satisfied to rest on past laurels, Meyer strove to make *Supervixens* "bigger" in every way than any of his previous films. Whereas films like *Common-Law Cabin* had employed the promotional gimmick of the "Big 6"—that is, *three* actresses with identical measurements—Meyer painstakingly searched for *six* women of monumentally outrageous proportions to star in *Supervixens*. After an exhaustive search Meyer had found only five with dimensions outsized enough to meet his rigorous standards (Shari Eubank, Christy Hartburg, Deborah McGuire, Uschi Digard, and Sharon Kelly). Production was nearly delayed until Roger Ebert suggested the reincarnation angle which permitted Eubank to return from the dead in the guise of SuperVixen and thereby round out the cast. Meyer included a memorable cameo appearance by Chicago-born stripper Ann Marie, but it is so short he refused to count her in his total of six "superwomen."

The result of Meyer's insistence on a larger, physically bigger female cast for *Supervixens* is a sense of unreality that pervades the film. The women, always of impressive physical stature in his films, now finally enter the realm of the fantastic and seem to have no relation to their flesh and blood counterparts. Ann Marie tapes in at a mind-boggling 67-25-36! What were merely "superwomen" in the earlier films like *Lorna* and *Faster, Pussycat! Kill! Kill!* have now evolved into parody and caricature. This trend towards larger breasts, begun in earnest with *Supervixens* and continued through every subsequent film, ends naturally with Meyer's unreleased autobiographical epic archly entitled *The Breast of Russ Meyer*, as of early 1990 in postproduction.

Underscoring *Supervixens'* physical sense of parody and caricature is a plot that revolves around the picaresque sexual misadventures of a young, fresh-faced gas station attendant named Clint Ramsey (Charles Pitts), falsely accused of the murder of his wife, SuperAngel (Shari Eubank). While on the run from a psychotic sheriff, Harry Sledge (Charles Napier), who in reality was the murderer of the young hero's bitchy wife, Clint encounters an array of sexually voracious women before finding true happiness with SuperVixen, the reincarnation of SuperAngel.

Meyer, who had in the turgid and overblown sexual melodramas of his third period tortuously explored the themes of violence, adultery, rape, and sexual dissatisfaction, often to the point of unintended humor, here turns the material back on itself and shares a laugh at himself with his audience. Perhaps this decision to abandon drama for comedy came from Meyer's conviction that he had finally exhausted the dramatic possibilities of the genre. It is certain that *Supervixens* merrily parodies Meyer's past themes and bluecollar characters in an impressive literary context which loosely combined elements of Voltaire's *Candide* with the plucky young heroes borrowed from Horatio Alger.

Like every other element of this "comeback" film that promised more of everything, even Meyer's signature cinematic technique is more consciously evident. In no previous film is Meyer's rapid-fire editing quicker. Never has he relied more heavily on cross- and intercutting. So numerous are the edits that several critics have rightly noted the film's cartoon-like quality. The actresses, already anatomical exaggerations of "normally" constructed women, are photographed from extreme angles that further accentuate their outrageous dimensions. Meyer continually experimented with the technical aspects of filmmaking, but *Supervixens* marks a major advance in the "Russ Meyer" style that has become synonymous with his name.

Adding greatly to the film's success (it grossed over $17 million worldwide on a $221,000 budget) was the standout performance of Charles Napier as the psychotic sheriff, Harry Sledge. Meyer, who never forgets a friend or a good performance, had used Napier in *Cherry, Harry & Raquel* and again in *BVD* and *The Seven Minutes*. For Meyer, Napier is the synthesis, the physical embodiment of all the previous men in his films. An imposing physical presence at 6′3″, 220 pounds, Napier's jutting brow, piercing eyes, and square jaw perfectly fit into Meyer's cinematic image of the brooding, intellectually limited "man's man" whose behavior is largely motivated by unbridled lust for the other essential component of the filmmaker's formula: dominant women with big bosoms. Napier's most unusual physical characteristic, the one Meyer most prizes, is his remarkable facial mobility. Gifted with the ability to project menace or invite confidence by simultaneously snarling out of one corner of his mouth and smiling out of the other, Napier also possesses, according to Meyer, "six more teeth than Burt Lancaster!"

The physical impression Napier creates perfectly captures the essence of Meyer's square-jaw, he-man look, but Napier can also act. As the crazed cop, Harry Sledge, Napier introduces an unsettling element of pure homicidal rage into a film that is in all other respects broad fantasy and satire. Napier's ability instantaneously to drop the mask of sanity and reveal the monster lurking beneath is nowhere more apparent than in the infamous bathroom murder scene which critics have heavily condemned for its graphic violence. Sledge, insulted by SuperAngel and taunted for his inability to perform sexually, attempts to break into the bathroom where she has locked herself. In one of the few protracted shots in the film, Meyer concentrates the camera on Napier without editing save an occasional intercut to SuperAngel, and allows him slowly to build his anger until he finally explodes into demoniac fury.

At the climax of the scene, a rage-blinded Sledge breaks down the door, stomps the woman into insensibility in the bathtub and electrocutes her by tossing a radio into the bloody bathwater. Despite Meyer's defense of the scene as a parody of violence, many viewers and critics fail to see the humor in its brutality. The kinetic intensity of Napier's performance under Meyer's deft direction transformed any satiric potential the scene may have had into one of gut-wrenching suspense and horror. It may be the most famous single scene in a Meyer film, and its emotional impact and technical merit have been favorably compared with the shower sequence in Hitchcock's *Psycho*. Napier, who has achieved greater theatrical success than any other Meyer performer, went on to costar with Sylvester Stallone as the corrupt CIA agent Murdoch in *Rambo: First Blood Part II* (1985) and to do numerous television roles.

Reviewers of *Supervixens*, in spite of the almost universal outcry over its violence, were uncharacteristically positive. While most critics welcomed Meyer's triumphant return to the genre, some criticized him for a "failure to grow" as a filmmaker by choosing merely to parody his own themes and style. The ever-philosophical Meyer rebutted the charges by asking, "Who else am I to parody?" With *Supervixens*, Meyer *had* successfully returned with the "vengeance of a mad Visigoth lusting to regain his throne." Much like Hitchcock and other directors whose artistic explorations had expanded and defined a film genre, Meyer realized that his audience expected a specific type of film from him and would accept no other. Meyer summed up his position in 1975 when he tersely noted, "If you create the Monster, you'd better damn well feed it." After *Supervixens*, the Monster had found a name: the "Russ Meyer Genre."

Up! and *Beneath the Valley of the Ultravixens* expand and refine the formula of big bosoms and square jaws that Meyer codified in *Supervixens*. Though nowhere as financially successful upon their theatrical release as *Supervixens*, both films represent Meyer the craftsman at his best. Like that 1975 smash, both *Up!* and *Beneath* are parody-satires that unfold in budget-dictated remote settings, populated with the traditional Meyer arch stereotypes of sexually rapacious women and lust-driven men engaged in feverish ruttings. What distinguish these films from *Supervixens* are the manner in which Meyer frames the stories and the literary devices he uses to comment on the plot while simultaneously propelling it forward.

A Greek Chorus of one, enthusiastically played by Francesca "Kitten" Natividad, introduces the characters of *Up!* In a prose style that sounds like Shakespeare on LSD she comments on the film's action while becoming involved in it. The commentary combined with Natividad's placement in incongruous natural settings (perched in trees, straddling logs) and extreme closeup photography of various parts of her body, produces an often amusing, and always visually interesting effect. Meyer, who suggested the character of the single-member Chorus, was ably assisted by Roger Ebert (alias "Reinhold Timme" in the credits), who wrote all her dialogue.

Ebert is similarly credited for cowriting with Meyer the screenplay for *Beneath* under his Meyer-inspired pseudonym "R. Hyde" (as in "Dr. Jekyll and...").

Beneath easily rates as the most literary of Meyer's work, utilizing and satirizing the device of the omniscient on-stage narrator made famous in Thornton Wilder's play *Our Town.* In *Beneath,* Stuart Lancaster plays the narrator, the Man from Small Town U.S.A., who comments on the action while periodically intruding upon it. The character, beyond his storytelling function, is a conscious homage to Meyer's formative years as an industrial filmmaker. The relaxed, on-camera narrator who folksily informed Standard Oil employees about the company's annuity plan in the late forties and early fifties comments in 1979 in a similarly down-home style on the sexual hangups of the citizens of Small Town U.S.A.

Beneath is photographed and edited like an industrial, with Meyer utilizing an establishing shot, a quick cut to an extreme closeup, then a quick cut back to a medium shot. The phallic imagery, like the omnipresent radio transmitter tower, strongly suggests the mechanical equipment featured in industrial films. Watching *Beneath* with a knowledge of Meyer's professional roots, the viewer becomes aware that by substituting closeups of whirring machinery for the frenetic scenes of lovemaking of the film, *Beneath* could easily be a glossy industrial.

Up! and *Beneath* continued to explore themes which by now were as instantly recognizable to Meyer's audience as his signature style. The films abound with dominant women, klutzy men, lust, greed, violence, murder and mayhem. For good measure they also include Nazis, whom Meyer parodied in *BVD* and *Supervixens,* the latter of which featured Nazi marching music and a gas station owner named Martin Bormann. Nazis figure prominently in *Up!* (Adolph Schwartz and Eva Braun, Jr.) and *Beneath* (Martin Bormann reprised). Meyer's fascination with Nazis and his knowledge of the subject date from his duty in the European Theatre. They represent another facet of the man who has largely eschewed Hollywood friendships and retained his ties to his army buddies. Cinematically, Meyer's Nazis permit him the pyschological luxury of satirizing a sociopolitical group he abhors.

In *Up!,* Meyer sought to avoid the heavy critical flak he received over the violence in *Supervixens.* He attempted to make it a more obvious parody. Violence abounds—homosexual sadomasochism, a piranha attack, rape, and a chainsaw murder—but in the most graphically violent scene, the chainsaw murder, Meyer tried to make the events leading up to it so fantastically unbelievable that they defused any possible criticism.

During the rapes of undercover policewoman Margo Winchester (Raven De La Croix) and Sweet Li'l Alice (Janet Wood), sheriff Homer Johnson (Monte Bane) sinks an axe into the back of their assailant, the moronic, but mammoth lumberjack Rafe (Bob Schott). Despite his serious wound, he manages to pull the axe from his back and lodge it squarely into Homer's chest. Geysering blood, Homer pulls the axe from his chest, grabs a chainsaw and chases Rafe, who is carrying both abducted women under his arms, into the woods. Bloodier confrontation follows. Homer and Rafe, locked in a death grip with the McCullough between them tearing full-throttled into the giant lumberjack, plunge over a cliff to certain death. The two hysterically frightened women, brought together by the carnage, turn to one another for comfort, with Sweet Li'l Alice realizing in a sexual epiphany that she is attracted to the curvaceous cop.

Despite the ludicrousness of the situation and Meyer's attempt to hedge his bets by adding a chorus of outlandish sound effects, critics still found the sequence and the film too violent. Believing that the criticism hurt *Up!* at the box office, Meyer turned away from linking sex and violence in *Beneath.* Blood is spilled only in fistfights, and even then it flows in a rainbow of colors, symbolic of the moral character of the injured. The eager-to-please, black Uncle Tom character Zebulon (De Forest Covan) bleeds white, while the blood of the lascivious homosexual dentist Asa Lavender (Robert Pearson) is hot pink. Only the manly, hard-loving Mr. Peterbuilt (Pat Wright) bleeds all–American red.

The content of *Up!* and *Beneath* was unarguably "harder" than any of his previous films, since they include fairly explicit sadomasochism and anal intercourse, respectively. *Up!* is particularly "hard," and critics have noted that it probably represents the outer edge of what can be considered "softcore" (see entry **964**). While *Beneath* contains none of the shocking violence of *Up!,* the young wife's attempts to cure her husband of his predilection for anal intercourse, here treated as a heinous sexual deviation requiring "divine intervention" to correct, make a more explicit story than any previous Meyer creation.

In the late sixties and early seventies Meyer had told several interviewers that he seldom included "perversion" in his films because he considered it to be "unamerican," but by 1979 he was featuring it as the central theme of *Beneath.* This contradiction is partially a reaction to hardcore, which represented a lessening, but still lucrative market. It is equally valid, given Meyer's sexploitation roots and the structural integrity of his wacky film world, to interpret the "perversion" in *Beneath* in a different manner. Any good "socially redeeming" sexploitation film seeks to pique public, but not judicial interest. "Sin" occupies most of the movie, but the redeeming grace of retribution with its attendant moral lesson appears in the final moments of the last reel. *Beneath* operates on this classic principle. It traces the attempts to cure the hapless Lamar Shedd (Ken Kerr) of his sexual hangup, while simultaneously showing his frustrated wife fulfilling her sexual needs with men like Mr. Peterbuilt.

As witnessed in numerous films like *Lorna* and *Faster, Pussycat! Kill! Kill!,* a rigid code of morality exists in the Meyer universe, and that code must be strictly observed if it is to function properly. "Normal" heterosexual sex is the primary component of this universe. It guarantees its harmony. In film after film any character who disrupts this harmony by breaking Meyer's moral laws is punished. Lorna, the adulteress, and Varla, the loveless lesbian, are both punished because of their deviance from the moral norm. In *Beneath,* Lamar's sexual problem poses a threat as great as adultery or homosexuality. His sexual reclamation from the "perversion" of buggery to the restoration of "normal" sexual relations with his wife reestablishes his marriage as well as Meyer's moral order.

The significance of *Up!* and *Beneath* for the filmmaker, who after *Supervixens* had become a genre unto himself, lay not so much in theme or story as in the continued development of his technical craftsmanship. Beyond their value as entertainment, the films are exercises in technical virtuosity and vivid testaments to what an independent filmmaker could accomplish on a late seventies budget of under $250,000 per film. As in *Supervixens,* Meyer's technical control over both films is total. The garish primary color photography is of pinup quality. The camera setups are varied and inventive. The editing is quick and precise, boasting fully twice as many edits as traditional "non–Meyer" films of the period. Such editing creates a breakneck pace, a rush of action that adds to the cartoon-like quality of his later films. Meyer spent 16 months in postproduction on *Beneath*, seven on editing and five on sound effects. The result is a production sheen often absent from multimillion-dollar studio efforts. Meyer is understandably proud of his technical achievements. He is equally proud of the track record of his films, which have successfully stood toe-to-toe with the product of the majors.

The release of *Beneath* in 1979 marked Meyer's twentieth year as an independent filmmaker. His unique style had transformed and ultimately transcended the narrow confines of the sexploitation genre. In the two decades between *The Immoral Mr. Teas* and *Beneath,* Meyer had explored the psychic landscape of his own sexual fantasies and produced such landmark films as *Teas, Lorna,* and *Vixen,* all the while accurately gauging the commercial winds.

Despite assertions that his work represented his filmed fantasies, Meyer had only occasionally blurred the line between reality and fantasy by appearing in a few of his films, albeit in small, anonymous roles. That he should figure prominently in the climax of *Beneath,* his last theatrically released film, is instructive. He appears as himself. Who else? The filmmaker who had so seamlessly integrated his life experiences and sexual interests into his films reached in *Beneath* a logical conclusion. Meyer's ten minute appearance, during which he totes a camera, directs his off-screen lover, Francesca "Kitten" Natividad, and delivers the film's "moral," shattered the thin and shifting line between fantasy and reality which he had previously maintained, however tenuously, in his cinema. Meyer's appearance in *Beneath* made *explicit* his intensely personal identification with his work. It also permanently laid to rest any speculation that anyone but Meyer was the true star of his films. In a puckish twist that confirmed Meyer and Ebert's conception of *Beneath* as a parody-satire, John Furlong, a talented impersonator and character actor who appeared as Calif McKinney in *Mudhoney,* dubs Meyer's voice.

Meyer has not theatrically released a film since *Beneath* for a variety of reasons. Though produced for the paltry (by industry standards) sum of $239,000, that film struggled to recoup its investment in spite of a vigorous city-to-city promotional campaign by Meyer and Natividad. Only after Meyer went alone to Chicago to exhaustively promote the film did it catch fire and make money. Its success proved Meyer's name still meant something to his particular audience and to cinema cognoscenti impressed by the sheen and style he could achieve working nearly alone on a minimal budget. But it was clear that the harsh economic realities of filmmaking were making it increasingly difficult for Meyer to work as an independent in his genre. Costs for raw film stock, laboratory processing, prints, advertising, and distribution were simply too high. Compounding the problem was the expense involved in finding a decent venue in which to exhibit his films, a must for Meyer who refused to exhibit his films in "scumbag" theatres. Not for the first time in his career, Meyer stood at the crossroads. Steadfastly refusing to cross over into hardcore pornography, he was equally averse to relinquishing total control over a property by seeking an alliance with a major studio. While Meyer pondered his predicament, a technological development appeared to resolve his problems.

Few filmmakers occupied the favorable position Meyer found himself in when the video revolution hit. As an independent filmmaker who had largely bankrolled each of his projects out of the profits of his previous effort, Meyer owned the sole rights to most of his films. The notable exception was his personal favorite, the 20th Century–Fox *Beyond the Valley of the Dolls,* of which he owned only ten percent. Setting up a video company, a division of his RM Films International, Meyer carefully selected and released 13 of his titles under the "Bosomania" banner. The complete control Meyer always exercised over making a film and the enthusiasm he brought to this effort continue with his total involvement in the production, promotion, and sales of these videos. He promotes his product by manning the RM Films International booth at the annual Video Software Dealers of America show in Las Vegas and, as likely as not, will answer his Los Angeles–based company's order phone.

The video revolution introduced Meyer to a new generation of film fans who would probably never have seen his work outside an occasional university showing or film society retrospective. It is for these new admirers, confirmed or potential, that Meyer spends so much time and energy in personally promoting his videos and managing his company. For the officially childless Meyer, his films represent his legacy and he derives from them the same intimation of immortality other men experience in producing offspring. For this reason and to put his life into some kind of perspective, he has conceived one of the most ambitious film projects ever attempted in the history of cinema — *The Breast of Russ Meyer.*

Originally envisioned in 1979 as a compilation of the best scenes from all his features, *BRM* as he calls it, has evolved into a 3¾-hour documentary of his life and career. Between condensations of his films, Meyer has interwoven on-camera interviews with old friends, enemies, actors, and past and present lovers to produce the rough fabric of himself as both a man and a filmmaker. He revisited the scenes of his greatest triumphs and bitterest defeats (Europe and Cincinnati, respectively) to shoot on-location footage for the personal epic he will narrate. Not satisfied with the past alone, Meyer will introduce in *BRM* a new generation of "superwomen," including the Hungarian sensation Tundi and the Atlanta-based burlesque queen Tami Roche.

Meyer answers criticism that a theatrical market no longer exists for this type of film by categorically stating that he does not care if anyone sees it. The film is being made by Meyer *for* Meyer. That he has been approached by international film societies and institutions like the Cinémathèque Française and the National Film Theatre in London to exhibit the film in a festival setting is immaterial. That video offers the possibility of profit in the long term for an epic which has to date cost $1.7 million does not matter. Meyer's only wish is to create a film *exactly* the way he wants it without answering to anyone but himself. His *BRM* is the ultimate expression of a filmmaker's passion for independence and the final integration of life and art which Meyer had only gingerly approached in *Beneath the Valley of the Ultravixens.* When complete, *The Breast of Russ Meyer* will *"be"* Russ Meyer. It will be Russ Meyer the artist and Russ Meyer the businessman, since he plans to release *BRM* serially on three videocassettes.

Meyer has temporarily suspended work on *BRM* to complete a two-volume print autobiography, *A Clean Breast: The Life and Loves of Russ Meyer.* Although there are two substantial biographies of the filmmaker by foreign writers (see entries 1 and 4), Meyer feels both are inaccurate and fail to capture the spirit of his life and films. Using his vast personal collection of newspaper clippings, interviews, film reviews, and other sources to aid his memory, Meyer has spent more than three years writing a "warts and all" memoir which promises to be an intriguing blend of erotica and cinema history. With over 2,300 photographs and drawings, a detailed filmography and a synopsis of each film written in the inimitable Meyer style, it is a work of characteristic lushness. Privately printed and limited to 5,000 signed and numbered copies, the book will only be available by mail order through RM Films International. When he completes both the film and print autobiographies, Meyer will have provided enthusiasts and cinéastes alike with a treasury of personal documentation they may use to fix his place in film history.

We have come full circle back to the original question: Is Russ Meyer an American *auteur?* Critical contention rages, as it usually does, but the facts are irrefutable. Films like *The Immoral Mr. Teas, Lorna,* and *Vixen* significantly altered the sexploitation genre, changed its content, determined its development and influenced mainstream films. Despite no-name casts, four of his films, *Vixen, Cherry, Harry & Raquel, Beyond the Valley of the Dolls,* and *Supervixens* are among the Top 100 all-time film rentals as tallied by *Variety.* Meyer's softcore fantasies have competed with box office distinction against the products of mainstream Hollywood. His name above the title guarantees an audience. If Meyer's ability to redefine a genre and his commercial success do not qualify him as an *auteur,* his consistent vision does. His style is his signature, as recognizable and as outrageous as his themes, his techniques, his humor and his dull-witted men perpetually in pursuit of sexually voracious, superabundant women. Finally, Meyer continues to be honored with numerous international retrospectives, the latest held in July 1989, at the Moscow Film Festival. *Auteur* or hack? Perhaps Roger Ebert (see entry 131) speaks best for those who see in Meyer's work a wondrous and unique film heritage: "What is his ultimate place in film history? Although he works in the disreputable genre of the soft-core skin flick, I believe the serious film historians of the future will discuss him with such other radical structuralists as Mark Rappaport, Chantal Ackerman, Sergei Eisenstein and Jean-Luc Godard. That's if they can see past the heaving bosoms."

II. BIOGRAPHIES

1 Jackson, Jean-Pierre. *Russ Meyer, ou, Trente ans de cinéma erotique à Hollywood.* Paris: PAC, 1982.

Jackson's ambitious and well-meant biography/appreciation of Meyer is unfortunately riddled with numerous printer's errors that cast doubt on the accuracy of the entire work. For example, several photo captions are misnamed with a shot of black actress June Mack of *Beneath* incorrectly identified as Erica Gavin! Jackson, president of Sinfonia Films and Meyer's distributor in France, is an extremely knowledgeable Meyer scholar and one can only surmise that he was not given an opportunity to proofread the galleys of the book prior to its final printing. (Illus.)

2 Jackson, Jean-Pierre. "Special: Russ Meyer." *Ciné-Zine-Zone,* No. 8, 1981.

A special seventy-page issue of the French film journal *Ciné-Zine-Zone* is dedicated to Meyer with chapter headings entitled "Immoral Mr. Teas," "Russ Meyer 'King of the Nudies'," "Roughies and Kinkies," and "Russ Meyer's Touch." (Illus.)

*3 Meyer, Russ. *A Clean Breast: The Life and Loves of Russ Meyer.* Hollywood, Calif.: Hauck Pub. Co., [1990?].

Meyer's highly personal and explicit reflections on his films and life are an absolute must for any fan, film student, film library, or lover of erotica. Envisioned as a two-volume set containing a definitive filmography and over 2,300 photos, Meyer presents a "warts and all" portrait of himself that leaves the reader wondering how so much living could have been compressed into a single lifetime. Self-published by Meyer who insisted upon complete autonomy over its content, the limited edition set of 5,000 numbered and signed copies is available directly from RM Films International. (Illus.) For a discussion of this book see entries **1145–1148.**

4 Thissen, Rolf. *Russ Meyer, der König des Sexfilms.* Munich: W. Heyne, 1987.

Interestingly, this large biography on Meyer written by German author Thissen served as the impetus for the filmmaker's autobiography *A Clean Breast: The Life and Loves of Russ Meyer.* According to Meyer, after compiling over forty pages of factual corrections on Thissen's manuscript, he became convinced that no one could tell his story, but him. Meyer was also successful in obtaining a court order against the book to prevent its distribution outside of Germany. (Illus.)

An asterisk next to an entry number denotes a work of particular merit.

III. INTERVIEWS

*5 Ashmun, Dale. "Mondo Russo: Russ Meyer Interview." *Film Threat*, 15:10–16, 1988.

Although a 90 percent rehash of his earlier, mid-1986 *Screw* interview (see entry 6), Ashmun's expanded interview here is valuable for Meyer's assessment of actors Stuart Lancaster, Charles Napier, and Haji. Highly recommended. (8 illus.)

*6 Ashmun, Dale. "Tits 'R' Russ." *Screw*, 906:4–7, July 14, 1986.

In a surprisingly subdued and informative interview conducted for the sex tabloid *Screw*, Meyer discusses his early career as an industrial filmmaker, the major stylistic influences on his films (Al Capp, Horatio Alger, W.C. Fields), and his current film and literary projects. Highly recommended. (11 illus.) For an expanded version, see entry 5.

7 Bahadur, Raj. "Russ Meyer Re-Visited." *Scene*, p. 13, Oct. 23–29, 1980.

A largely unedited conversation with Meyer in which the filmmaker discusses in detail the banning of *Vixen* in Ohio, the Russ Meyer style, the acting ability of his stars, his involvement with the Sex Pistols, and his personal thoughts about the group and their manager, Malcolm McLaren.

8 Bennett, Alex. "*Screw* Interview with Russ Meyer: The Barnum of Boobs." *Screw*, 411:4–7, Jan. 17, 1977.

Alex Bennett, producer of *Screw*'s cable television program *Midnight Blue's America*, interviews the filmmaker on several aspects of his career before finally focusing on a graphic discussion of the anatomical dimensions of the male cast members in Meyer's current production *Up!* (7 illus.)

*9 Berkowitz, Stan. "Russ Meyer: Sex, Violence and Drugs—All in Good Fun!" *Film Comment*, 9(1): 46–51, Jan./Feb. 1973.

In an August 1972 interview Meyer discusses in detail his upcoming parody of black exploitation films, *Blacksnake!*, and offers his thoughts on a wide range of topics including his attitude on Women's Liberation, his favorite directors, and the censorship problems of *Vixen*. The filmmaker also touches on the plot and production aspects of his next proposed film venture, *Foxy*, as well as on a planned production entitled *Beyond... Beyond*, which Meyer describes as not a sequel, but "a similar picture" to his 1970 hit *BVD*. Recommended. (1 illus.)

10 Boz. "Beyond the Valley of Russ Meyer: A Talk with Russ Meyer." *Suburban Relapse*, 13:9–12, July 1985.

The music fanzine *Suburban Relapse* interviews Meyer on a wide variety of topics which include his censorship problems, the autobiographical work in progress, *The Breast of Russ Meyer*, and the music in his films. Boz notes that several of "today's hip music makers" are interested in Meyer's films with the band the Cramps covering the title song from *Faster, Pussycat! Kill! Kill!*, Redd Kross doing a version of "Look on Up at the Bottom" from *BVD*, and the Bangles often playing anonymous gigs in Los Angeles as the Carrie Nations (the girl band featured in *BVD*). (16 illus.) See entry 537.

11   Charles, Jody. "Russ Meyer: 'Lawrence Welk of the Skinflicks'." *Gent,* 21(8):20–23, Aug. 1980.

Interviewed by the men's magazine *Gent* while in Miami promoting *Beneath,* Meyer discusses the portrayal of women in his films and his proposed changes of the Motion Picture Association of America's ratings system. (1 illus.)

*12   Eyman, Scott. "Pensees of a Porno Prince." *Take One,* 5(3):7–8, Aug. 1976.

Eyman turns on a tape recorder and lets Meyer talk about his war experiences, shooting still photos on the set of *Giant* (1956) and his relationship with its star, James Dean, and his career up through the filming of *Up!* Eyman's decision to exclude himself from the interview and to let Meyer speak in the first person results in a fine biographical piece that is accurate and readable. Recommended. (2 illus.)

13   Gavron, Laurence. "Le Walt Disney du Porno: Entretien avec Russ Meyer." *Cahiers du Cinéma* (Le Journal des cahiers section), 341: vi–vii, Nov. 1982.

In a standard interview that notes Meyer is practically unknown in France, the filmmaker likens his movies to comic strips and describes the view the Hollywood Establishment holds of him as "the lost sheep from their flock." (2 illus.)

14   Glassman, David. "Director Meyer Gives Thanks for the Mammaries." *UCLA Daily Bruin,* 107(14):16–17, Jan. 24, 1980.

In one of several interviews he has given to university newspapers throughout his career, Meyer discusses the role of women in his films and a possible career path he might have chosen in lieu of filmmaking. (2 illus.)

*15   Golab, Jan. "Return from Beyond the Valley of the Dolls." *Los Angeles,* 31(12):224–228, 230, Dec. 1986.

Golab visits the "Museum," Meyer's memorabilia-filled home in the Hollywood Hills, and discusses with the filmmaker his current projects: the five-hour compilation film, *The Breast of Russ Meyer,* and his massive autobiography, *Russ Meyer: The Rural Fellini* (since retitled *A Clean Breast: The Life and Loves of Russ Meyer*). Describing the tome as "the most important thing I've ever done," Meyer believes that it will clearly show how he was "able to honestly integrate my sexual lust with my lust for filmmaking." Tundi, the Meese Commission's effect on his video sales, and his upcoming film, *The Jaws of Lorna* are also discussed. Includes filmography. Highly recommended. (4 illus.)

16   Jackson, Jean-Pierre; Romer, Jean-Claude; and Lenne, Gérard. "L'Amérique à outrance: Russ Meyer." *Revue du Cinéma,* 379: 41–48, Jan. 1983.

In three small articles linked together under a unifying title, Meyer is interviewed and his body of work examined by, among others, his French distributor Jean-Pierre Jackson. Meyer's films are described as "monuments of sexual energy, violence and bad taste." Includes a filmography compiled by Jackson. (9 illus.)

17   Kelly, Matthew. "The Breast of Russ Meyer: *Swank* Salutes the King of Softcore Porn." *Swank,* 28(5):42–45, May 1981.

Interviewed in the men's magazine *Swank,* Meyer discusses his obsession with breasts, his current film project *(The Breast of Russ Meyer),* and the reasons he has resisted crossing over into the triple-X rated film market. (18 illus.)

18   Koch, Maureen. "Inter/View with Russ Meyer and Edy Williams." *Andy Warhol's Interview*, 19:22–23, Feb. 1972.

In an interview conducted shortly after the release of *The Seven Minutes,* Meyer, accompanied by wife Edy Williams, expresses his belief that the public is now disinterested in traditional sex films. Citing the popularity of movies like *Willard,* Meyer plans to enter the horror film genre. Two proposed directorial assignments for 20th Century–Fox, *Choice Cuts* and *Eleven,* are also discussed. (2 illus.)

19   Lovece, Frank. "Up Front with Russ Meyer." *Oui,* pp. 90–91, Sept. 1983.

A short interview that concentrates on the early days of Meyer's career as a cheesecake and TV still photographer, a cameraman on the late 1940's film *The Desperate Women,* and the shooting of the 1950 "lost" film *French Postcards (The French Peep Show)* for El Ray burlesque theatre owner Peter DeCenzie. In a more contemporary vein, Meyer also discusses his future film projects *Mondo Topless 2, The Breast of Russ Meyer,* and *The Jaws of Lorna.* (15 illus. est.)

*20   Lowry, Ed, and Black, Louis. "Russ Meyer Interviewed." *Film Comment,* 16(4):44–48, July/Aug. 1980.

An excellent interview arranged under various subheadings like *"Vixen," "Cherry, Harry & Raquel," "BVD,"* "Warner Brothers," etc. Also discussed are the reasons why the Sex Pistols film *Who Killed Bambi?* was never made. Highly recommended. (6 illus.)

*21   Morton, Jim. "Interview: Russ Meyer." *Re/Search: Incredibly Strange Films,* 10:76–85, 1986.

In one of the best interviews ever conducted with the filmmaker, Meyer talks in depth about *The Breast of Russ Meyer,* his wives (Eve Meyer and Edy Williams), the women in his films (Haji, Shari Eubank, Tura Satana, Uschi Di-

gard), his past personal relationship with Francesca "Kitten" Natividad, and the closeness he still shares with his old army friends. Highly recommended. (9 illus.)

22   Ollive, Thierry. "Russ Meyer." *Ciné Eros Star,* 5:3–15, Sommaire 1981.

Meyer is interviewed by Ollive for a French men's magazine devoted to "a review of erotic cinema" and answers questions concerning his stature as an *auteur,* his disdain for hardcore films, his assessment of French versus American striptease, and his admiration for the young Anita Ekberg who symbolized to him "perfection in feminine anatomy." Includes filmography. (38 illus.)

23   Reid, Craig. "Interview/Russ Meyer." *Adam,* 25(5):14–16, 26, 73, May 1981.

A 1981 interview distinguished from numerous other interviews granted by Meyer to men's magazines by the intelligence and perception of the questions. While much of the interview treads over ground worn bare by other interviewers—Meyer's thoughts on screen violence, his audience, the women in his films—Reid's observation on Meyer's historical willingness to fight costly censorship battles in court enables the filmmaker to reflect on the new wave of political and moral conservatism he feels promises to sweep the country in the wake of Reagan's recent election to the presidency. (3 illus.)

*24   Ross, Gene. "Russ Meyer: The Brains Beneath the Brest, Bormann and Beyond." *Adult Video News,* 2(4):86–92, June 1987.

An excellent and highly informative article on the strain of unexpected moralism in Meyer's cinema, his actresses, and his work in progress, *The Breast of Russ Meyer.* Ross offers respectful commentaries on several films and includes a filmography of Meyer titles currently available on videotape. Meyer also mentions his latest discovery, the Hungarian-born Tundi, who will appear in both *The Breast of Russ Meyer* and in a 22-minute short entitled *Soul Too* which the filmmaker shot in Germany late in 1986. Highly recommended. (11 illus.)

25 Simon, Robert. "Meyer and Ultra-vixens: A Candid Interview." *Westword*, 2(26):12, Aug. 17–Sept. 7, 1979.

Among other subjects, Meyer speaks out against censorship of any kind (excluding the personally taboo topics of child porn and animal abuse) and accuses the Motion Picture Association of America with being a de facto censorship board which forces filmmakers to edit their films in order to obtain a desired rating. (1 illus.)

*26 Teicholz, Tom. "Movies: Tit for Tat: Russ Meyer." *Interview*, 16(1): 70–73, Jan. 1986.

A highly recommended interview conducted in Meyer's memorabilia-filled Hollywood Hills home which director John Waters has dubbed "The Russ Meyer Museum." Topics discussed include Meyer's war years, the international market for his films, and various aspects of his personal life. (2 illus.)

*27 Turan, Kenneth, and Zito, Stephen F. "King Leer: An Interview with Russ Meyer." *Sinema: American Pornographic Films and the People Who Make Them*, pp. 26–35. New York: Praeger, 1974.

A classic interview with Meyer that traces his life and career up through *Blacksnake!* Co-written by Kenneth Turan, presently a film critic for the *Washington Post*, the interview captures a relaxed Meyer discussing his commitment to the investors in his films, the halcyon war years, and his disdain for hard-core sex films. The interview concludes with Meyer questioning whether there is anything left for him to do since his films fall short of hardcore, but are being eclipsed by major studio productions like *Last Tango in Paris*. Highly recommended as is the book, *Sinema* in which the interview appears as Chapter 3. (12 illus.)

*28 Waters, John. "Two Masters." *Shock Value*, pp. 191–212. New York: Dell, 1981.

Baltimore's favorite filmmaker, John Waters, director of such camp classics as *Pink Flamingos* and *Female Trouble*, makes no secret of his respect for Meyer, and in particular, his adoration of *Faster, Pussycat! Kill! Kill!* which he feels is "the best movie ever made." In this chapter from *Shock Value*, Waters discusses the film's effect on him, synopsizes it in his own inimitable prose style, and even talks with the film's star Tura ("Varla") Satana. The heart of the chapter, however, is a fascinating 4-page interview with Meyer and paramour Francesca "Kitten" Natividad in which the filmmaker candidly answers off-beat questions posed by Waters on such diverse topics as *Faster, Pussycat!*, *Beyond the Valley of the Dolls*, the recruitment of big-bosomed actresses, and the Sex Pistols. The other "Master" interviewed by Waters in the chapter is gore film specialist Herschel Gordon Lewis. Highly recommended. (5 illus.)

*29 Winegar, Karin. "Porn King: Russ Meyer Still Up-Front with Films and 'Fillies'." *Minneapolis Star*, sec. C, pp. 1, 4, July 2, 1979.

An excellent interview with Meyer distinguished by Winegar's non-threatening feminist approach to the filmmaker and her wide range of interesting, and sometimes, pointed questions. The numerous topics discussed include Meyer's breast fixation, his feelings for "Kitten" Natividad, and the things which emotionally move him. Highly recommended. (5 illus.)

30 Yakir, Dan, and Davis, Bruce. "An Interview: Beyond the Big-Breast—Can Russ Meyer Keep It 'Up!'" *The Thousand Eyes Magazine*, 2(4): 6–7, 16, Dec. 1976.

In a lengthy interview which focuses on his current film *Up!*, Meyer discusses a variety of topics including his unique cinematic moralism and his attitudes on screen violence and "message" films. Having been called "a moralist in a field where few expect to find one," Meyer acknowledges that the idea of retribution, the violent destruction of the moral transgressor, has been a recurring theme in his work since *Lorna* and is continued in *Up!* (3 illus.)

IV. MISCELLANEOUS

*31   Ansen, David. "Russ Meyer: Auteur of Sleaze." *The Real Paper,* 4(30):18–19, July 30, 1975.

In a marvelous article, Ansen characterizes Meyer as "a bonafide auteur, as authentic in his fashion as Grandma Moses," but also an individual whose narrow social attitudes towards women and gays demonstrate his limitations as a filmmaker. For now *Newsweek* film critic Ansen, Meyer's insistence on portraying these groups as unsympathetic stereotypes betrays his fear as a director "to step out of the self-protective shade of parody" which is the hallmark of his films. Highly recommended.

32   Bacon, James. "Ups and Downs of Film Rating." *Los Angeles Herald-Examiner,* sec. C, p. 2, Mar. 26, 1973.

Based upon his past experiences with the X-rated *Beyond the Valley of the Dolls* and the R-rated *Blacksnake!,* Meyer contends that ratings are determined by the direction of on-screen pelvic movements. Meyer's formula: "North and south...mean an X—east and west an R."

33   Bernstein, Richard. "Meyer: Put More on the Screen Per Dollar Than Anyone Else." *Independent Film Journal,* UNKNOWN, Feb. 4, 1970.

Rather than pay exorbitant salaries to name actors, Meyer's formula is to "put it into something that a moviegoer will see up there on the screen." Pointing to pace and plot as the most important elements in movies, Meyer sees a major studio trend toward the "sensibly budgeted highly exploitable film." (1 illus.)

34   Brode, Douglas. "Russ Meyer: Soft Porn, Hard Sell." *Syracuse New Times,* p. 10, Aug. 8, 1979.

Meyer is portrayed as a filmmaker whose cinematic artistry has enabled him to transcend the sexploitation genre he prefers to work in. The filmmaker also discusses the making of *Beyond the Valley of the Dolls,* his respect for moviemaker Radley Metzger ("Henry Paris"), and some proposed changes of the current rating system. (1 illus.)

35   "Busenpabst Russ Meyer Packt aus: Wozu BHs gut sind—und wozu nicht." *Lui,* 9:50–51, Sept. 1987.

The "Pope of the Bosom" offers his advice and experience to German readers on the best methods to remove a stubborn bra. Meyer also relates shared incidents concerning bras that involved "Kitten" Natividad and Tundi. (9 illus.)

36   Carnes, Jim. "Russ Meyer: The Disney of Sex." *Sacramento Union,* sec. C, p. 5, Sept. 14, 1979.

Carnes' article quotes Meyer extensively on such topics as the filmmaker's proposed revision of the MPAA's ratings code, his motivations for making movies, and how the Hollywood Establishment views him. (1 illus.)

37 Christner, D.L. "Mister X." *Newsweek*, 75(6):9, February 9, 1970.

An irate female reader angrily responds to the editor of *Newsweek* concerning its "Mr. X" article on Meyer (see entry **557**). The Dallas, Texas, resident berates the magazine for wasting a page on Meyer and questions how people who probably have "rotten personal lives" can succeed in pushing "their trash down the American public's throats!"

38 Chute, David. "Saying 'No Thanks' to the Ratings." *Boston Phoenix*, sec. 3, pp. 5, 25–26, Dec. 11, 1979.

In an exceptionally informative article Meyer, George Romero *(Dawn of the Dead)*, and Bill Sargent *(Richard Pryor—Live in Concert)*, discuss the inequities they perceive to exist for independent filmmakers under the present Motion Picture Association of America's rating system. Jack Valenti, President of the MPAA, presents that organization's stand on the issue with which reporter Chute seems to agree. (2 illus.)

39 Cook, J. "Look at All the Naked Ladies." *Forbes*, 122:92, Sept. 18, 1978.

On the strength of his unparalleled financial success as an independent filmmaker, Meyer is dubbed by Cook "the Hugh Hefner of the adult-movie business." (1 illus.)

*40 Dante, Joseph J. "The Phenomenon of Russ Meyer." *Film Bulletin*, 39(7):10–11, 14, Apr. 6, 1970.

With Meyer's prestige presently at "an all-time high" thanks to his own efforts, Dante traces the filmmaker's rise to his current status as a director making *Beyond the Valley of the Dolls* for 20th Century–Fox. Dante, who later came to direct *Gremlins*, says of Meyer's direction that at best it "has a riveting vitality and imagination comparable to that of Sam Fuller." Highly recommended. (2 illus.)

41 "Debate Whether Women Exploited by Russ Meyer." *Variety*, 284:6, Oct. 20, 1976.

A brief newspaper account (datelined San Antonio, Oct. 19) of a debate between Meyer and feminist Massachusetts State Representative Elaine Noble on the topic "X-Rated Films: Exploiters of Women?" Co-sponsored by the Student Activities Board of Trinity University and Santikos Theatres.

42 "Director Disputes Film, Crime Link." *Lynchburg News*, Sec. C, pp. 1–2, Sept. 30, 1973.

Speaking at a conference on pornography at the College of William and Mary, Meyer denies that any demonstrable relation exists between the explicit depiction of sex on film and any social ill like crime.

43 Dittman, Stevan C. "Mr. X." *Newsweek*, 75(6):9, Feb. 9, 1970.

In a letter to the editor responding to the January 19, 1970, "Mr. X" article (see entry **557**), a reader thanks Meyer for tapping into "the hearts of the American conscience" by providing cinematic violence and perversion which afford the silent majority an escape from reality "in the form of a woman's breast."

44 Dudek, Duane. "Legitimacy Aim of Porno Prince." *Milwaukee Sentinel*, sec. Let's Go!, p. 22, May 9, 1975.

Dudek portrays Meyer in passing as a sexploitationist concerned with gaining respectability and legitimacy.

45 Eagan, Gary. "Skinflick King Explains Movies." *Record Searchlight*, p. 22, Sept. 22, 1979.

Meyer champions the "A" (Adult) rating as a buffer between the current "X" and "R" ratings set down by the Motion Picture Association of America. The filmmaker also explains his preference for the terms "limbercore" or "raucous comedies" as descriptions of his softcore sex films. (1 illus.)

*46 Ebert, Roger. "...And a Critic." *Wall Street Journal*, 171(91):16, May 8, 1968.

In the letter to the editor of the *Wall Street Journal* which served as the basis of his friendship with the film-maker, Roger Ebert commends the newspaper for "recognizing the unsung talent of Russ Meyer" and likens him to action directors like Howard Hawks and Henry Hathaway. Prophetically, Ebert asks why a major studio has yet to sign the independent Meyer who can produce "technically . . . alive and interesting work" for a fraction of a studio budget. Highly recommended. See entry 77.

*47   Ebert, Roger. "Russ Meyer: King of the Nudies." *Film Comment,* 9(1):34–45, Jan./Feb. 1973.

In what is surely one of the finest articles ever written on the filmmaker, film critic-collaborator-friend Roger Ebert traces Meyer's long career up through preproduction on *Blacksnake!* Interwoven with this excellent chronology are incisive comments on Meyer's directorial style, his "symbolism," and Ebert's own perceptions of working with the filmmaker on *Beyond the Valley of the Dolls.* Includes a "Russ Meyer Filmography." Absolutely essential reading. (3 illus.) For an update of this article see entry **48.**

*48   Ebert, Roger. "Russ Meyer: King of the Nudies (1973)." *Kings of the Bs: Working Within the Hollywood System,* pp. 110–132. Ed. by Todd McCarthy and Charles Flynn. New York: Dutton, 1975.

Ebert's January 1973 *Film Comment* piece (see entry **47**) is reprinted here with an added "Postscript, 1974" that briefly mentions the box office disappointment *Blacksnake!,* the initial shooting on *Supervixens,* and Ebert's "in-progress" script for the proposed *Beyond, Beyond.* Highly recommended. (1 illus.)

*49   Ebert, Roger. "Why Meyer Is King of the Skin Flicks." *Chicago Sun-Times,* sec. 5, pp. 1, 4, Feb. 16, 1969.

Days before the opening of *Vixen* in Chicago, Ebert convincingly argues that Meyer, "the last great undiscovered American director," deserves *auteur-*status for the "consistent artistic vi-

sion (that) dominates" his films. Meyer's impact on film is discussed with Ebert pointing out that the director invented the American "roughie," *Lorna,* and has now crashed through the ranks of respectable first-run houses with *Vixen* and *Finders Keepers, Lovers Weepers!* An excellent, early article that Ebert has expanded upon throughout his many thoughtful appreciations on Meyer. Highly recommended. (1 illus.)

50   Edwards, Ellen. "Russ Meyer: Money, Sex Keep 'King Leer' Making Movies." *Miami Herald,* sec. B, p. 7, Nov. 17, 1976.

Among other topics, Meyer reminisces about his tenure at 20th Century–Fox, his marital history, and how the motion picture Establishment perceives him. (2 illus.)

51   "Even 'Teas' Prod. Upset by 'Curious'." *Variety,* 255(5):5, June 18, 1969.

Responding to the financial success of and hardcore erotica in *I Am Curious (Yellow),* Meyer concedes that while he is against censorship, he feels that in portraying cinematic sexual depictions something should be left to the filmgoer's imagination.

52   "Feminist, Meyer to Debate Porn." *San Antonio Express-News,* sec. C, p. 8, Oct. 9, 1976.

The Trinity University–sponsored debate between Meyer and Elaine Noble, a State Representative of Massachusetts, on the topic of whether X-rated films exploit women is announced. (1 illus.)

53   Flores, Michael. "Target USA." *It's Only a Movie,* 2(6):3, 1987.

In Chicago for the Consumer Electronics Show, Meyer emcees a "Leave It to Cleavage" contest at the Limelight, a popular Windy City nightspot.

54   Fredericks, Ronald. "Celebrity Balling." *Man's World,* 23(9):16–18, Sept. 1977.

In a men's magazine survey, Meyer (along with several other sex celebrities including the late Althea Flynt, Al Goldstein, and Blaze Starr) was asked who he fantasized about being intimate with. His straightforward reply: "I've had the best. Why settle for less?" (6 illus.)

*55 Fugett, Steve; Holmes, Pat; and Holm, Douglas. "Interview with Russ Meyer." *Cinemonkey*, 5(2): 57–59, Spring 1979.

Meyer is questioned concerning stylistic influences his early years as a military newsreel photographer and industrial filmmaker have exerted on his later sex films. Examples of industrial filmmaking techniques in *Up!* and *Beneath* are discussed. Recommended.

56 Goosenberg, Ellen. "Supervixen Russ Meyer." *The Drummer*, p. 13, July 29, 1975.

Meyer discusses the reasons people attend his films, the controversy caused by his work in feminist circles, and his reasons for not making hardcore films. (2 illus.)

57 Haber, Joyce. "Celebrities Pick Their Favorite Sexpots." *Los Angeles Times*, sec. Calendar, p. 13, Jan. 28, 1973.

Asked to name the "sexiest woman in the world," Meyer picks Israeli prime minister Golda Meir because of his admiration and respect for her as a stateswoman. Wife Edy Williams chooses Dr. Aaron Stern, president of the Motion Picture Association Code and Ratings Board, whom she describes as "cool sex." (Illus.)

58 Habinski, Harald. "Meyer: Shining Beacon of Free Enterprise; Specialist in Producing Cinematic Sludge." *The South End*, p. 3, July 18, 1975.

Habinski accuses Meyer of producing "cinematic sludge" that panders to the "lowest common denominator" in people. For Habinski, Meyer's ability to provide what the market demands makes the filmmaker "a shining beacon in the annals of free enterprise." (1 illus.)

*59 Harmetz, Aljean. "Oh, Those Beautiful Dolls!" *New York Times*,

sec. II, p. 17, Dec. 21, 1969.

Written during the production of *Beyond the Valley of the Dolls*, Harmetz' personality piece on Meyer is strikingly rich in biographical detail and highly recommended. (2 illus.)

60 Hernon, Fran. "Naughty But Nice." *London Daily Mirror*, pp. 13–14, Oct. 9, 1980.

A biographical article that incorrectly identifies Meyer's second wife and long-time business partner, Eve Meyer, as Edy Williams. Reflecting back over his career-to-date, Meyer states that he has reached every goal he has ever set for himself. (3 illus.)

61 "His Pix Extend His Fantasies; She Says, 'You're Adolescent'." *Variety*, 284:34, Oct. 27, 1976.

An article reporting on the Trinity University–sponsored debate between Russ Meyer, "producer of X-rated Mammalia motion pictures," and the feminist State Representative Elaine Noble of Massachusetts on the topic "X-Rated Films: Exploiters of Women?"

62 Hoskyns, Barney. "Thanks for the Mammaries." *New Musical Express*, p. 19, Jan. 22, 1983.

An unfocused survey touching on various aspects of Meyer's life and career. Meyer's discussion of his "drive-in Steinbeck" period which featured such films as *Motorpsycho!* (1965) and *Faster, Pussycat! Kill! Kill!* (1966) is useful as are his thoughts on the disastrous *Who Killed Bambi?*, the failed Sex Pistols film. (2 illus.)

63 Huddy, John. "In Meyer's Case Trash Pays Cash." *Miami Herald*, sec. A, p. 20, Oct. 17, 1979.

Huddy assesses Meyer's films as "trash, but well-photographed trash." (1 illus.)

64 Hunt, Don. "Emotions Flare in Sex Debate." *Norfolk Virginian-Pilot*, sec. B, p. 3, Oct. 1, 1973.

A sparsely attended conference on pornography and the law held at the College of William and Mary provoked heated discussion among the panelists who included Ronald Garst, publisher of the *National Ball;* Robert K. Dornan, national spokesperson for Citizens for Decency Through Law; Gerard Damiano, director of *Deep Throat;* and film critic Judith Crist. While Meyer sat on the panel and is pictured, the article fails to mention him. (4 illus.)

65 Jacaway, Taffy. "X-Rated Producer Lets Hair Down, Down, Down, Down." *Tacoma News-Journal,* p. 6, July 4, 1975.

Meyer discusses the European market for his films and states what Jacaway terms his "philosophy in a nutshell": never replace a fine bosom with a fine actress. (1 illus.)

66 "Jackson Revives Meyer Sexers, Waters Pics, for Paris Reprise." *Variety,* 313:23, Dec. 28, 1983.

The impressive commercial success of Meyer's films in France, especially Paris, is discussed in a biographical piece on the filmmaker's French distributor and biographer, Jean-Pierre Jackson of Sinfonia Films. Jackson's efforts to distribute the films of another American independent filmmaker, John Waters, are also discussed.

*67 Kahrl, William L. "Peep Show Becomes Fine Art: The Transmogrification of Russ Meyer." *World's Fair,* 2(4):1–6, Fall 1982.

An excellent article that convincingly argues that Meyer's high quality softcore satires of American sexual preoccupations effectively preserve and nurture the innocent "thrill of the peep show." The impact of *The Immoral Mr. Teas* and *Lorna* is discussed with Kahrl likening the world created in Meyer's films to that of *L'il Abner.* Meyer was so impressed by this article that he chose to reprint it in its entirety as the preface to the filmography in his autobiography, *A Clean Breast: The Life and Loves of Russ Meyer.* Highly recommended. (4 illus.)

68 Knoblauch, Mary. "Russ Meyer: Master of the Skin Flick 'Put On'."

Chicago Today American, sec. Now, pp. 1, 10, Mar. 22, 1970.

A nice biographical piece which discusses Meyer's recent entry into mainstream filmmaking as well as his past career as a successful independent producer of "skin-flicks." Knoblauch admits that Meyer's gentlemanly demeanor and articulately presented theories on filmmaking shattered her preconception of him as the "typical 'Grade B' movie dirty old man." (1 illus.)

69 Koch, Ruth. "'Walt Disney of Skinflicks': Russ Meyer Revels in His Role." *Sun-Tattler,* sec. D, pp. 2, 29, Nov. 19, 1976.

Meyer states that after having been called everything from the "Walt Disney of the Skin Flick" to the "Chaucer of the 70's," he now revels in his title of the "King of porno movies." (1 illus.)

70 Kupcinet, Irv. "Kup's Column." *Chicago Sun-Times,* p. 54, July 13, 1970.

On Kup's talk show, Meyer relates a war story in which General George Patton ordered the assassination of Adolf Hitler and Hermann Goering because he feared no court would sentence them to death.

71 Lague, Louise. "Russ Meyer: Back in the Soft Core Business." *Washington Star,* sec. H, pp. 1, 12, June 29, 1975.

A standard example of one of the numerous articles written around the opening of *Supervixens* reporting on Meyer's happiness at returning to the milieu he created; the world of independently produced softcore sex films.

72 Lazare, Lewis. "Russ Meyer Analyses His Own Films, 'No Losers'." *Variety,* 296:22, Sept. 26, 1979.

Meyer assesses himself as an *auteur* whose independently produced sex films compete directly with those of the major studios.

73 Lees, David, and Berkowitz, Stan. "Into the Valley of the 'Ultravixen'." *Washington Post,* sec. H,

p. 9, Mar. 18, 1979.
Same as entry 74.

74 Lees, David, and Berkowitz, Stan. "Russ Meyer, One-Man Movie Machine, Is at It Again." *Los Angeles Times,* sec. Calendar, pp. 18–19, Jan. 7, 1979.

On location in Rosamond, California, to do some insert shots for *Beneath,* Meyer (accompanied by "Kitten" Natividad) talks about the challenges of independent film production which include dealing with actors, labor unions, and the press. Former Meyer actors Charles Pitts *(Supervixens),* Phyllis Davis *(Beyond the Valley of the Dolls),* and Uschi Digard (*Cherry, Harry & Raquel* ... [et al.]) also reminisce about working with the filmmaker. (1 illus.)

75 Lenne, Gérard. "Les Gros Roberts illustrés." *Lui,* 225:64–66, 150, 158, 160, 162, Nov. 1982.

A long, but somewhat disappointing article on Meyer that provides basic biographical information on the filmmaker touching on his international censorship problems (France denied *Vixen* an import license) and noting the fact that it has taken seven years for *Supervixens* (1975) to appear in Paris. (1 illus.)

76 Losano, Wayne A. "Romance and Irony in the Films of Russ Meyer." *Journal of Popular Culture,* 4(1): 286–291, Summer 1970.

An application by Professor Losano of the principles outlined in Northrop Frye's book *Anatomy of Criticism* to a consideration of the romantic and ironic elements in three Meyer films—*Vixen, Common-Law Cabin,* and *Cherry, Harry & Raquel.* This article posits as an explanation for the success of the three films under discussion, Meyer's "skillful blending of romantic archetypes and irony." Losano concludes by denigrating Meyer's latest film, *Beyond the Valley of the Dolls.*

*77 Lovelady, Steven M. "King Leer: Top 'Nudie' Film-maker, Russ Meyer, Scrambles to Outshock Big

Studios." *Wall Street Journal,* pp. 1, 25, Apr. 24, 1968.

A landmark article that succeeded in bringing public recognition to Meyer beyond the narrow field of film enthusiasts. In it, Meyer's influence on the sexual explicitness featured in major studio films is discussed as is the huge financial success his films have enjoyed in relation to their minuscule budgets. Besides being one of the first "legitimate press" studies on Meyer, this piece also served to introduce the filmmaker to Roger Ebert when the critic wrote to the paper applauding its story and praising Meyer's directorial style (see entry 46). Highly recommended.

*78 Mahar, Ted. "Director's Billing Reflects New Fan." *The Oregonian,* sec. 1, p. 13, Sept. 21, 1970.

An excellent article that discusses Meyer's name recognition among the general public as witnessed by its prominent display on two downtown Portland movie marquees for his films *Beyond the Valley of the Dolls* and *Cherry, Harry & Raquel.* Mahar's thoughtful assessment of the structure ("like musicals"), themes ("punishment," "puritanism"), and technical aspects in Meyer's cinema is also of importance. Highly recommended. (1 illus.)

79 Malina, Martin. "Better Than Volleyball." *Montreal Star,* sec. Entertainments, p. 47, Mar. 7, 1970.

A good historical article that traces the evolution of Meyer's career from the "nudies" *(The Immoral Mr. Teas)* through the "roughies" *(Lorna)* and finally up to the present with his acceptance by the Hollywood Establishment, 20th Century–Fox, to direct *Beyond the Valley of the Dolls* and three other films. (1 illus.)

*80 Martin, James. "Film Talk." *Hustler,* 2(3):23, Sept. 1975.

With box office receipts for triple-X films sagging, the uncertain trend in the adult film industry toward either hardcore or softcore eroticism is examined with filmmakers Gerard Damiano *(Deep Throat)* and Meyer representing the two respective trends. While Damiano blames the sluggish box office on the lack of production quality in hardcore films, Meyer believes an audience exists for both hard and softcore if it is done well although he personally feels that the depiction of penetration is unerotic and "best left to the imagination." Recommended.

81 McGillivray, David. "Q & A." *Films and Filming,* 24(4):46, Jan. 1978.

Biographical material and a filmography are offered in response to a reader's request for information on Meyer. Of note, none of the director's films were publicly shown in Britain until *Fanny Hill* in 1964. Note: the film did not play in the U.S. until 1965.

82 McIntyre, Dave. "Front Row." *San Diego Evening Tribune,* sec. B, p. 18, May 7, 1969.

The Motion Picture Association of America's rating system is reviewed and Meyer contends that the organization has not been strict enough in applying its ratings to major studio releases *(Candy, The Fox, Blow-Up)* which depict nudity and aberrant sexual behavior. Citing the competition of the majors, Meyer admits that the inclusion of more sensational material in his self-imposed X-rated *Vixen* is his reaction to the trend of the times which he assesses as "Permissiveness is the rule of the day."

*83 Meisel, Myron. "Over, Around, Through and Beyond the Valley of the Super-Meyers." *Reader: Los Angeles Weekly,* 1(24):7, 14, Apr. 13, 1979.

Meisel's literate examination of Meyer's film style compares and contrasts his editing practices with those of D.W. Griffith, Alfred Hitchcock, and Sergei Eisenstein. The negative impact Meisel feels scriptwriter Roger Ebert *(Beyond the Valley of the Dolls)* has exercised on Meyer's subsequent films is also examined. Recommended. (1 illus.)

84 Melcher, R. "Tundi: Le Bombe de Russ Meyer." *Newlook* (French ed.), 43:63–73, Mars 1987.

Much of the talk in this French men's magazine interview with Meyer centers around Tundi, his 19-year-old Hungarian discovery, whose multi-page pictorial here acts as a teaser for her appearance in his autobiographical opus *The Breast of Russ Meyer.* Meyer also speaks of losing his virginity with the help of Ernest Hemingway, his days in industrial filmmaking, and his financial support of agencies fighting cancer. (18 illus.)

85 "Memories for Meyer." *Daily Variety,* 146(27):3, Jan. 15, 1970.

The press preview of *Patton* holds many fond memories for Meyer, a former combat photographer, whose uncredited World War II action footage is intercut into the film.

86 "Mensch Meyer." *High Society* (German ed.), 6:64–66, Juni 1986.

Meyer talks about the women in his films and likens them to "superbly made cartoons" that do not threaten most women because their outrageous figures make them "beyond women." (10 illus.)

87 Merrick, Hélène. "Russ Meyer: Starflesh! Sexe, violence et génie." *Starfix,* 20:22–23, Nov. 1984.

In Paris for the belated opening of *Hollywood Vixens (Beyond the Valley of the Dolls),* Meyer is asked his thoughts on being a director and to expand on the sexual elements in his work. Meyer answers that as a director he is "eager to get into the mud," i.e. to become involved in every aspect of the film. He prefers to express "erotic tension" and the escalation of violence through light, settings, and ambiance rather than through explicit hardcore. Merrick notes the influence of both Faulkner and Erskine Caldwell on Meyer in his presentation in numerous films of "poor whites." (3 illus.)

*88 Meyer, Russ. *The Glamour Camera of Russ Meyer.* Louisville,

Ky.: Whitestone Publications, 1958.

Described by Meyer as the culmination of his work in "tittyboom," this rare pulp publication features some beautiful pinup shots of Anita Ekberg, Tina Louise, Sabrina, and Meyer's second wife, Eve, who is prominently featured in a chapter entitled "Nearly All About Eve" in which he describes their meeting, marriage, and professional relationship. A real treasure. (Hundreds of illus.)

89 Meyer, Russ. "Hits Censorship Sees Film Erotica Passing." *Entertainment Today,* UNKNOWN, Dec. 30, 1970.

Meyer predicts that the "extreme sexuality in films will pass" because viewers will become bored by it. The filmmaker also airs his views on censorship, which he calls "persecution," and notes that his production *The Seven Minutes* will make a serious point about "politically inspired" censorship. (1 illus.)

*90 Meyer, Russ. "The Low-Budget Producer." *The Movie Business: American Film Industry Practice,* pp. 179–182. Ed. by A. William Bluem and Jason E. Squire. New York: Hastings House, 1979.

Meyer discusses the economics of low-budget film production using his $72,000 *Vixen* as an example of how his films start with and maintain a "budgetary formula ... through direct economies during production and post-production." The importance of guaranteed distribution for the independent film producer is also discussed with Meyer explaining the structure and significance of his distribution network composed of 19 regional representatives. A primer for the independent filmmaker. Highly recommended.

91 Meyer, Russ. "My Friend Cleavage." *Oui,* 5(8):54–56, 96, Aug. 1976.

Meyer's satirical paean to cleavage could easily be subtitled "Everything You Always Wanted to Know About Cleavage, But Were Afraid to Ask." Filled with his fond remembrances of its manifestations on schoolmates, countergirls, French hookers, and various "rutting partners," the article also traces the historical development of cleavage from its Hollywood heyday in the forties and fifties to its almost virtual disappearance from the pages of the top contemporary fashion magazines. (8 illus.)

92 "Meyer and 2 Feminists Exchange Barbs at Yale." *New York Times,* p. 38, Mar. 4, 1970.

A brief report on a verbal exchange between Meyer and two New York feminists during the two day "Russ Meyer Film Festival" at Yale. The women, Lucy Kosimar of the National Organization of Women (NOW), and Nanette Rainone, producer of "Womankind" on WBAI radio, denounced Meyer for portraying sex as something "sinful and evil."

93 "Meyer Meets Mello in Cleavage 'Bordello'." *Adult Video News Confidential,* 1(29):26, Sept. 1987.

While in Chicago to attend the Consumer Electronics Show, Meyer serves as an emcee for the "First Annual Leave It to Cleavage" bosom festival at the Limelight nightclub.

94 Minson, John. "Bazoom Lens." *Time Out,* 770:12, May 23–29, 1985.

An article appearing in the London entertainment guide, *Time Out,* that profiles Meyer as "the last great Hollywood maverick." (2 illus.)

*95 Morton, Jim. "Russ Meyer Biography." *Re/Search: Incredibly Strange Films,* 10:86–87, 1986.

Featuring a detailed discussion of several key films, Morton traces the evolution of Meyer's career from his early days as a "nudie-cutie" director up through his last film, *Beneath.* Morton concludes, "...Meyer remains a genuine character and true original who—at his best—is unbeatable. His position in film history is assured." Highly recommended.

96 Ornstein, Bill. "Russ Meyer Praises Stern and the MPAA Rating System." *Hollywood Reporter,* 218 (14):12, Oct. 7, 1971.

Meyer does an about face and praises Dr. Aaron Stern, administrator of the Code & Rating System, after several sessions spent with him discussing proposed changes in *Vixen* and *Beyond the Valley of the Dolls* that would alter their X-ratings to more financially lucrative R-ratings resulting in an estimated 2000 additional playdates for *Beyond the Valley of the Dolls* and a $2 million profit added to its $8 million gross-to-date.

97 Petryni, Mike. "Scrambling Xs, Rs." *Arizona Republic,* sec. B, p. 11, Apr. 19, 1977.

Uncharacteristically, Meyer complains that the liberalization of the Motion Picture Association of America's ratings code (which has resulted in several of his films being changed from "X" to "R") has forced him to be even more inventive and bold in depicting simulated sex in order to retain the desired X-rating.

98 "Pionier der Fleischeslust." *Hollywood,* 8:28–32, Aug. 1986.

A biographical piece on the "uncrowned King of the Sexfilm," which is of minor interest because it briefly discusses his first wife, Betty Valdovinos, as well as his other two wives, Eve Meyer and Edy Williams. (5 illus.)

99 Pittner, Hanno. "Mit Großen Busen macht Meyer Millionen." *Quick,* 11:103, 106, Mar. 5–11, 1981.

A standard personality piece on Meyer that discusses his wives, films, and breast fixation. (7 illus.)

100 "Porn Producer Is Not Ashamed of His Films." *Fresno Bee,* sec. H, p. 8, Sept. 21, 1979.

Meyer explains the strategy he employs to answer critics who charge him with corrupting youth and degrading women is to simply agree with them.

101 Porter, Bob. "Russ Meyer: He's the Father of Mainstream Movie Nudity." *Dallas Times Herald,* sec. C, pp. 1, 6, Mar. 19, 1979.

Meyer is identified as the "Father of Mainstream Movie Nudity," and credited with bringing first-rate production values and humor to the depiction of screen nudity. (1 illus.)

102 Rayns, Tony. "Dolls, Vixens, and Supervixens in the Films of Russ Meyer." *Late Night Video,* 2(2): 32–35, 1983.

A biographical sketch on the filmmaker Rayns dubs "the ultimate Tit man" which traces Meyer's cinematic transition from sex comedies to sex cartoons. Each film is briefly discussed with Meyer offering comments on the more historically important films like *The Immoral Mr. Teas* and *Lorna.* (12 illus.)

103 "The Remarkable Russ Meyer." *Show,* 2(4):42–44, June 1972.

Meyer's "remarkable" career is superficially treated in an unremarkable article. (6 illus.)

104 Riley, Miriam K. "Criticism..." *Wall Street Journal,* 171(91):16, May 8, 1968.

A West Lafayette, Indiana, resident reacts angrily to the *Wall Street Journal* article (see entry 77) featuring Meyer and condemns the newspaper's editor for providing "free publicity" to a smut peddler. Ebert's letter supporting Meyer (see entry 46) appeared with this response.

105 Rosenbaum, David. "The Man Behind the Casabas." *Boston Phoenix,* 4(31): sec. 2, p. 3, Aug. 5, 1975.

Meyer is discussed in a tongue-in-cheek manner as an *auteur* with a consistent filmic vision. (1 illus.)

106 "Russ Meyer Speaks Tonight at Irvine." *Daily Variety,* 151(26):8, Apr. 12, 1971.

Meyer is set to address a University of California at Irvine Cinema Arts class on "The Role of Contemporary Films in Modern Society."

107 "Russ Meyer Talks to Young Couples in Encino." *Hollywood Reporter*, 213(2):12, Sept. 24, 1970.

Meyer, set to begin production on *The Seven Minutes* for 20th Century–Fox on October 12, is scheduled to address The Young Couples Club of the Temple Valley Beth Shalom in Encino on the topic, "Censorship and Right of Free Expression in Films."

108 "Russ Meyer Titles Added to the Ivy Film Catalog." *Boxoffice*, 113 (7):11, May 22, 1978.

Recognizing Meyer's "auteur" status, a spokesperson for New York–based Ivy Film announces that the firm has acquired exclusive non-theatrical rights to all of Meyer's films. The company's catalog now contains over 1200 feature films.

109 "Russ Meyer's Next Film to Be Made in Georgia." *Boxoffice*, 95 (7):SW-4, June 2, 1969.

Jack Vaughn, president of Jack Vaughn Productions (the Atlanta distributor for Eve Productions), discloses Meyer's intention to begin an October shooting in the north Georgia mountains on a film tentatively titled *Billie Jo*. According to Vaughn, another possible Meyer project with the working title *Moonshine Massacre* will also be filmed in Georgia.

110 Russell, Candice. "This Man Has Wild Fantasies." *Miami Herald*, sec. H., pp. 1, 5, Nov. 30, 1975.

Though admitting his films document his own outrageous fantasies, Meyer denies that they actually reflect his behavior in reality. (1 illus.)

111 Sabatier, J.M. "Mondo Erotico." *Revue du Cinéma*, 309–310:243, Oct. 1976.

Though the distributor of *Mondo erotico* bills this as a "Russ Meyer film," none of his work is represented except a few excerpts from *Fanny Hill*. In actuality, it is a feeble attempt to survey screen eroticism by stringing together clips from various blue movies and using the star value of Meyer's name to exploit this Purity Pictures production. The film fails, for Sabatier, because it is "too timid."

112 Sasso, Joey. "Russ Meyer … King of X." *Swingle*, 2(5):22–23, 68–69, July 1971.

Though rife with factual errors, Sasso's career piece on Meyer in the men's magazine *Swingle* contains the filmmaker's comments on his diverse film audience and the effects his past marital history have exerted on the portrayal of women in his films. (2 illus.)

113 Smith, Desmond. "Pop Sex Among the Squares." *Nation*, 209(5):142–145, Aug. 25, 1969.

The social and financial phenomenon of "pop pornography" is examined by Smith as represented by the works of Meyer, Jacqueline Susann, Al Goldstein of the sex tabloid *Screw*, and *Playboy* publisher Hugh Hefner. The 1957 Supreme Court decision of Roth vs. the United States which allowed local community standards to determine what is obscene is cited as providing the impetus for pop pornographers to expand. (1 illus.)

114 Taylor, Robert. "Filmmaker Can't Explain Appeal." *Oakland Tribune*, sec. B, p. 9, Sept. 25, 1979.

As the title suggests, Meyer is at a loss to explain the popular appeal of his films although he admits to making them only to appeal to his own prurient interest. (2 illus.)

115 Themal, Harry F. "Meyer Is Auteur of Sex Films." *News Journal*, sec. F, pp. 1–2, July 17, 1983.

Meyer is discussed as an American *auteur* in a career article which focuses heavily on Meyer's experiences in World War II and the continued relationships he enjoys with his former service friends.

116 Thien, Alex. "Meyer More Than Porno Prince." *Milwaukee Sentinel*, pt. 3, p. 1, Nov. 8, 1976.

A biographical article that reports on the dramatic split in the public's perception of Meyer as either an opportunistic pornographer or else a gifted filmmaker whose movies accurately reflect the times. (1 illus.)

117 Thistle, Frank. "King Leer." *Adam Film World,* 7(6):10–14, 66, Sept. 1979.

A below average men's magazine article seemingly compiled from various other published sources which offers nothing new on Meyer. (7 illus.)

118 Trigger, Craig. "Russ Meyer Keeps Few Secrets: 'I'm in Business for Greed, Lust'." *Miami Hurricane,* p. 8, Nov. 19, 1976.

A personality piece on Meyer that comments on his candidness and straightforward honesty in answering questions ranging from his sexual fantasies, film career, and former marriages. (1 illus.)

119 Waters, John. "John Waters' Tour of L.A." *Rolling Stone,* 452/453:55–56, 58, 60, 62, July 18–Aug. 1, 1985.

John Waters, cult director of films like *Pink Flamingos* and *Polyester,* escorts the reader on a specialized tour of Los Angeles featuring such highlights as Frederick's of Hollywood and the Pet Haven Cemetery-Crematory. The so-called "Russ Meyer Museum" (as dubbed by Waters) containing the director's extensive collection of memorabilia documenting the entirety of his film career is discussed as is the Other Ball, a strip club where some of his actresses have been discovered, and Maureen of Hollywood, the costume designer for many of Meyer's later films. (8 illus.)

120 Weaver, Emmett. "Meyer, King of Nudie Films, Visits City." *Birmingham Post-Herald,* sec. A, p. 10, Aug. 14, 1975.

A biographical article touching on several well-known aspects of Meyer's filmmaking career. (1 illus.)

121 White, Ron. "Battle of Sexes Goes X-Rated in Debate Over Meyer's Films." *San Antonio Express-News,* sec. B, p. 5, Oct. 12, 1976.

A detailed report on the October 11, 1976, Trinity University–sponsored debate between Meyer and feminist Elaine Noble, Democratic state representative from Boston, on the topic of whether or not X-rated films exploit women.

122 White, Ron. "Exploit? Of Course Art Exploits." *San Antonio Sunday Express-News,* sec. H, p. 7, Oct. 17, 1976.

In the wake of a Trinity University–sponsored debate between Meyer and Massachusetts State Representative Elaine Noble on the topic of whether X-rated films exploit women, White explores the concept of exploitation as it is manifested in "art" and "popular culture." (1 illus.)

123 Winakor, Beth. "People . . . and Things." *Chicago Sun-Times,* p. 75, Nov. 17, 1976.

Meyer comments on the women in his life (Edy Williams, Raven De La Croix) and those he admires (Jeanne Moreau, Germaine Greer). (5 illus.)

V. FESTIVALS AND RETROSPECTIVES

124 Assayas, Olivier. "Russ Meyer a-t-il sa place ici?" *Cahiers du Cinéma* (Le Journal des cahiers section no. 14), 322: ix, Apr. 1981.

A short personality piece on Meyer prompted by the upcoming Avignon Festival which will honor him, Billy Wilder, and Orson Welles with film retrospectives. Assayas notes that Meyer's humor is inherited from both the Marx Brothers and *Mad* magazine.

125 Berry, Jeff. "Bosom Buddies: Russ and Roger in a Trip Down Mammary Lane." *UCLA Daily Bruin,* 103(10):18–19, Oct. 5, 1978.

A few days before a Russ Meyer festival at the Nuart Theatre in Los Angeles, UCLA student Jeff Berry interviews the filmmaker and his friend/collaborator Roger Ebert concerning *Beyond the Valley of the Dolls* and the soon-to-be-released *Beneath.* Speaking candidly, Meyer ascribes his artistic success and current recognition as an *auteur* to his lifelong love for and obsession with breasts adding that while he does not have the capability to make "The Great Movie," he does have "a hell of a good time" filming his fantasies. (3 illus.)

126 Bockover, Linda, and Elliott, Stuart. "Russ Briefs His Fans on 'B.V.D.' Film." *Daily Northwestern,* 92(8):4, Oct. 1, 1971.

Following the showing of *Beyond the Valley of the Dolls,* the Russ Meyer Film Festival concludes with a panel discussion composed of Meyer, his attorney Elmer Gertz, and film critic Roger Ebert. Despite Gertz's announcement that the Illinois Supreme Court had reversed the city of Danville's suit finding *Vixen* to be obscene, Meyer maintained the decision would not alter his plans to leave skinflicks "for mystery-horror-violence movie production." The counter-movie festival staged by the Pink Pigs, persons protesting Meyer's appearance at Northwestern, is also reported on. (1 illus.) See entry **135.**

127 Bone, Harold. "Russ Meyer at Yale: 'Know Little About Porno, My Atty. Sez'." *Variety,* 258(3): 6, Mar. 4, 1970.

Bone reports on the two-day "Russ Meyer Film Festival" sponsored by the Yale Law School Film Society and notes that in Meyer's address to the group he purposely avoided the word "pornography" on advice of counsel.

128 Dexter, Jim. "Meyer Moves the Mountains to NU." *Daily Northwestern,* 92(9):5, Oct. 5, 1971.

Dexter, associate editor of the *Daily Northwestern,* did not attend the Russ Meyer Film Festival because of a past disappointment with a Meyer triple bill shown at a local theatre. In concluding his commentary, Dexter summarizes all of Meyer's films as "the same old bump and grind."

129 Dubson, Geof. "Russ Meyer—Sex Films Can Be Fun to Make." *Daily Illini,* p. 21, Apr. 2, 1971.

While the attending student body of the University of Illinois apparently had raucous fun at the Cinemaguild's Russ Meyer Film Festival, Dubson expresses regret that Meyer, "an engaging and talented individual," was not accorded "more serious consideration" during the question and answer period which followed the showing of *BVD.*

*130 Ebert, Roger. "The King of the Nudies: Recognition Finally Arrives for Russ Meyer." *St. Louis Post-Dispatch,* sec. Sunday, pp. 14–15, Feb. 20, 1983.

The British Film Institute's recognition of Meyer at a National Film Theatre retrospective of his work marks for Ebert a "personal vindication" of his long-time interest in and respect for the filmmaker he considers a true American *auteur.* Initially attracted to Meyer's work by its physically abundant female stars, Ebert later recognized the filmmaker's style and ultimately admired his movies because he saw in them "a sly, farcical intelligence at work." In conclusion, Ebert suggests that the "key to the work of Russ Meyer" is to be found "in the man himself." One of the best articles on Meyer that is absolutely essential to an understanding of him both as a man and as a filmmaker. Highly recommended.

*131 Ebert, Roger. "Russ Meyer Busts Sleazy Stereotype." *Chicago Sun-Times,* pp. 39–40, Nov. 15, 1985.

The honoring of Meyer by the Chicago International Film Festival affords Ebert the opportunity to reflect upon the recurrent themes in the filmmaker's work and to assess "his ultimate place in history" which the critic believes will be among "other radical structuralists" like Jean-Luc Godard, Mark Rappaport, Chantal Ackerman, and Sergei Eisenstein, despite the "disreputable"

softcore genre Meyer has chosen to work within. Highly recommended. (2 illus.)

132 Elliott, Stuart. "Coming to NU: Russ Meyer Speaks Wednesday." *Daily Northwestern,* 92(3):1, Sept. 24, 1971.

The Northwestern University Film Society announces the Russ Meyer Film Festival to be held on campus September 28–30. Scheduled throughout the three-film, three-day program are a discussion by *Chicago Sun-Times* film critic Roger Ebert on "the Americanization of the skinflick," a personal appearance by Meyer, and a panel discussion featuring Ebert, Meyer, and attorney Elmer Gertz who is representing Meyer in a current obscenity case against *Vixen.*

133 Elliott, Stuart. "'Engrossed' Students Lend Legitimacy to Meyer Pix." *Daily Northwestern,* 92(9): 5, Oct. 5, 1971.

Interviewed while at Northwestern University for the Russ Meyer Film Festival, Meyer said that he would never refuse an opportunity to exhibit his work at colleges because they lend his films an air of "legitimacy and recognition." Meyer also discussed the plot of his next movie, *The Eleven.* (1 illus.)

134 Elliott, Stuart. "Nudies King Russ Meyer Plans to Renounce Throne." *Daily Northwestern,* 92 (7):1, Sept. 30, 1971.

Following a sold-out screening of *Vixen* on the second of a three-day Russ Meyer Film Festival at Northwestern University, Meyer told an appreciative audience that his decision to make his next independent production a "mystery-violence" film was based on the decline in popularity of skinflicks and the ongoing legal attempts to censor them. (1 illus.)

135 Elliott, Stuart. "Porno Picketed." *Daily Northwestern,* 92(6):1, Sept. 29, 1971.

Wielding picket signs reading "Do you want your daughters to marry Russ Meyer" and "Sex is beautiful—

exploitation is ugly," three protesters calling themselves "The Pink Pigs" verbally "taunted a sell-out crowd" entering an auditorium where a showing of *Cherry, Harry & Raquel* kicked off the Russ Meyer Film Festival at Northwestern University. Following the movie, film critic Roger Ebert informally lectured on the Americanization of the skinflick and noted that Meyer's work represented a "straightforward, All-American sort of pornography" not designed to arouse, but to amuse.

136　Erhert, Jan. "Meyer Says Sex in Films Has Declined." *Champaign-Urbana Courier,* sec. A, p. 24, Mar. 28, 1971.

Noting a three-year decline in the depiction of sex in cinema, Meyer predicts that future audiences will demand a return to escapist, "action-type pictures." In Champaign-Urbana to appear at the Russ Meyer Film Festival sponsored by the University of Illinois Cinemaguild, the filmmaker also criticized screenwriter Roger Ebert for failing to defend their collaborative effort *Beyond the Valley of the Dolls.*

137　"Flesh King Has Fourth Festival." *Hollywood Reporter,* 218(6):8, Sept. 27, 1971.

The three-day Russ Meyer Film Festival to be held at Northwestern from Sept. 28–30 marks the fourth time the director has received university recognition (Yale, University of Illinois, and the University of California) and is but one of several other festivals scheduled by institutions like the Museum of Modern Art, Georgia State University, and Princeton.

138　Gardner, Paul A. "Russ Meyer Retro Too Raunchy; M.P. Raps Film Institute Taste." *Variety,* 287:38, June 15, 1977.

Parliamentary and governmental controversy erupts over a proposed Russ Meyer retrospective to be presented by the Canadian Film Institute at the National Film Theatre.

139　Grant, Lee. "A Salute to Russ Meyer at USC." *Los Angeles Times,* sec. IV, p. 22, May 25, 1979.

Meyer is saluted at the University of Southern California with a two-hour film clip retrospective of his work and a presentation by Delta Kappa Alpha, a national cinema fraternity, making him an honorary member. (3 illus.)

140　Hieronymus, Stan. "King of the Nudies Russ Meyer Says They've Shown All There Is to Show." *Champaign-Urbana News Gazette,* sec. 1, p. 2, Mar. 28, 1971.

Speaking at a press conference prior to his appearance at the Russ Meyer Film Festival at the University of Illinois, Meyer takes UI graduate Roger Ebert to task for letting his fellow critics intimidate him concerning his screenplay for the financially successful *Beyond the Valley of the Dolls.* Also discussed are the legal problems facing *Vixen* in Danville, Illinois, and Meyer's next project for Fox, *The Seven Minutes.* (1 illus.)

141　Hinckley, David. "Russ Meyer Go-for-Bust Flick Fest." *New York Daily News,* sec. Friday, p. 14, Sept. 21, 1984.

Hinckley announces the "Russ Meyer Film Festival: Lust and Greed Together" which runs from September 21 through October 4 at New York City's Bleecker Cinema. Though noting that Meyer produces films "that make Ken Russell look like Frank Capra," Hinckley admits that by comparison with other directors Meyer "was always one piece of flesh ahead of his time." (1 illus.)

142　Horton, Robert. "Beyond, Beneath, and Up!" *The Informer: Monthly Newsletter of the Seattle Film Society,* p. 14, June 1983.

An announcement for a Meyer triple bill at the Neptune Theatre in Seattle on July 4, 1983. Entitled by Meyer "Robust American FUN Movies," the program consists of *Vixen, Supervixens,* and *Beneath.* A lengthy plot synopsis (often inaccurate) and exposition are offered for each film. (1 illus.)

143 Kehr, Dave. "Our Critics' Best Bets." *Chicago Tribune,* sec. 2, p. 2, Nov. 30, 1988.

Kehr announces that *The Immoral Mr. Teas* will kick off "a month-long series of Meyer's engagingly garish sex comedies" at Chicago's Film Center of the Art Institute. Time, Kehr assesses, has transformed the eroticism in Meyer's work into "furiously self-engaged satires on America's oversized tastes in sex and violence."

144 Kimmel, Daniel M. "Controversial Russ Meyer Reflects on Long Career." *Sunday Independent South,* p. 12, Oct. 11, 1987.

Attending a marathon retrospective of his films at the Boston Film Festival, Meyer discusses the history of *The Immoral Mr. Teas,* reminisces about burlesque comedienne Princess Livingston *(Mudhoney, Beyond the Valley of the Dolls),* and states his belief that the commercial outlook for hardcore films is bleak due to product oversaturation. (1 illus.)

145 "Meyer as Yale's Prof. of Porn." *Variety,* 258(2):6, Feb. 25, 1970.

Details are given on the eight-picture, two-day Russ Meyer Film Festival to be held on campus under the auspices of the Yale Law School Film Society.

146 "Meyer Film Fest." *Hollywood Reporter,* 215(13):3, Mar. 5, 1971.

In the interim between completing *The Seven Minutes* for Fox and beginning the studio's *The Big Steal,* Meyer will be honored by the University of Illinois at Champaign with a two-day festival of four of his films set for March 26–27.

147 "Meyer Retrospective Set for Northwestern." *Variety,* 264(5): 7, Sept. 15, 1971.

The Cinema Arts Department of Northwestern University will present a Russ Meyer retrospective followed by a seminar in which he will participate.

148 "New York Museum Honors Russ Meyer." *Hollywood Reporter,* 216

(6):8, May 5, 1971.

Lawrence Kardish, curator and director of New York's Museum of Modern Art, announces a July 1971 Russ Meyer retrospective featuring six films.

149 "Panama Official's Death Postpones Nation's Film Fest." *Daily Variety,* 157(52):1, Nov. 17, 1972.

The sudden death of a Panamanian official postpones the Tenth Annual Panama Film Festival incommoding planned attendees Meyer, Edy Williams, and Elia Kazan.

150 Parsons, Roger. "Profile: Confessions of a Breastfed Man." *Time Out,* 646:9, Jan. 7–13, 1983.

A fun personality piece written during the time Meyer was in London to present a Guardian Lecture at a National Film Theatre restrospective of his films. Topics covered include Meyer as *auteur,* his candid thoughts on the retrospective, and his sexual assessment of "Kitten" Natividad. (1 illus.)

*151 Ressner, Jeffrey. "Russ Meyer Readies 17-Hour, Nine-Cassette Home Vid Epic." *Hollywood Reporter,* 248(50):4, 8, Sept. 18, 1987.

While in Boston for a major retrospective of his work at the Boston Film Festival, Meyer discusses his 17-hour "tone poem," *The Breast of Russ Meyer,* and his plans to not only release the film directly to the home video market, but also to exhibit it at the Cinémathèque Française and London's National Film Theatre. Among other film projects, Meyer also touched upon his upcoming acting role in John Landis' new movie *Amazon Women on the Moon,* his music video directorial debut for the rock band Faster Pussycat!, and his proposed new film *Blitzen, Vixen and Harry* to be shot in Germany in 1988. Recommended.

152 Ross, Alex. "Why Roger Ebert Is Beyond Shame." *Chicago Sun-Times,* p. 39, Nov. 15, 1985.

A *Chicago Sun-Times* colleague of Ebert's humorously reports on the

Since first being honored by the Yale University Law School Film Society in 1970, Meyer has been the recipient of several international awards and retrospectives. Here, Meyer is honored in 1985 at the 21st Chicago International Film Festival.

showing of *Beyond the Valley of the Dolls* as part of the Chicago Film Festival. In attendance are Ebert and Meyer who had not seen the film together for fifteen years. (2 illus.)

153 "Russ Meyer at Yale." *Hollywood Reporter*, 209(19):4, Jan. 9, 1970.
Meyer accepts an invitation from Yale to be present at a seminar on his work to be conducted March 2–3, 1970.

154 "The Russ Meyer Faithful Brave Rain for Marathon." *Variety*, 328:28, Oct. 7, 1987.
A *Variety* report on the 17 ½-hour Russ Meyer marathon which served as a "sidebar event" to the Boston Film Festival. Among other topics, Meyer also discusses *The Breast of Russ Meyer*, his dispute with 20th Century–Fox over their seeming reluctance to video release

Beyond the Valley of the Dolls in the U.S., the success of his "Bosomania" videocassette series, and his proposed next film, *Blitzen, Vixen and Harry* to begin shooting after the 1988 release of Part I of *The Breast of Russ Meyer*. The filmmaker's rock video directorial debut for the Warner/Elektra group *Faster Pussycat!* is also mentioned.

155 "Russ Meyer Festival Starts Sunday at Yale." *Film and TV Daily*, 136(66):8, Feb. 26, 1970.

In the first film festival ever held at Yale since its founding, the Yale Law School Film Society honors Meyer with an eight-picture, two-day-long retrospective which also features a panel discussion, "Sex in American Cinema."

156 "Russ Meyer Film Festival." *Daily Illini*, p. 22, Mar. 24, 1971.

Following closely upon the heels of a restrospective held at Yale, the University of Illinois is the site for a two-night Cinemaguild Russ Meyer Film Festival to be attended by Meyer and his Chicago-based attorney, Elmer Gertz, who in light of the banning of the allegedly obscene *Vixen* in Danville will speak on cinema censorship. The sources of many of the cited photographs are incorrect. (7 illus.)

157 "Russ Meyer Retro at Illinois U." *Hollywood Reporter*, 214(7):3, Dec. 14, 1970.

Meyer accepts an invitation from Cinemaguild, University of Illinois for a March 19–20, 1971 retrospective of his films.

*158 Schickel, Richard. "Porn and Man at Yale." *Harper's*, 241:34, 36–38, July 1970.

Schickel's perceptive article on the Russ Meyer Film Festival held at Yale in late February 1970 and what it actually *meant* to the students and to Meyer alike is essential reading. Though Meyer's "technical facility" should not be confused with art, Schickel does liken the filmmaker's preoccupation with budget, his "concern for and identification with

Middle America," and his ability to film his fantasy life to those of another movie figure honored by Yale in 1938 . . . Walt Disney. Highly recommended.

159 Stanley, John. "Russ Meyer Gets Respect in the Real Movie World." *San Francisco Sunday Examiner & Chronicle*, sec. Datebook, p. 36, Dec. 11, 1983.

A biographical/appreciation piece written to provide background information for an eight-film Meyer restrospective to be held from 12:30 P.M. to midnight at the Strand Theater in San Francisco. (1 illus.)

160 Tozian, Greg. "Director's X-Rated Films Make Him King of Kink." *Tampa Tribune*, sec. D, pp. 1–2, Jan. 25, 1980.

A featured filmmaker in the director's showcase series of the Miami International Film Festival, Meyer, following a screening of *Beyond the Valley of the Dolls*, answers a wide variety of audience questions concerning his career and films. (1 illus.)

161 "Vixen's Director Honoured at Yale." *Canadian Film Weekly*, 35(7):2, Feb. 27, 1970.

Details are given for the eight-film, two-day-long Russ Meyer Film Festival held under the auspices of the Yale Law School Film Society.

162 Voedisch, Lynn. "Rock 'n' Psycho Fest Will Feature Classy Trash." *Chicago Sun-Times*, p. 3, Apr. 18, 1986.

Faster, Pussycat! Kill! Kill! is among the "fun-filled trash-with-flash films" scheduled for the Rock 'n' Psycho Festival sponsored by Chicago's Psychotronic Film Society. (1 illus.)

163 "Women's Org. Pickets Russ Meyer Filmfest." *Daily Variety*, 189(53):22, Nov. 20, 1980.

Three dozen members of the Sacramento, California, Women's Collective picket a one-day Russ Meyer filmfest on the grounds that his films "perpetuate sexual myths." Meyer, noting that such protests sell tickets, filmed the scene for inclusion in his upcoming autobiographical film, *The Breast of Russ Meyer.*

164 X, Mrs. "A 'Curious' Study Comes to an End." *Chicago Tribune,* sec. 2, p. 13, Feb. 19, 1971.

A humorous look, using *Vixen* and the Russ Meyer Film Festival at the Oriental Theater as focal points, at the type of persons who patronize "dirty movies."

165 "Yale to Honor Meyer." *Los Angeles Herald-Examiner,* sec. B, p. 7, Feb. 27, 1970.

Particulars are given on the eight-picture, two-day-long Russ Meyer Film Festival sponsored by the Yale Law School Film Society. The February 29th event represents the first film festival ever held at Yale.

VI. WIVES

Eve Meyer

166 "Eve Meyer, Mike Simon Among Plane Crash Victims." *Daily Variety,* 175(18):19, Mar. 30, 1977.

Eve Meyer is among the estimated 574 people killed in the March 27 aviation disaster in the Canary Islands.

167 Grant, Hank. "Rambling Reporter." *Hollywood Reporter,* 239(9):2, Dec. 1, 1975.

Grant reports that Eve Meyer is completing a book about her years of collaborating with ex-husband Meyer entitled *This Doll Was Not X-Rated.*

168 "Obituaries: Eve Meyer." *Variety,* 286(9):127, Apr. 6, 1977.

Meyer's second wife, Eve (née Turner), is tragically killed on March 27, 1977, in the Tenerife, Canary Islands, aviation disaster. Meyer was 44.

169 Teeman, Larry. "How Eve Meyer Was Changed into Cheesecake." *Modern Man,* 8(3):10–13, 46, Sept. 1958.

While principally a photo layout on Eve Meyer, "a girl who has curves in places most girls don't even have places," a lengthy accompanying article details her initial meeting with Meyer, their eventual marriage, and her transformation by Meyer into one of the top cheesecake models of the late 1950s. (12 illus.)

***170** Wilson, Jane. "What's a Nice Girl Like You Doing in a Business Like This, Eve? (Well, Maybe Crying All the Way to the Bank)." *Los Angeles Times,* sec. WEST Magazine, pp. 16–19, May 9, 1971.

A fine biographical article on Eve Meyer presents the filmmaker's late second wife as a hardworking, self-made career woman. Meyer's career is traced from her early days as Meyer's cheesecake model and lead actress in *Eve and the Handyman* up through her behind-the-camera involvement as co-owner of Eve Productions, the production company and distributor for the number of films produced by Meyer during 1958 and 1969. The article concludes with Meyer's description of the market problems confronting the independent film distributor and the status of her current relationship with ex-husband Meyer. Highly recommended. (5 illus.)

Edy Williams

171 Bacon, James. "Have Rings, Are Wed." *Los Angeles Herald-Examiner,* sec. B, p. 6, Oct. 15, 1974.

Edy Williams writes Bacon from Rome that enthusiastic fans there are actually stripping her bare on the street. Williams, behind a massive publicity campaign, has recently signed for her first Italian film, *Sin in the Family.*

Eve Meyer (circa 1955), the filmmaker's second wife and favorite camera subject, in a "sweater shot" taken by Meyer and reminiscent of glamor queens Lana Turner and Marilyn Monroe. Together, photographer and model, helped define the look and essence of cheesecake photography in the fifties.

172 Coy, Kimberley. "Skin Flick Producer's Wife: Mrs. Russ Meyer— Once a Shy Teen?" *Atlanta Constitution*, sec. B, p. 1, July 13, 1971.

Actress Edy Williams is showcased in a short biographical piece reporting on how she first met husband Meyer. Williams, accompanied by Meyer, was in Atlanta promoting *The Seven Minutes*. (1 illus.)

173 Cassyd, Syd. "Backstage." *Boxoffice*, 102(7):W-2, Nov. 27, 1972.

Edy Williams discusses her early life, career, and involvement in the upcoming Meyer film *Foxy*, set to begin shooting in Hollywood on December 6, 1972. The actress notes that while critics are important they often fail to recognize what "turns the kids on." Meyer, however, according to Williams, respects his audience and strives to give them "something unusual."

174 "Edy Williams Warns Actresses About Sexpo." *Daily Variety,* 171 (13):4, Mar. 24, 1976.

Speaking at a Film Advisory Board luncheon, Edy Williams warns young actresses that appearing in sex-ploitation films could have adverse effects on their careers. Williams claims that following her *Beyond the Valley of the Dolls* role, she was "branded" and found it nearly impossible to obtain work in non-pornographic productions.

175 London, John. "Edy Williams Is Five Feet Eight Inches Tall, with Tawny, Dark Auburn Hair, Sensuous Lips and Titillating Hips, Who Says So? Edy Williams." *London Evening News,* sec. C, p. 5, Feb. 12, 1972.

Interviewed in London, Edy Williams discusses her meeting with Meyer and her initial reluctance to uninhibitedly perform a love scene with Wayne Maunder in *The Seven Minutes* directed by Meyer. The actress praises her husband's industrious nature, but feels he is sometimes "mean" when he neglects her for work. (1 illus.)

176 Grant, Hank. "Rambling Reporter." *Hollywood Reporter,* 227(11):2, July 16, 1973.

The recent release of Edy Williams from a hospital for treatment of a "pinched nerve in her backside" sustained in a rear-end collision with a Bentley and the fact that her license plate reads, SXY EDY, lead Grant to quip "that any doll who can't spell can't be all bad."

177 Mahar, Ted. "Sex-Bomb Reaps Revenge on Men." *The Oregonian,* sec. 3, p. 6, Aug. 26, 1970.

Edy Williams, interviewed in Portland during a promotional tour for *Beyond the Valley of the Dolls,* speaks unflatteringly of men in general, with the exception of husband Meyer. Mahar wonders if comments from the actress comparing men to dogs could be "as big

a put-on" as *Beyond the Valley of the Dolls* and spoken only to promote the film. (1 illus.)

178 Manners, Dorothy. "Edy Williams Giving Up Sex Symbol Status." *Los Angeles Herald-Examiner,* sec. F, p. 4, Mar. 14, 1971.

Edy Williams, denouncing her sex symbol image, believes her husband Meyer can help do for her what Carlo Ponti did for his wife, Sophia Loren ... cast her in roles that showcase her acting ability. (1 illus.)

179 Manners, Dorothy. "Edy Williams Sends Money Back." *Los Angeles Herald-Examiner,* sec. B, p. 2, Oct. 19, 1971.

An appreciative Edy Williams repays sponsor Irv Kupcinet the $500 cash prize she won five years ago as a recipient of the Karyn Kupcinet drama award given to the year's "most promising young known actress." (1 illus.)

180 Moss, Morton. "Have Pity for a Poor Sex Object." *Los Angeles Herald-Examiner,* sec. B, p. 7, Sept. 9, 1971.

Besides lamenting her status as a sex symbol who has yet to be given the chance to act dramatically, Edy Williams describes the initial antagonism between her and Meyer on the set of *Beyond the Valley of the Dolls* which eventually culminated in their marriage. (1 illus.)

181 Pile, Susan; Moran, John; and Close, Patrick Tilden. "Getting Intimate with Edy Williams." *Andy Warhol's Interview,* 34:16–18, 41, July 1973.

In a rambling, disjointed interview conducted during the time of her marriage to Meyer, Edy Williams talks openly about the impact the union could have on her acting career. Williams' thoughts on *Blacksnake!* and *Foxy* are also presented. (2 illus.)

182 Prelutsky, Burt. "What's a Sex Symbol to Do?" *Los Angeles Times,* sec. Calendar, p. 20, April 28, 1974.

Lovely Edy Williams (circa 1970), Hollywood's "last starlet" and Meyer's third wife, from June 27, 1970, to November 5, 1975. (Movie Star News.)

Edy Williams, aspiring actress and Meyer's third wife, discusses her insatiable appetite for publicity and her dismay at being stereotyped as a sex symbol. Meyer is not mentioned in this article although Williams' performances in *Beyond the Valley of the Dolls* and *The Seven Minutes* are noted.

183 Scott, Marlena. "Edy Williams Takes Her Love & Sex Seriously." *National Insider*, 20(25): UNKNOWN, June 18, 1972.

In a 1972 interview with the gossip tabloid *National Insider*, Edy Williams outlines the qualities she likes in men and praises Meyer, "the connoisseur of super-ample women," for his casual, yet dynamic style. (1 illus.)

184 Stark, John. "Famous for Her Nude Romps in the World's Pools, Edy Williams Tries to Make One More Hollywood Splash." *People Weekly*, 26(26):88–91, June 29, 1987.

Edy Williams, "Hollywood's perennial starlet," is featured in a biographical piece which concentrates on her self-promotion and long-time desire to become a major film star. Ex-husband Meyer, who directed her in *Beyond the Valley of the Dolls*, is blamed by Williams for having stereotyped her as a "porn star" which has subsequently barred her from serious consideration for dramatic roles. (5 illus.)

185 Terrill, Ann. "Filmdom's Most Unlikely Lady Militant." *Register*, UNKNOWN, Nov. 7, 1971.
Edy Williams insists that despite Meyer's desire to have her stay at home or else appear in sexpot movie roles, she has a strong wish to become a serious actress. Acknowledging that she agrees with the fundamental tenets of Women's Liberation, Williams states that she would like to play the role of suffragette Victoria Woodhall. Terrill believes the actress' natural beauty will be enough to make her a star. (3 illus.)

186 Williams, Edy. "Why Does the World Revolve Around a Man?" *Citizen News*, pt. II, p. 11, Dec. 16, 1971.
Career woman Edy Williams' feminist manifesto declares that a woman can be sexy and feminine, yet still possess "an ambitious, independent brain." In addition to analyzing the operative dynamics in male-female relationships, the actress enumerates the qualities she feels make a man sexy, concluding that Meyer, the "famous connoisseur of super-ample women," embodies them all. (2 illus.)

187 Zec, Donald. "All About Edy: (Front Girl for the New Fifties)." *London Daily Mirror*, p. 9, Feb. 14, 1972.
British columnist Zec characterizes Edy Williams as a glamorous "creature right out of the Fifties" who credits Meyer and her mother with being the two great influences in her life. The personality piece also reports on her frustration with Meyer over his refusal to star her in *Blacksnake!* (1 illus.)

Edy Williams — Divorce

188 "Actress Fights for Property." *Los Angeles Herald-Examiner*, sec. A, p. 2, Oct. 16, 1975.
The legal battle continues in the Meyer-Williams divorce as the actress contests the community property value of their Mulholland Drive mansion and seeks to share in the profits of *Supervixens*. (1 illus.)

189 "Actress Denied Share of X-Rated Movie's Profits." *Los Angeles Times*, pt. 1, p. 20, Nov. 6, 1975.
The bitter divorce of Meyer and Edy Williams ends with the actress being denied profits from *Supervixens*, but awarded half of their $220,000 home and some limited support.

190 "Actress' Scuffle with Cameraman Explained." *Valley News*, UNKNOWN, Oct. 17, 1975.
A brief explanation of the fracas between Edy Williams and a news photographer which occurred after a divorce court session in which Meyer accused the actress of threatening to shoot him.

191 Austin, John. "Uncensored Interview: Marriage Isn't for Sex Symbols Says Edy Williams Who Would Rather Play the Field." *National Police Gazette*, 179(2): 3, 38, Feb. 1974.
The actress is interviewed poolside at her Mulholland Drive mansion in Beverly Hills concerning her recent separation from Meyer and her desire to transcend her status as a sex symbol to become a serious actress. Meyer is portrayed as a jealous, possessive husband too busy with his own career to promote hers. Williams is described as "Hollywood's most beautiful sexpot, who unfortunately arrived on the scene about ten years too late." (3 illus.)

192 Bacon, James. "Entertainment."
Los Angeles Herald-Examiner,
sec. B, p. 8, July 9, 1973.

In an open letter to celebrity columnist James Bacon, Edy Williams
writes that since she is not by nature a
"promiscuous lady" she felt that morally
she should be divorced from Meyer
before taking a lover. The actress blamed
Meyer's tendency to overwork with ruining their marriage.

193 Bacon, James. "Bikinied Edy
Waits for the Sheriff." *Los Angeles Herald-Examiner,* sec. B, p.
6, July 1, 1975.

A bikini-clad Edy Williams waits
at her Mulholland Drive estate to be
served Meyer's eviction notice by sheriff's
deputies.

194 Batchelor, Ruth. "Edy Williams:
'I Think They Censor the Films
Too Much'." *L.A. Free Press,* 12
(23), no. 568, sec. Adult Entertainment, p. T, June 6–12, 1975.

Edy Williams discusses her stormy
four-and-a-half year marriage to Meyer
and her subsequent film career. Williams
characterized the filmmaker as a "bossy"
ex-sergeant who did not care that she
wanted to be an actress. (1 illus.)

195 Castleman, Brad. "Edy Williams
Sheds Mate Who Made Her Star
of Nude Movies." *National Insider,* p. 19, Aug. 19, 1973.

Estranged wife Edy Williams
berates Meyer and relates to Castleman
how she manipulated the filmmaker into
twice proposing marriage. Williams also
discusses how difficult it is for a sex symbol to be married. (3 illus.)

196 Clapton, Diane. "Foxy Lady Edy
Williams: Linda Lovelace with
Lockjaw?" *Bachelor,* 14(2):24, 64,
Dec. 1973.

A men's magazine article detailing the chronology of Williams' tempestuous relationship with Meyer. The actress' thoughts on a variety of topics
(lifestyles, contemporary religion, sex
symbols, etc.) are also presented. (2 illus.)

*197 "Edy Williams' Dirty Divorce."
Modern People, p. 3, Jan. 4, 1976.

An emotionally and financially
devastated Edy Williams shares the story
of her divorce from Meyer with readers of
the tabloid *Modern People* "so that the
next girl who marries a producer will
maybe be a little smarter." In her version
of the divorce she characterizes the
filmmaker as a satanic "smut peddler"
who "planned the divorce like he was
Hitler." Highly recommended. (2 illus.)

198 Frederick, Don, Jr. "Speaking of
People." *The National Observer,*
p. 6, July 7, 1973.

Sex symbol Edy Williams, accusing husband Meyer of "disappearing
acts," files for divorce.

199 Grant, Hank. "Rambling Reporter." *Hollywood Reporter,* 221
(33):2, June 7, 1972.

Denying rumors that she and
Meyer are separating, Edy Williams explains that the filmmaker is on location
in the Bahamas filming a non-sex film
with an all–British cast. Grant incorrectly
refers to the film as *The Eleven* rather
than *Blacksnake!*

200 Grant, Hank. "Rambling Reporter." *Hollywood Reporter,*
232(19):2, July 24, 1974.

Meyer's estranged wife, Edy Williams, is spotted on Rome's Via Veneto
walking hand in hand with British actor
Richard Johnson.

201 Grant, Hank. "Rambling Reporter." *Hollywood Reporter,*
232(22):2, July 29, 1974.

In Rome with British actor Richard Johnson ("the first man to really
make love to me"), Edy Williams complains that the Italian press constantly
misspell her first name.

202 Grant, Hank. "Rambling Reporter." *Hollywood Reporter,"*
233(7):2, Sept. 17, 1974.

Edy Williams and former basketball great Wilt Chamberlain are seen
making the rounds of night spots on
Rome's Via Veneto.

203 Grant, Hank. "Rambling Reporter." *Hollywood Reporter,* 237(7):2, July 3, 1975.

A soon-to-be-evicted Edy Williams complains that it is not easy moving her pet menagerie and 134 bikinis from the Beverly Hills mansion she shared with Meyer. The divorce is final July 22.

204 Haber, Joyce. "Edy and Russ—Is Something Wrong?" *Los Angeles Times,* pt. IV, p. 11, June 25, 1973.

Haber reports on a hospitalized Edy Williams and notes the absence of husband Meyer and the delay in starting *Foxy,* to star Williams, as proof that their marriage is in trouble. (1 illus.)

205 "Judge Denies Edy Williams Any Profits in 'Vixens' Film." *Hollywood Reporter,* 238(44):4, Nov. 7, 1975.

Superior Court Judge Paul G. Breckenridge, in granting Meyer and Edy Williams an interlocutory divorce, rules that the actress is not entitled to either Meyer's production company or profits from *Supervixens* because they were not the result of "community efforts."

206 "No Film Profits for Edy." *Los Angeles Herald-Examiner,* sec. A, p. 20, Nov. 6, 1975.

Superior Court Judge Paul G. Breckenridge grants an interlocutory divorce decree that denies Edy Williams any profits from Meyer's film *Supervixens,* but does award her $900 a month

alimony through June 1976 and half of the profits from the sale of their Mulholland Drive mansion.

207 Oliver, Myrna. "Now She Wants to Shed Mate [Seeks New Role]." *Los Angeles Times,* pt. II, p. 2, Oct. 17, 1975.

One day after a fracas with a news photographer covering her divorce from Meyer, Edy Williams, clad in a "Free! Almost" tee-shirt, vows never again to appear nude in films. The actress accused Meyer of exploiting her body and refusing to showcase her acting ability. (1 illus.)

208 "Sexpot, Skinflick Director Break Up." *Dayton Daily News,* p. 40, Nov. 6, 1975.

Details are given on the November 5, 1975, divorce of Meyer and his third wife Edy Williams. (1 illus.)

209 Trenwick, Van. "Skin Flick King Russ Meyer's Wife Edy Dating Black Actor." *National Insider,* 21(2):UNKNOWN, July 9, 1972.

Hollywood insiders are amazed that Edy Williams would jeopardize her marriage to estranged husband Meyer by publicly flaunting her interest in black actor Ed Hall who can do nothing to further her career aspirations. (4 illus.)

210 Van Gelder, Lawrence. "Notes on People: This Book May Be Dangerous." *New York Times,* p. 55, June 28, 1973.

Edy Williams explains the motivating factors underlying her divorce from Meyer.

VII. ACTRESSES

June Wilkinson

211 "Beauty and the Bust." *Adam,* 3(1):43–45, 1959.

June Wilkinson, the 43-21-36 British pinup queen of the late 50s and 60s, is featured in a lengthy *Adam* pictorial centering on a Russ Meyer photo shoot of her fitting at Paulette's Custom Made Training Brassiere factory and emporium. In addition to detailed biographical information on Wilkinson, the article contains extensive quotes from Meyer on her bright Hollywood future. Interestingly, *Adam* photographer Meyer states that Wilkinson is the third model he has found who will make him a fortune. Eve Meyer (his wife) and Diana Webber are identified as the other two. (11 illus.)

Lorna Maitland

212 "Lorna: Part 1." *Fling,* 10(1): 42–45, Mar. 1967.

In the initial installment of a two-part photo layout and personality piece featured in the men's magazine *Fling,* Lorna Maitland, the 42C-24-36 star of *Lorna,* discusses her personal interests, professional ambitions, and initial meeting with Meyer. (8 illus.)

213 "Lorna: Part 2." *Fling,* 10(2):2, 22–31, May 1967.

In the second and final installment of a featured pictorial, Maitland

discusses her initial reticence to do the film's nude scenes. On a critical note, the article's uncited author praises Meyer's "photographic wizardry," but concludes *Lorna* "is about as exciting as watching four hours of home movies." The article contains several candid shots of Meyer photographing the film's fantasy and rape sequences. (45 illus.)

Uschi Digard

214 Craven, Michelle. "Uschi: My Life as a Goddess." *Cheri,* 4(8): 66–72, 103, Mar. 1980.

Legendary nudie film queen and softcore sex star Uschi Digard is featured in a 1980 interview/pictorial in the men's magazine *Cheri* in which she discusses her association with Meyer both as an actress and later as an associate producer for *Up!* and *Beneath.* (13 illus.)

215 "She's Supersoul in 'Supervixen'." *Chicago Daily Defender,* p. 21, Apr. 28, 1975.

Uschi Digard, actress, jewelry sales expert, linguist, and a "devout member of a Los Angeles nudist club," is featured in a short biographical sketch. (1 illus.)

216 Williams, Ken. "Swedish Actress Has Charm, Brains." *Journal-News,* sec. Leisure, p. 22, Apr. 26, 1975.

Multi-lingual actress Uschi Digard promotes a non–Meyer R-rated sex comedy, *If You Don't Stop It You'll Go*

Blind, in Cincinnati and answers questions concerning her film career, thoughts on nudity, and her assessment of Women's Liberation. According to the article, Meyer "discovered" her when she appeared in *Penthouse.* (1 illus.)

Erica Gavin

217 "Erica as Vixen." *Fling,* 13(1):2, 20–23, Mar. 1970.
A photo layout of Erica Gavin, star of *Vixen,* appearing in the men's magazine *Fling.* The stills, taken exclusively from the film, are accompanied by a thin plot synopsis. Critical comments are confined to citing the "Meyer trademark of some exceptional color camera work." (13 illus.)

Candy Samples

218 Fishbein, Paul. "Interview: Candy Samples." *Adult Video News,* 1 (13):1, 9–10, Apr. 1984.
Candy Samples, famed adult model and stripper, discusses her lengthy and varied career as well as her professional relationship with Meyer. Samples, who briefly appeared in *Up!* and *Beneath,* will also appear in two Meyer films currently in production: *The Breast of Russ Meyer* and *Mondo Topless II.* (1 illus.)

219 Stewart, Rick. "Mammaries Are Made of This." *Screw,* 764:13, Oct. 24, 1983.
A report on "porn's senior sex symbol," Candy Samples, during her striptease engagement at New York City's Show World, makes note of Meyer's cameo appearance in her first hardcore feature film, *Candy Samples Presents All the Way In.* Samples also relates an anecdote regarding her painful acting assignment in Meyer's upcoming production, *Mondo Topless II.* (7 illus.)

Shari Eubank

220 Baker, Robert. "Farmer City Girl Appears in New Russ Meyers [sic] Film." *Daily Pantagraph,* sec. A, p. 7, Apr. 26, 1975.
Shari Eubank, former homecoming queen at Farmer City High School in 1964 and star of *Supervixens,* is featured in a "local-girl-makes-good" piece in a Bloomington-Normal, Illinois, newspaper. (1 illus.)

221 Thomas, Jason. "The Development of Supervixen." *Chicago Sun-Times,* p. 135, May 1, 1975.
A detailed biographical piece on *Supervixens* star Shari Eubank. (1 illus.)

Ann Marie

222 Parker, P.J. "More Than Just a Well-Filled Bra." *Las Vegas Panorama,* p. 62, Feb. 4, 1977.
Burlesque headliner and Meyer actress Ann (67-25-36) Marie is featured in a *Las Vegas Panorama* article that reports on her successful engagement at the Cabaret. (1 illus.)

Raven De La Croix

223 Baumoel, Lois. "'Up!' Star Raven De La Croix Says She Wants to Make More Pictures." *Boxoffice,* 110(8):ME-1, Nov. 29, 1976.
With Meyer in Cleveland to promote *Up!,* Raven De La Croix, once the highest paid stripper at the Purple Lion in Hollywood, expresses her desire to appear in more feature films. (2 illus.)

*224 DeKom, Otto. "Late-Blooming Raven Rejects Hardcore Porn." *Wilmington Morning News,* p. 29, Dec. 21, 1976.
Raven De La Croix, interviewed while in Wilmington, Delaware, to promote *Up!,* insists that *everything* about her life and anatomy is real. For those interested in De La Croix's biography, this

Exotic dancer Raven De La Croix emotes in a publicity shot for *Up!*

article supplies several details. Recommended. (1 illus.)

225 Swindle, Howard. " 'Up' with Texas for Russ' Raven." *Dallas Times Herald,* sec. B, p. 10, Oct. 10, 1976.

Raven De La Croix, star of *Up!,* recounts her discovery in a Hollywood restaurant by a woman in the casting department at 20th Century–Fox. (1 illus.)

Francesca "Kitten" Natividad

226 Bailey, Dian. "Kitten by Russ: Russ Meyer Presents His Pick of the Pecs." *Partner,* 2(9):87–91, 96, Feb. 1981.

"Kitten" Natividad is lovingly photographed by Meyer in a pictorial/feature on the Mexican-born stripper/

Opposite, left: Legendary queen of softcore sexploitation and men's magazine pictorials, Uschi Digard occupies a special place in Meyer's heart and films. Appearing in three of them *(Cherry, Harry & Raquel, Beyond the Valley of the Dolls* (uncredited), and *Supervixens),* Digard also served as an associate producer on *Up!* and *Beneath the Valley of the Ultravixens.* *Right:* Fondly remembered by Meyer as the best actress ever to appear in any of his films, university trained drama major Shari Eubank strikes a playful pose for *Supervixens* publicity.

Premier exotic dancer, comedienne, and one-time Meyer love interest Francesca "Kitten" Natividad in *Beneath the Valley of the Ultravixens* (1979).

actress who appeared as the "Greek Chorus" in *Up!* and in the dual role of "Lavonia" and "Lola Langusta" in *Beneath*. The personal and professional relationship between Meyer and the actress is explored with the filmmaker commenting on the two aforementioned films. (8 illus.)

227 Craven, Michelle. "Catnips: (*Beneath the Valley of the Ultravixens* Star Kitten Natividad Describes Life with and without Russ Meyer)." *Cheri*, 4(2):36–43, 89, Sept. 1979.

In a 1979 interview/pictorial appearing in the men's magazine *Cheri*, Francesca "Kitten" Natividad, stripper and star of *Beneath*, discusses elements of her professional, and later, personal relationship with Meyer. (15 illus.)

228 Irving, Lee. "Interview: Kitten Natividad." *Adult Video News*, 1(35):36, 38, Feb. 1986.

Francesca "Kitten" Natividad, premier stripper and actress, discusses her recent professional activities and long-time personal relationship with Meyer including the reasons for their decision not to marry. (2 illus.)

229 Midnite, Susi. "Kitten Lets It All Hang Out." *Las Vegas Panorama,* sec. A, p. 25, Nov. 25, 1977.

Striptease artist "Kitten" Natividad is interviewed between performances at the Cabaret Club in Las Vegas where she denies hating Meyer, for whom she worked on *Beneath.* While he was a tough and demanding director whose personal antagonism of the cast was designed to get the most from his actors, Natividad considers him a friend. Though presently estranged from him, she plans to be in Meyer's punk rock film *Anarchy in the U.K.* (a.k.a. *Who Killed Bambi?*). (1 illus.)

230 Millar, Jeff. "Actress Measures Up to Role." *Houston Chronicle,* sec. 6, p. 1, Mar. 23, 1979.

A personality piece on Francesca "Kitten" Natividad written while she and Meyer were in Houston to promote *Beneath.* (2 illus.)

231 Van Arsdol, Ted. "Meyer Brings Kitten to Promote Newest Sex Film." *The Columbian,* p. 36, Apr. 29, 1979.

"Kitten" Natividad is featured in an article written while she and Meyer were in Vancouver, Washington, promoting *Beneath.* The stripper/actress reports on her proven main-street walk method of generating publicity while Meyer believes she has the potential to be a comedienne in the Charo vein. (1 illus.)

Tami Roche

232 Merrill, Hugh. "Tami Tell Me True." *Atlanta Journal,* sec. Atlanta Weekly, pp. 10–11, 13, Mar. 13, 1983.

Atlanta-based burlesque queen and stripper Tami Roche is featured in a lengthy and colorful biographical piece that mentions her scheduled role as "the Bolivian Bombshell" in Meyer's *Blitzen, Vixen and Harry.* (3 illus.)

Miscellaneous

233 "Russ Meyer's Bosom Buddies." *Fling,* 14(1):2, 15–19, Mar. 1971.

Three Meyer stars—Lorna Maitland *(Lorna, Mudhoney),* Veronica Reed *(Fanny Hill, Beyond the Valley of the Dolls),* and Candy Morrison *(Mondo Topless)*—are featured in a *Fling* pictorial replete with minimal biographical information. For Meyer purists, the model identified in the article as Veronica Reed appeared under the name Erica Erickson in *Fanny Hill* (1964) and as Veronica Erickson in *Beyond the Valley of the Dolls* (1970). The article incorrectly cites Candy Morrison as appearing in the 1967 Meyer film *How Much Loving Does a Normal Couple Need?* (a.k.a. *Common-Law Cabin*) whereas she actually appeared under the name Darlene Grey as one of the featured strippers in *Mondo Topless* (1966). (19 illus.)

234 "The Ultra-Ultra Girls." *Oui,* 6(12):112–119, Dec. 1977.

The women from *Beneath the Valley of the Ultravixens*—June Mack, "Kitten" Natividad, Sharon Hill, Ann Marie—are featured in a *Oui* pictorial that also includes brief interviews in which they discuss their personal histories and perceptions of Russ Meyer. (8 illus.)

VIII. CHARLES NAPIER

235 Atkins, Eric. "Local Boy Makes Good—Gets Plenty of Exposure." *St. Petersburg Times,* sec. D, p. 1, Nov. 24, 1969.

A vicious open letter to Charles Napier, a former Pinellas County, Florida, art school teacher, sarcastically berating him for his "exposure" in *Cherry, Harry & Raquel* while reminding him that he once played the title role in *Becket* in a local theatre company production. (2 illus.)

236 Ebert, Roger. "Interview: This Is the Man 'Rambo' Fans Hate." *Chicago Sun-Times,* sec. Sunday, p. 19, June 30, 1985.

Charles Napier, "Harry Sledge" in *Supervixens* (1975) and more recently seen as "Murdock" in *Rambo: First Blood Part II* (1985), is featured in a detailed biographical piece which discusses the actor's past career struggles and current popularity. Crediting his roles in Meyer films as providing his first career breaks, Napier is quick to defend his association with the man "who always stood by me." (3 illus.)

237 "'King of Skin Flicks' Shoots Film Near Yuma." *Arizona Daily Star,* sec. B, p. 13, Dec. 13, 1974.

Actor Charles Napier takes precedence over Meyer in an article reporting on the location filming of *Supervixens* near Quartzsite, Arizona, in the Kofa Mountains. Meyer's favorite leading man discusses his entry into films and his past career frustrations. (2 illus.)

238 Lees, David, and Berkowitz, Stan. "Villains' Worst Crime: Stealing the Show." *Los Angeles Times,* sec. Calendar, pp. 40–42, Feb. 5, 1978.

Charles Napier, the psychotic sheriff "Harry Sledge" in *Supervixens,* is one of several character actors featured in an article on movie bad-guys. (7 illus.)

Charles Napier, seen here as the psychotic cop in *Supervixens* (1975), is the quintessential "Meyer man": a square-jawed, he-man with an I.Q. of 40 motivated solely by lust. Napier, the only Meyer star to crack the Hollywood mainstream, supported Sylvester Stallone in *Rambo: First Blood Part II* (1985), portraying the psychotic C.I.A. agent "Murdock."

IX. SEXPLOITATION

239 Carroll, Kent E. "N.Y. Over-Seated for Sex: Cheapies Fear Class Sin Pics." *Variety*, 255(7):1, 70, July 2, 1969.

Carroll asserts that the entry of "elite" producers and directors into the U.S. sexploitation market could spell extinction for the low-budget American produced erotic film. Major studio releases like *Candy* and *The Killing of Sister George* not only compete directly with independently produced sex films, they also create a "moral backlash" that Lee Hessel, president of the independent Canbist Films, feels is responsible for the community and police pressure aimed at sex films, especially in the suburbs. Hessel's proposed solutions to the problems confronting independent sex film producers include advising them to release two versions of a film with one being more tame than the other, the more careful targeting of films for a specific nudie market, and the caution that if the industry is to survive the production values in most films must be upgraded. Meyer's *Vixen* is cited by Hessel as an example of a low-budget "quality movie" which received both critical and commercial success. Based on this success, Carroll concludes that a lucrative market still exists for economically produced, high quality sexploitation films.

*240 Chute, David. "Wages of Sin, (I)." *Film Comment*, 22(4):32–39, 42–48, Aug. 1986.

Chute's initial interview with David F. Friedman, legendary sexploitationist and president of Entertainment Ventures Incorporated, traces the prehistory of exploitation from its roots in the 1920s up through the 1930s and the band of exploitationists known as the Forty Thieves, concluding with a detailed discussion of genre classic *Mom and Dad* (1944) produced by premier showman Kroger Babb. Herschel Gordon Lewis, director of the 1960s "Blood Trilogy," is also discussed. Friedman, a fascinating and roguish character, stands alone in his knowledge of the sexploitation field and his thoughts on the genre Meyer helped define and expand are essential reading. (20 illus.)

*241 Chute, David. "Wages of Sin, II." *Film Comment*, 22(5):56–61, Sept.-Oct. 1986.

Chute's interview with David F. Friedman concludes with the outspoken producer describing the Los Angeles exploitation scene in the 1960s and his involvement with the film *Ilsa, She-Wolf of the S.S.* (1974). Friedman also discusses his entry into hardcore and predicts that the genre will eventually destroy sexploitation because it is essentially documentary in nature. The article includes a Friedman filmography that is useful. Highly recommended in that it places Meyer squarely in a genre he helped to expand and legitimize. (3 illus.)

242 Crawley, Tony. "History of the Blue Movie: [Part 1]." *Marilyn*

Chambers' Best of Club, 15:4–6, 20, 36, 44, 62, 76, 82, 1981.

Part one of Crawley's screen treatment of the historical development of the blue movie traces the genre from its earliest roots in the Latin American blue reelers of the early twentieth century through the arrival on the American scene in the twenties of the Forty Thieves, the independent producers of low-budget sexploitation films that skirted the Will Hays Motion Picture Production Code. David Friedman, Chairman of the Board of the Adult Film Association of America and a direct historical/spiritual descendant of the Forty Thieves, discusses their importance and films. (7 illus.)

243 Crawley, Tony. "A History of Blue Movies. Part Two: Azure Like It or Not." *Game,* 2(6):41–43, 85–88, June 1975.

In part two of his screenplay treatment tracing the historical development of the blue movie, Crawley discusses Meyer's breakthrough films *Lorna* (1964) and *Vixen* (1968) in terms of their impact on and contribution to the genre. (33 illus.)

244 Crawley, Tony. "History of the Blue Movie: Part Four: The Nudie Cuties." *Club International,* 5 (4): 6–8, 23, 28, Apr. 1981.

Crawley's "cinematic" history of the blue movie continues with the focus on *The Immoral Mr. Teas* (1959), the landmark sexploitation film which launched the "nudie cuties" cycle by spawning countless imitators like David Friedman's *The Adventures of Lucky Pierre,* Ted Paramore's *Not Tonight Henry,* and Bob Cresse's *Once Upon a Knight.* (3 illus.)

245 Crawley, Tony. "History of the Blue Movie: [Part 5]." *Marilyn Chambers' Best of Club,* 15:48–50, 61–62, 76, 82, 1981.

In the fifth installment of his history of the blue movie, Crawley chronicles the quick death of the "nudie

cuties," notes the rise of the "ghoulies" (David Friedman's blood and flesh opuses), and focuses on Meyer's second breakthrough film, *Lorna,* a sexy melodrama that rivalled the European films of that period in its earthiness. Meyer's career is traced through *Vixen* with the financial success of that film convincing a near-broke 20th Century–Fox that sex, when produced by Meyer, can sell. Of note, director Radly Metzger (called by Friedman "the only genius working in sexploitation") is also discussed. (3 illus.)

246 Crawley, Tony. "History of the Blue Movie: Part Six: Show 'Em." *Club International,* 5(6):5–6, 23, 29, 44, June 1981.

Crawley's series concludes with an examination of Michelangelo Antonioni's 1966 *Blow-Up,* the first major film to show pubic hair and a discussion of Meyer's profound influence on the depiction of sexuality in mainstream movies. Commenting upon Meyer's and his own considerable influence in the genre, pioneer sexploitationist David Friedman flatly states that the independent producers have done more to fight censorship and to expand that which can be shown on the screen than all the major Hollywood studios combined. (7 illus.)

247 Hyams, Joe. "Rash of Trash Films Stirs a Hollywood Debate on Nudity." *Chicago Sun-Times,* sec. 2, p. 18, Sept. 25, 1961.

Are nudie pictures made by independents "more or less immoral" than films made by major Hollywood studios? Three independent filmmakers — Meyer *(The Immoral Mr. Teas),* Robert Cresse, producer of *Once Upon a Knight,* and Jay Sheridan *(The Touchables)* — offer their opinions. The furor raised by nudie films among the Los Angeles City Council and the Hollywood trade unions and guilds is also noted.

248 Kane, Joe. "I Remember Soft-Core." *Genesis,* 7(4):40–42, 100–101, Nov. 1979.

"Soft-core savant" Joe Kane pays

tribute to the "inspired sleaze" of the fifties and sixties skinflick. Though focusing on such memorable films as *White Slaves of Chinatown* (1964) and his personal favorite, *Tricks of the Trade* (1968), Kane notes that Meyer's *Lorna* (1964) did effectively parody the genre's "puritanical bent." (2 illus.)

*249 McDonough, Jimmy. "Sexposed." *Film Comment*, 22(4):53–61, July-Aug. 1986.

A good article that seeks to explain sexploitation, "one of the most forgotten genres in film history," and to trace it from its roots in stag films up through its "death" in 1970 with the advent of hardcore. Meyer's major contributions to the genre are discussed (*The Immoral Mr. Teas* [1959] and *Lorna* [1964]) with McDonough noting that pioneers Meyer and Radley Metzger "eclipsed the genre." The article includes a useful filmography of "representative" sexploitation films which lists *Mondo Topless* (1966). Recommended. (12 illus.)

250 Ross, Gene. "Sexploitation Films: The 60's Sexplosion!!!" *Adult Video News*, 2(1):82–84, 86, Mar. 1987.

The current revival of interest in the 1960s sexploitation film as witnessed by numerous festivals in New York and Los Angeles prompts Ross to examine the genre's availability on video and to briefly discuss two of its highest artistic achievements: *Mudhoney* and *Lorna*. (2 illus.)

*251 "Sexpix of $25,000–45,000 Negative Cost See Bright, Not Clouded, Future." *Variety*, 255 (9):17, July 16, 1969.

Variety reports that the sexploitation market composed of non-art sex films costing around $75,000 to produce is quite healthy with 75 to 100 such films being produced each year. Meyer's high quality, low-budget softcore sex films are identified as the industry standard by which distinctions are made between "cheapies" (budget under $15,000) and hardcore (explicit sexual depiction). The financially lucrative Meyer product is also cited as possessing a quality equal to or surpassing that of the art-sex films which boast redeeming social value. Recommended.

*252 Wasserman, John L. "The Wild Variety in S.F.'s Sexy Films." *San Francisco Chronicle*, p. 6, June 10, 1969.

Wasserman contends the dramatic increase in the number of sex films being produced and correspondingly exhibited in legitimate houses has obliterated the line between "clean and dirty theaters." The directorial styles of Roger Vadim *(And God Created Woman, Barbarella)*, Meyer, Radley Metzger *(Therese and Isabelle, The Dirty Girls)*, and Whit Boyd *(The Sex Shuffle, The Office Party)* are contrasted to illustrate the widely diverse artistic range to be found in the sex field genre. Meyer is described as an "intellectual primate" who distinguishes himself from the other directors as "the best of all sex film makers in terms of technique." Recommended. (1 illus.)

253 "Where Have All the Boobies Gone?" *Adam*, 11(11):4–5, 22–25, Nov. 1967.

Adam traces the evolution of "skinpix" from their birth in 1959 with the "blatant nudity" of *The Immoral Mr. Teas* (and its numerous technically inferior imitators) up to the end of the genre signalled in 1964 by the release of *Lorna* in which a frank treatment of sex first "rivalled the art house product from Europe and Japan." The changing moral climate of the times which permits easy access to nudity in topless bars and other venues is identified as the major causative factor responsible for the now-unprofitable theatrical exhibition of nudie films. (8 illus.)

X. THE FILMS

Teas (1959)

PRODUCTION NOTES

254 "Adam Goes on Location with the Cast and Crew of . . . The Immoral Mr. Teas." *Adam,* 3(2): 22–27, 1959.

While primarily a photo layout on the women of *The Immoral Mr. Teas,* the article also contains several candid shots of an unidentified Meyer directing and photographing the film. Though Meyer is not cited in the piece, a brief mention is given to producer Pete DeCenzie of PAD Productions and the film's star, W. Ellis Teas. The film itself is described as "a satirical comedy in the tradition of the great Chaplin movies or the hilarious French comedy, 'Mr. Hulot's Holiday'." (18 illus.)

255 Knickerbocker, Paine. "He Scorns Nudity Bare of Humor." *San Francisco Chronicle,* p. 32, July 7, 1961.

Bill Teas, star of *The Immoral Mr. Teas,* discusses the production of that film and his collaboration with producer Pete DeCenzie and photographer/director Meyer. While the financial success of the film has spawned numerous imitators, Teas sees a danger in presenting too much film nudity, commenting that "if these pictures are to have any lasting appeal, the accent has to be on a subtle sort of humor." A sequel, *Mr. Teas Goes to Paris,* is planned. (1 illus.)

256 Snider, Burr. "The Blue Movie That Started It All." *San Francisco Examiner,* sec. E, pp. 15–16, Nov. 18, 1981.

W. Ellis ("Bill") Teas, star of *The Immoral Mr. Teas,* reminisces about the making of the film and his longtime association with Meyer. (4 illus.)

*257 Turan, Kenneth. "'Immoral Mr. Teas' in Retrospect." *Washington Post,* sec. B, p. 13, Mar. 23, 1973.

A retrospective showing of *The Immoral Mr. Teas* at the Dupont Circle Theatre in Washington, D.C., affords *Washington Post* film critic and erotic film historian Kenneth Turan an opportunity to discuss the film's production history and its subsequent seminal influence on the evolution of erotic cinema. Highly recommended. (1 illus.)

*258 Turrell, Roger. "Portrait of a Burlesque Producer." *Adam,* 3(1): 60–65, 1958.

Pete DeCenzie, one-time owner of Oakland's El Ray burlesque theatre and producer of *The Immoral Mr. Teas,* is featured in an *Adam* biographical piece that pre-dates the 1959 release of that landmark film. The now "lost" *French Peep Show* featuring stripper Tempest Storm which DeCenzie produced in collaboration with photographer Meyer and movie cameraman Chuck Schelling is also discussed. The "in the works" *Teas* is obliquely referred to as an "off-beat movie with a sex theme ... which may prove even more sensational than *French Peep Show*." An important article in that it discusses DeCenzie's tactic of personally promoting the film in each city which Meyer later successfully adopted to publicize his own independently produced films. Recommended. (22 illus.)

MISCELLANEOUS

259 "The Nudeniks." *Time,* 87(26): 51, June 23, 1961.

The financial success and numerous West Coast bookings for low-budget nudie movies like *Not Tonight Henry* and *The Immoral Mr. Teas* are discussed with *Henry*'s producer Edward E. Paramore commenting that the field suffers from "amateurs ... who use nudity for nudity's sake." *Time* suggests "Girlie Photographer Russ Meyers" (sic) may fall into this category.

260 "A Report on 'Immoral Mr. Teas'." *Variety,* 223(8):14, July 19, 1961.

A 1961 report on the continued financial success of sexploitation films at a time when the film establishment faces threatened Code censorship for its depiction of "adult excesses." Meyer's currently running *The Immoral Mr. Teas* and *Eve and the Handyman* are cited as examples. Also discussed are Meyer's thoughts on ratings and his desire to do "straight" films, perhaps even a biopicture on W.C. Fields.

261 Snider, Burr. "Through the Open Door." *San Francisco Examiner,* sec. E, p. 15, Nov. 18, 1981.

Questioned as to the state of contemporary pornography, Bill Teas of *The Immoral Mr. Teas* fame stated that while he had no objections to it on moral grounds, he found it to be even more boring and repetitive than the landmark film in which he starred.

262 "Thief Finally Gets 3rd Reel of Mr. Teas." *Seattle Times,* p. 5, Dec. 19, 1960.

After an unsuccessful initial attempt to steal a print of *The Immoral Mr. Teas* from the Guild 45th Theater in Seattle where it has played for 19 weeks, an unidentified thief finally succeeds in taking the third reel of the film.

263 Thomas, Bob. "Film Makers Find Money in Nudes." *Oakland Tribune,* p. 28, Sept. 20, 1961.

The Immoral Mr. Teas and *Not Tonight Henry* are cited as examples of the new wave of cheaply made, highly profitable nude films currently sweeping the country and setting box office records in their wake. Typically filmed in secluded settings with casts composed of professional models and strippers, the Screen Actors Guild has refused contracts with nudie producers, arguing that their films "reflect ill on the movie industry."

264 Thomas, Bob. "'Nude Film' Industry Drawing Large Crowds." *Arkansas Democrat,* p. 4, Sept. 18, 1961.

Thomas notes that nudie films like *The Immoral Mr. Teas* are not just playing skid row theatres, but are often now exhibited in respectable art houses in nice neighborhoods. The Supreme Court's decision proclaiming "freedom of the screen" is partially blamed for hampering state and local authorities from censoring these types of films.

265 "28,810 for 'Mr. Teas'." *Hollywood Reporter,* 165(2):11, Apr. 26, 1961.

After two years in release, *Teas* sets a new house record in its seventh week at the 1037 seat Paris Theatre in Los Angeles. The Paris Theatre run has outgrossed every previous engagement with the exception of the film's initial weeks in 1959 at the Monica Theatre. On May 5, 1961, *Teas* will move to the Vista-Continental to make way for Meyer's new production *Eve and the Handyman.*

The Immoral Mr. Teas (1959): Shot in five days on a budget of $24,000, Meyer's landmark film is alternately praised and damned for having opened the floodgates of screen sexual permissiveness. The first "nudie-cutie," *Teas* marked a radical departure from the nudist colony films of its day by having a coherent, if fanciful, plot.

266 Williams, Dick. "Nude-Girly Films Multiplying into a Tawdry Vogue." *Los Angeles Mirror*, pt. 4, p. 11, July 6, 1961.

Williams points with alarm to the impending flood of "cheaply made, cornily-acted nude-girly films" sure to follow in the wake of the financially successful *The Immoral Mr. Teas* which started the trend in 1959. While recent court cases have paved the way for screen nudity, Williams states that *Teas* was not pornographic, merely "bovine." For Meyer's reaction, see entry 267.

267 Williams, Dick. "Nudie Movies Defended As a Job Source." *Los Angeles Mirror*, pt. 2, p. 5, July 26, 1961.

Responding to an earlier Dick Williams article condemning the current vogue of nudie films, Meyer defends *The Immoral Mr. Teas* and concludes that many men "admire large breasted women" despite Williams' charge that the women in *Teas* were "bovine." Williams' reply accuses Meyer of being "hard up for something to film." (1 illus.) See entry 266.

Bill Teas, the Everyman voyeur, in Meyer's breakthrough movie *The Immoral Mr. Teas.*

CENSORSHIP

268   Meyer, Russ. "The Naked Ear." *Show Business Illustrated*, 1(6):5, Nov. 14, 1961.

Meyer's letter to the editor responding to the inaccuracies of an article entitled "The Naked Ear" identifies *The Immoral Mr. Teas*, not *Not Tonight Henry* as the film having faced censorship difficulties in Philadelphia and Los Angeles. The "naked ear" of the article's title refers to an ear-nibbling scene in *Teas* censored in Los Angeles. See entry **269**.

269   "The Naked Ear." *Show Business Illustrated*, 1(3):5–6, Oct. 3, 1961.

A report on the rash of financially successful "flesh-in-the-pan" nudie quickies being made by independent film producers in Hollywood. *The Immoral Mr. Teas* is identified as being responsible for initiating the nudie trend which has spawned scores of imitators like *Not*

Tonight Henry which the article mistakenly cites as having faced censorship problems in Philadelphia and Los Angeles (it was in fact *Teas*). Interestingly, Meyer's creative philosophy as reported in this 1961 article has remained remarkably unchanged to this day: "I take advantage of sex . . . But I treat it humorously." For the filmmaker's response to this article, see entry **268**.

REVIEWS

*270   Fiedler, Leslie. "A Night with Mr. Teas." *Show*, 1(1):118–119, Oct. 1961.

The first serious review of any Meyer film by a major critic focuses on the elements of antipassion and pathos in *The Immoral Mr. Teas*. Fiedler argues that the unfulfilled voyeurism of the character "Teas" serves as a striking metaphor for the similarly unfulfilled consumer desires consciously manufactured by the mass media. Like their stylized counterparts in advertising, the women in *Teas* are all unblemished, unreal pinups who exist solely to be looked at and desired, but never actually touched or attained. For Fiedler, despite the film's unpretentious good humor, herein lies "the sadness of 'Mr. Teas'." Highly recommended.

271 "The Immoral Mr. Teas." *Playboy*, 7(11):99–101, Nov. 1960.
The Immoral Mr. Teas is featured as representative of a wave of low-budget American-produced movies featuring nudity, not sex, that are beginning to compete commercially with the more explicit European art films. The recent liberal attitude of the federal courts toward censorship, as manifested by several cited examples, is credited with making the U.S. exhibition of these films possible. Meyer's film is described as "a good-natured, if heavy-handed, comedy." (9 illus.)

272 Knickerbocker, Paine. "Long-Run Nudes on Market Street." *San Francisco Chronicle*, p. 31, Jan. 18, 1961.
Knickerbocker attributes the long San Francisco run of *The Immoral Mr. Teas* to its tongue-in-cheek view of nudity which offers a refreshing change from the self-righteous pretensions of nudist colony movies like *This Is My Body* that sanctimoniously promote the virtues of sun worship. All aspects of the production are praised with the only criticism being the film's one joke is stretched too thin over 63 minutes.

273 Peary, Danny. "The Immoral Mr. Teas." *Guide for the Film Fanatic*, p. 208. New York: Simon & Schuster, 1986.
Peary acknowledges the historical importance of *Teas* for the adult film industry and voices his suspicion that the title character was in fact patterned after Jacques Tati's "Mr. Hulot."

274 Rimmer, Robert. "The Immoral Mr. Teas." *The X-Rated Video-*

tape Guide, pp. 97–98. New York: Arlington House, 1984.
Rimmer credits *The Immoral Mr. Teas* with having created the adult film industry. Rimmer suggests that perhaps a more sexually contemporary sequel could be filmed entitled *Son of Mr. Teas.*

275 Ron. "The Immoral Mr. Teas." *Variety*, 217(9):6, Jan. 27, 1960.
Reviewer Ron. compares the film to a "perverted 'Mr. Hulot's Holiday'" which rises above the ranks of other burlesque films "only by the reaction shots of Mr. Teas himself." Meyer's Eastman color photography is termed "amazingly good" and both he and actor Bill Teas are praised for creating "a rather interesting and amusing character." As an interesting historical footnote, playing to a Hollywood audience of "unashamed adults only," the film broke the Monica Theatre's house record on its opening night.

276 Stinson, Charles. "'Immoral Mr. Teas' Ends Era in Movies." *Los Angeles Times*, pt. 1, p. 18, Jan. 26, 1960.
In one of the earliest reviews, Stinson declares that with *The Immoral Mr. Teas* the Peep Show has "finally moved across the tracks from Main Street." While stopping just short of being a stag movie, Stinson considers it to contain enough risqué material "to add up to about a year's subscription to *Playboy* magazine."

Eve and the Handyman (1960)

PROMOTION

277 Henaghan, J.M. "Rambling Reporter." *Hollywood Reporter*, 165 (7):2, May 3, 1961.
The first 10,000 patrons to attend the Paris Theatre showings of *Eve and the Handyman*, a "naughty" tale about a

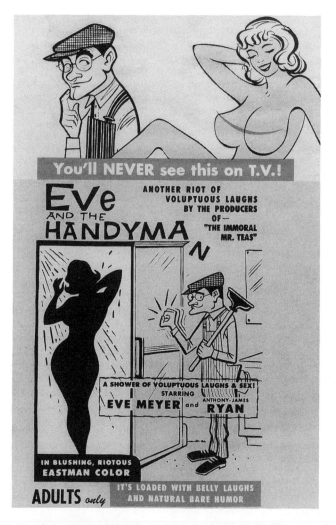

Eve and the Handyman (1960): The episodic follow-up to the classic *The Immoral Mr. Teas* featured Meyer's photogenic second wife, Eve, and army buddy Anthony James Ryan.

plumber, will receive free bathroom plungers.

278   "Rambling Reporter." *Hollywood Reporter,* 165(7):2, May 3, 1961.

To promote the May 5, 1961, opening of *Eve and the Handyman,* the Paris Theatre in Los Angeles will give free bathroom plungers to the first 10,000 customers.

MISCELLANEOUS

279   "'Eve and the Handyman'; One-Man Project in Bow." *Hollywood Reporter,* 165(7):4, May 3, 1961.

Eve and the Handyman, "a satire that pokes fun at medicine, modeling, wasteful technology and modern art," has its world premiere at the Paris Theatre in Los Angeles on May 5, 1961.

Handyman Anthony James Ryan is enamored of secretary Eve Meyer in an expressionistic publicity shot for Meyer's second venture into the "nudie-cuties" genre, *Eve and the Handyman*.

280/1 "'Eve,' New Film Comedy, Due." *Los Angeles Times*, pt. IV, p. 15, May 4, 1961.

The "adults only" satire *Eve and the Handyman* will be world premiered May 6, 1961, at the Paris Theatre in Los Angeles.

REVIEWS

282 "'Eve' All Smirk, No Smoke." *Los Angeles Examiner*, sec. 4, p. 6, May 8, 1961.

Eve and the Handyman is termed a "ghastly goulash" which suffers intellectually and artistically by comparison with the old peep show *What the Butler Saw*. The article is signed "S.A.D."

283 "Stage and Screen." *Oakland Tribune*, sec. D, p. 16, July 3, 1961.

Even though *Eve and the Handyman* promises to fill Oakland's Parkway Theater with a large, albeit, masculine crowd, the film's one *Esquire* and *Playboy*-like joke "tends to become a staggering bore" after only a short while.

A man and his "camera" . . . Meyer mugs in the 1961 PAD-RAM production *Erotica*.

284 Tube. "Eve and the Handyman."
Variety, 222(11):6, May 10, 1961.
　　Though "roughly the cinematic
equivalent of one of the more sophisticated pose magazines," the film shows
Meyer has talent to possibly excel in other
more "reputable" genres.

Erotica (1961)

REVIEWS

285 "Erotica." *Filmfacts*, 5:364, 1962.
A short plot synopsis and partial

cast and credits list of Meyer's 1961 PAD-
RAM production *Erotica* (also known as
Eroticon).

Wild Gals of the Naked West! (1961)

REVIEWS

286 "Wild Gals of the Naked West."
Adam Film Quarterly, 2:23, June
1967.

Wild Gals of the Naked West! (1961): Meyer offers "the first real ART COMEDY that HOLLYWOOD has produced since the GOLDEN ERA of motion pictures!"—publicity.

A retrospective appreciation in the men's magazine *Adam Film Quarterly* of Meyer's 1961 Films Pacifica release *Wild Gals of the Naked West!* also known as *Naked Gals of the Golden West.* (4 illus.)

Europe in the Raw (1963)

CENSORSHIP — ILLINOIS

287 "Chi Film Censor Board Deadlocks Less Likely Now." *Daily Variety,* 123(62):2, June 1, 1964.

Chicago Mayor Richard J. Daley appoints a fifth member to the city's Motion Picture Appeals Board thus forestalling the possibility of a two-to-two deadlock. In the 18-month history of the Board only two films—*Not Tonight Henry* and *Europe in the Raw*—have been turned down with *Not Tonight Henry* resubmitted and approved in an edited version.

288 "Mayor Under Fire to Fill Vacancies on Chi Censor Bd." *Daily Variety,* 123(38):1, 10, Apr. 28, 1964.

Public pressure mounts for Chicago's Mayor Richard J. Daley to replace two members who resigned from the five-person Motion Picture Appeals Board, the censorship committee that decides which films can be shown in the city. The three remaining members are split two-to-one in favor of passing *Europe in the Raw,* Meyer's photographic essay on the

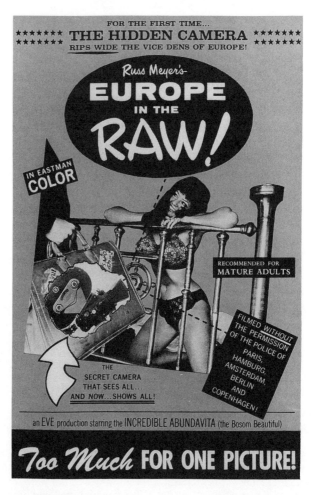

Europe in the Raw (1963): Armed with a loudly clanking camera hidden in a suitcase, Meyer "rips wide the vice dens of Europe!" This one-sheet, featuring "Baby Doll" Shawn Devereaux, shows the camera in action.

vice dens of Europe. The politically unaligned board requires a majority of three votes to enact any of its decisions.

289 Roth, Morry. "'Europe in the Raw,' Shot in Brothels, Banned in Chi." *Daily Variety,* 123(55):1, 15, May 21, 1964.

Upholding an earlier ruling of the police Film Review Section, the Chicago Motion Picture Appeals Board has denied *Europe in the Raw*, a film shot in European brothels, a permit to be shown in the city. The ruling, broadly based on Roth vs. U.S., stated that the reason for the Board's rejection was not the subject matter, but rather the manner in which the material was presented was designed solely to appeal to prurient interest.

REVIEWS

290 "Europe in the Raw." *Modern Man*, pp. 37–39, Winter 1963.

Heavenly Bodies! (1963): An "electrifying monument to feminine pulchritude," some ads for the film boasted that it "tops any nudie movie that has ever been produced."

This 1963 Eve Productions release is featured in a pictorial that credits the film's hidden camera gimmick and Meyer's sense of humor with elevating it "above the level of mere sensationalism." (11 illus.)

Bodies!, "a documentary that purports to show how glamor photogs like Meyer work with gorgeous nude models," serves as the basis for a brief sketch on the "nudie movie mogul." Gentry assesses Meyer's movie formula as "a maximum of color, comedy, and corn—and a minimum of clothes." (12 illus.)

Heavenly Bodies! (1963)

PRODUCTION NOTES

291   Gentry, Milt. "Russ Meyer: Nude Movie Mogul." *Modern Man,* UNKNOWN, Nov. 1961. A visit to the set of *Heavenly*

Lorna (1964)

PRODUCTION NOTES

292   "'Lorna' Set as Title." *Hollywood Reporter,* 177(47):6, Nov. 13, 1963.

Meyer checks the light reading on Althea Currier before filming *Heavenly Bodies!*

Meyer announces that the recently completed Eve Productions film starring curvaceous Lorna Maitland, "Hollywood's answer to foreign sexpots," has been retitled *Lorna*.

CENSORSHIP — FLORIDA

293 "Film Return Denied." *National Decency Reporter,* 6(1–2):14, Jan.-Feb. 1969.

The Florida Supreme Court denies an appeal to return a print of *Lorna* seized by police in March 1967 at the Gulf Follies Theater in Pensacola, Florida. The film, ruled obscene, has been ordered burned by the court.

294 "Three Movies Confiscated." *National Decency Reporter,* 5(9–10): 11, Sept.-Oct. 1968.

Lorna is one of three films confiscated from the Ritz Theater in Pensacola, Florida, in a raid conducted by County Solicitor Carl Harper. On September 20, 1968, the films, were judged to be obscene under Florida law and ordered by the court to be destroyed. Almost two years earlier, *Lorna* had been confiscated at another local theatre and following an unsuccessful district court appeal was ruled obscene.

CENSORSHIP — MARYLAND

*295 de Grazia, Edward, and Newman, Roger K. "Lorna." *Banned Films: Movies, Censors and the First Amendment,* pp. 276–277. New York: R.R. Bowker, 1982.

In 1964 the Maryland State Board of Censors refused to license *Lorna* for exhibition and after viewing it, the Circuit Court of Baltimore upheld the ruling. In October 1965 (Dunn v. Maryland State Board of Censors, 213 A. 2d 751 [1965]) the Maryland Court of Appeals reversed the lower court's order. The legal importance of this case rested upon the constitutional burden of the film censorship board to prove with evidence that a film was obscene prior to denying it a license. The court decided that "enlightening testimony" was necessary to determine if a film met constitutional standards. Recommended.

CENSORSHIP—PENNSYLVANIA

296 "Defense Attempt to Block Criminal Prosecution of 'Lorna' Thwarted." *National Decency Reporter,* 2(5):1–4, Jan. 31, 1965.

On December 10, 1964, a print of *Lorna* was seized by police from the State Theatre in Lebanon, Pennsylvania, and its manager charged with exhibiting an obscene film. Two days later, the corporate owners of the theatre initiated an action in the Court of Common Pleas "seeking to enjoin prosecution of the criminal action." Reprinted here in its entirety is the judge's opinion denying the injunction.

297 "State Theater Raided, Manager Arrested, Film Confiscated." *National Decency Reporter,* 2(3):9, Dec. 1964.

In a December 10, 1964, raid on the State Theater in Lebanon, Pennsylvania, 35mm prints of *Lorna* and the film's advertising are confiscated by detectives responding to numerous citizen complaints filed at the district attorney's office. A detective termed the film a "poor quality production" while other patrons described it as the type of fare "one could expect to see at stag smokers."

REVIEWS

298 Harford, Margaret. "'Lorna' Caricatures Adult Art Features." *Los Angeles Times,* pt. IV, p. 10, Sept. 18, 1964.

Harford refers to Meyer as a "Tennessee Truffaut" and criticizes *Lorna* as "an unintentional caricature . . . of the adult art film."

299 Murf. "Lorna." *Variety,* 239(13): 6, 18, Aug. 18, 1965.

Lorna is identified as Meyer's first serious effort after a string of six nudie films. Murf. deems Meyer's direction "good" and his photography and editing "excellent."

300 Peary, Danny. "Lorna." *Guide for the Film Fanatic,* pp. 248–249. New York: Simon & Schuster, 1986.

Lorna, Meyer's first attempt at serious filmmaking, "impressively" creates a "puritanical, backwoods environment" and effectively chronicles a young woman's repressed sexual impulses. Peary likens Lorna's character to that of Hedy Lamarr's in *Ecstasy,* but is disturbed that she becomes sexually excited and fulfilled by a rapist.

301 Rimmer, Robert. "Lorna." *The X-Rated Videotape Guide,* p. 101. New York: Arlington House, 1984.

This "not to be missed" film marks Meyer's "first blend of sex and violence." Incorrectly dated as 1959 instead of 1964, a typographical error suggests the video is available from F.M. International Films rather than RM Films International.

302 Topp, Gary. "'Lorna' (Cinepix)." *Canadian Film Weekly,* 35(10):4, Mar. 20, 1970.

A total cinematic cliché, but one that Meyer admirer Topp finds makes for "quite an enjoyable movie."

Fanny Hill (1964)

PRODUCTION NOTES

303 "Double Fanny." *Newsweek,* 63(22):83, June 1, 1964.

An amusing report on two simultaneous and competing film productions of John Cleland's novel *Fanny Hill,* one by theatrical producer David Pelham,

the other by producer Albert Zugsmith of *High School Confidential* (1958) fame. The general chaos plaguing the Zugsmith production is forcefully conveyed by the myriad difficulties encountered in casting the title role ultimately filled by Letitia Roman who director Meyer complained refused to cooperate with him. (1 illus.) For Zugsmith's letter rebutting the factual inaccuracies in this article see entry **305**.

*304 Stinnes, Jürgen. "Im Garten der Brüste." *Tip: Berlin Magazin,* 14(24):52, 54, Nov. 14–27, 1985.

With Hamburg distributor Endfilm-Verleih preparing to screen two newly revised prints of *Mudhoney* and *Supervixens* in conjunction with Meyer's 12-city promotional tour of Germany, Heinz Hölscher, cameraman on Meyer's 1964 German/U.S. coproduction *Fanny Hill,* reminisces about the experience. While little was known of Meyer in Germany at the time, Hölscher got along well with the director, stating that Meyer understood his job and worked according to traditional camera methods. Hölscher also notes that Renatte Hutte (later Rena Horten of *Mudhoney* fame), who had a small role in *Fanny Hill,* was "a nice modest, sweet Berlin girl, but not an actress." Highly recommended. (3 illus.)

305 Zugsmith, Albert. "Filming 'Fanny Hill'." *Newsweek,* 64(1): 3A-3B, July 6, 1964.

Albert Zugsmith, producer of *Fanny Hill,* responds to "untrue statements" concerning personnel difficulties on that production which appeared in a June 1, 1964, *Newsweek* article. See entry **303**.

306 "Zugsmith Sets 'Fanny' Co-Prod'n in Germany." *Hollywood Reporter,* 179(22):4, Mar. 2, 1964.

Artur Brauner, head of CCC studios in Spandau-Berlin, announces the March 1964 start of the German-American coproduction of *Fanny Hill: Memoirs of a Woman of Pleasure* to be produced by Albert Zugsmith and directed by Meyer.

307 "Zugsmith's German Co-Prod'n Deal to Film 'Fanny Hill'." *Daily Variety,* 122(60):3, Mar. 2, 1964.

Artur Brauner, head of CCC Studios in West Berlin, announces *Fanny Hill* will be a German/U.S. coproduction in association with Famous Players Corp. of Hollywood. Famous Players allegedly chose the German studio because British censors would not permit the shooting of the film in England.

REVIEWS

308 Crowther, Bosley. "Screen: Poor Fanny Hill!" *New York Times,* p. 48, Dec. 2, 1965.

In a highly negative review, Crowther contends there are literally no similarities between Cleland's novel and the film. (1 illus.)

309 Dale. "Fanny Hill: Memoirs of a Woman of Pleasure." *Variety,* 238 (4):6, Mar. 17, 1965.

A devastating review characterizing the film as "an insult to the integrity and sensibility of the Hollywood motion picture industry." Meyer's direction is termed "dull."

310 Durgnat, Raymond. "Fanny Hill." *Films & Filming,* 12(8):57, May 1966.

British critic Durgnat attacks film ("two hours of tatty medium") for violating the novel's integrity in order to make a quick profit.

Mudhoney (1965)

PROMOTION

311 Hanck, Frauke. "Zusammenstöße beim Football: Russ Meyer auf

---

Opposite: Two views of pneumatic Lorna Maitland from Meyer's second breakthrough film *Lorna* (1964). Note the strategically placed "tree branch" on the censored photo at right, typical of the manner in which his stills were "doctored" for lobby case exhibition.

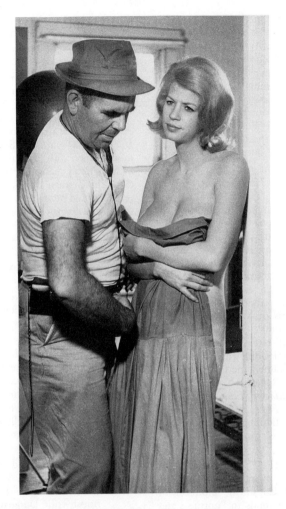

Lorna Maitland seems unimpressed by Meyer's last minute equipment check prior to rolling the cameras for one of the bedroom scenes in *Lorna*.

Deutschland-Tournee." *Film-Echo/Filmwoche*, 39(66):10, Nov. 23, 1985.

Promoting *Mudhoney* and *Supervixens* in Germany, Meyer talks about his plan to shoot scenes in the Black Forest and Munich for the upcoming film *Blitzen, Vixen and Harry*, and also for his magnum opus, *The Breast of Russ Meyer*. Of interest, Meyer also discusses his intention of shooting a music video for black French rock-rap-star Philipe Krootchey. (1 illus.)

312 Müller, Joachim. "Film: Russ Meyer." *Live*, 6(1):92–93, Jan. 1986.

The "Meyer Renaissance" in Germany, sparked by the twin release of *Mudhoney* and *Supervixens* and a biography of the filmmaker by Rolf Thissen, is bolstered by Meyer's tour of the country to promote the films. The article discusses

PASSION DEBASED BY LUST...

MUDHONEY

...LEAVES A TASTE OF EVIL!

...a film of ribaldry and violence made from the juice of life!

produced by RUSS and EVE MEYER
a EVE PRODUCTION

starring: hal HOPPER / antoinette CRISTIANI / john FURLONG / stu LANCASTER
rena HORTEN / frank BOLGER / princess LIVINGSTON / nick WOLCUFF / lee BALLARD
sam HANNA / mickey FOXX / f. rufus OWENS...directed by RUSS MEYER

featuring "THAT GIRL" from LORNA ...Lorna Maitland!
TOO MUCH for One Town!!
IF YOU MISS THIS PICTURE YOU'LL HATE YOURSELF IF YOU MISS THIS PICTURE

Mudhoney (1965): Considered by Roger Ebert to be Meyer's "overlooked masterpiece," the filmmaker admits that the film's sluggish box office reception was due, in part, to its complexities of theme and characterization, which were largely lost on sexploitation audiences of the time.

Mudhoney, "Meyer's neglected masterpiece," and theorizes that a lawsuit against Thissen for his book *Russ Meyer, der König des Sexfilms* may be brewing since Meyer has clearly expressed his distaste for it by refusing to autograph fans' copies. (3 illus.)

REVIEWS

313 Ebert, Roger. "Guilty Pleasures." *Film Comment*, 14(4):49–51, July-Aug. 1978.

Listed among Ebert's ten "guilty pleasures" (odd movies that are not boring and share an "insanely-inspired vision") is *Mudhoney*, "Meyer's overlooked masterpiece" that represents "melodrama taken to obsessed extremes." (6 illus.)

314 "Mud Honey." *Adam Film Quarterly*, 2:37–41, June 1967.
A lavishly illustrated *Adam Film Quarterly* pictorial/review which praises Rena Horten's performance as the deaf mute and calls the film "one of the better

Statuesque German actress Rena Horten, a.k.a. Renatte Hutte, poses in a publicity shot for *Mudhoney* **(1965). Meyer did not let her heavy Teutonic accent prevent him from using her in this Gothic drama set in Depression-era Missouri . . . he cast her as a mute!**

pieces of entertainment out of Hollywood in the past year." (9 illus.)

315 Murf. "Rope of Flesh." *Variety*, 239(13):18, Aug. 18, 1965.

Rope of Flesh, also exhibited under the title *Mudhoney*, is summarized as a "well-produced and directed" dramatic sexploitation film.

316 Peary, Danny. "Mud Honey/ Rope of Flesh." *Guide for the Film Fanatic*, p. 284. New York: Simon & Schuster, 1986.

Meyer "perfectly blends the sex, nudity, and violence" in a film Peary considers perhaps his best.

317 Rimmer, Robert. "Mudhoney." *The X-Rated Videotape Guide*, pp. 107–108. New York: Arlington House, 1984.

The mixture of sex and violence as the vehicle for retribution in *Mudhoney* provided the "basic direction for all . . . (Meyer's) . . . later films." Incorrectly dated as 1976 instead of 1965.

318 Sabatier, J.M. "Le Désir dans les tripes." *Revue du Cinéma*, 283: 125, Apr. 1974.

Sabatier praises *Mudhoney*, stating that one must see the film if only to understand that ten years ago an

In one of the few nude scenes in *Mudhoney*, the rustic mute "Eula" innocently bathes before "Sidney Brenshaw" (Hal Hopper) and "Brother Hanson" (Frank Bolger). *Mudhoney* clearly shows the influence of Al Capp's comic strip *L'il Abner* on Meyer's films: sexually rapacious women and strong, dumb men living and loving in squalor.

American "cinéma d'auteur" was working who had no ties to either Hollywood or the Underground. Noting Meyer's "expressionistic direction," Sabatier concludes that with *Mudhoney* the viewer is "much closer to Faulkner or Caldwell than to the traditional universe of the 'nudie'."

319 Trussell, Jake. "Making the Rounds." *Kingsville-Bishop Rec-*

ord-News, sec. B, p. 1, June 20, 1965.

Playing under the title *Rope of Flesh, Mudhoney* is described as "amazingly adult fare" that "makes *God's Little Acre* look like Walt Disney." Trussell praises the pulchritude of actresses Rena Horten and Lorna Maitland and states that while violent, the film delivers what it promises.

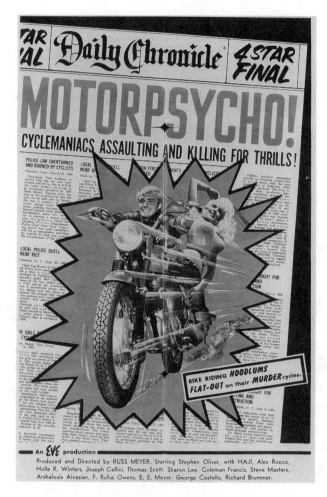

Motorpsycho! (1965): Meyer once again sets the Hollywood trend with *Motorpsycho!,* a tale of stressed-out Vietnam vets astride their "MURDER cycles" terrorizing an innocent populace. This film appeared one year before the American International Pictures release *The Wild Angels* (1966), which is usually credited with starting the sixties trend of outlaw motorcycle gang pictures.

Motorpsycho! (1965)

REVIEWS

320 Dunn, J.A.C. "Although Film-folk Switch the Pitch, 'Adult' Plot Is Still Skin and Sin." *Charlotte Observer,* sec. B, p. 7, Dec. 15, 1965.

Reviewer Dunn fails to understand why *Motorpsycho!* was advertised under the title *Motor Mods and Rockers.* The film's acting is described as "at least well-rehearsed" in this ironic and noncritical review.

321 "Motor Psycho!" *Boxoffice,* sec. Bookinguide, p. 2959, Sept. 20, 1965.

Geared towards the adult crowd in "more populous centers," *Motorpsycho!* is to be commended for Meyer's "directorial prowess" and the "stark realism" of its script. Exhibitors were recommended to invite sociologists and social workers to advance screenings in order to use their comments to promote the film in the news media.

322 "Motor Psycho!" *Adam Film Quarterly*, 2:30–35, June 1967.

A plot synopsis, written in the form of Beat generation fiction, of Meyer's 1965 Eve Productions release *Motorpsycho!* Published in the men's magazine *Adam Film Quarterly*, the article is signed "WR," the possible initials of frequent *Adam* magazine film reviewer William Rotsler. (8 illus.)

323 Murf. "Motor Psycho." *Variety*, 239(13):6, Aug. 18, 1965.

A well-directed and excellently photographed "rape-murder drama" that should prove to be highly exploitable though subject to censorship by "local bluenoses."

324 Powers, James. "'Motorpsycho!' Is Exploitable." *Hollywood Reporter*, 186(45):3, Aug. 13, 1965.

Powers contends that even though Meyer is "a gifted film-maker" his lack of judgment in failing to eliminate the film's "burlesque element" severely "undermines his stronger qualities."

Faster, Pussycat! Kill! Kill! (1966)

REVIEWS

325 "Faster, Pussycat! Kill! Kill!" *Filmfacts*, 9:244, 1966.

A lengthy excerpt from *Variety* reviewer "Murf.'s" February 9, 1966 critique of *Faster, Pussycat! Kill! Kill!* accompanies a detailed plot synopsis and cast/credits list. See entry 329.

326 "Faster, Pussycat! Kill! Kill! *Adam Film Quarterly*, 2:26–29, June 1967.

A men's magazine pictorial on the female leads of *Faster, Pussycat! Kill! Kill!* with skeleton plot synopsis and scant comments referring to it as "one of the most violent films ever made." (8 illus.)

327 Garel, Alain. "Faster, Pussycat! Kill! Kill!: Un Russ meilleur?" *Revue du Cinéma*, 405:34, Mai 1985.

Though Garel does not agree with John Waters' assessment of *Faster!* as being the best film ever made, he does feel it is a worthy effort by "this singular director." (1 illus.)

328 Hoberman, James. "Offbeat Genre Flicks." *Premiere*, 1(1):99, July/Aug. 1987.

Hoberman, film critic for *The Village Voice*, lists his ten favorite genre flicks on video, among them *Faster, Pussycat! Kill! Kill!* which he likens to having the "convoluted quality of a gothic novel."

329 Murf. "Faster, Pussycat, Kill! Kill!" *Variety*, 241(12):6, Feb. 9, 1966.

A technically well-made production marred by a muddled script that nevertheless demonstrates Meyer to possess "a directorial talent which belongs in bigger and stronger films."

330 Peary, Danny. "Faster, Pussycat! Kill! Kill!" *Guide for the Film Fanatic*, pp. 147–148. New York: Simon & Schuster, 1986.

An ideal drive-in movie made noteworthy by its fast-paced action sequences and its unique featuring of "three independent, aggressive, voluptuous females." Peary ranks Tura Satana ("Varla") second only to Erica Gavin ("Vixen") as "Meyer's best heroine."

331 Peary, Danny. "Faster, Pussycat! Kill! Kill!" *Cult Movies 3*, pp. 82–87. New York: Simon & Schuster, 1988.

Peary begins his critique of the film by pointing to Meyer's many directorial failings including his inability to

Faster, Pussycat! Kill! Kill! (1966): Meyer inverted the male gang formula of *Motorpsycho!* (1965) to create an all-female gang whose frank dominance and superiority over men served to presage the more "benevolent" sexual power displayed by Erica Gavin in *Vixen*.

make any film that is not a broad parody. Peary does admit, however, that *Faster!* is "the least objectionable of Meyer's films" and its violence can be forgiven because it is uncharacteristically not directed toward women. The scenes of violence "are all boldly directed" and reminiscent of scenes in Sam Fuller and Don Siegel films. (9 illus.)

332   Rimmer, Robert. "Faster Pussycat, Kill! Kill!" *The X-Rated Videotape Guide*, p. 90. New York: Arlington House, 1984.

More violent than most Meyer films, Rimmer states that "there's not much nudity" in it. In actuality, the film contains no nudity. Rimmer also incorrectly dates the film as 1977, not 1966.

*333   Rose, Cynthia. "Faster, Pussycat! Kill! Kill!" *Monthly Film Bulletin*, 48(575):243, Dec. 1981.

A retrospective review attempting to historically place the film into the "American trash aesthetic" and to assess its seminal influence on the evolution of the genre. Recommended.

334   Thomas, Kevin. "Sadism Rampant in Double Bill." *Los Angeles Times*, pt. IV, p. 11, Mar. 11, 1966.

The "ludicrously erotic and sadis-

Tura Satana, Haji, and Lori Williams take a break from their characterizations as the psychotic go-go girl gang in *Faster, Pussycat! Kill! Kill!* to pose for a painfully artificial publicity shot.

tic" double bill of *Faster, Pussycat! Kill! Kill!* and *Motorpsycho!* leads Thomas to conclude that both films are essentially "parodies of the entire genre of exploitation pictures."

335 Wasserman, John L. "Meyer's Amateurs: Two Films with But One Thought." *San Francisco Chronicle*, p. 41, Apr. 19, 1966.
     Meyer, "a graduate of the cudgel school of direction," delivers a duo of unique films to the Presidio Theatre: *Faster, Pussycat! Kill! Kill!* ("the worst script ever written") and *Mudhoney* ("the worst film ever made").

Mondo Topless (1966)

REVIEWS

336 Carruthers, Jeff B. "Sub-Lit Sex Set Sees Topless Scene." *Minnesota Daily*, 68(52):15, Nov. 10, 1966.

In the only known newspaper review of *Mondo Topless*, Carruthers reports for the University of Minnesota student newspaper that the film's "trite material is made aesthetically pleasing" by its photography and its imaginative juxtaposition of curvaceous women with starkly linear objects like high-tension towers. Academically, Carruther concludes, the film might appeal to anthropologists and sociologists interested in observing audience reaction. Also briefly noted is *Erotica*, which played as a second feature to *Mondo Topless*.

337 Rimmer, Robert. "Mondo Topless." *The X-Rated Videotape Guide*, p. 106. New York: Arlington House, 1984.
     Rimmer warns female videotape viewers with small breasts that they will not like this film. The film is incorrectly dated as 1976 instead of 1966.

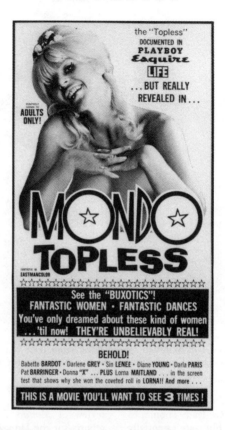

Mondo Topless (1966): "Go-go girls—in and out of their environment—are revealed in scenes that can only be called a swinging tribute to the unrestrained female anatomy! Go, baby! Go!"—Publicity.

Common-Law Cabin (1967)

REVIEWS

338 "How Much Loving Does a Normal Couple Need?" *Filmfacts*, 10:437, 1967.

A brief plot synopsis with cast and credit listings for Meyer's 1967 Eve Productions release *How Much Loving Does a Normal Couple Need?*, more popularly known as *Common-Law Cabin*.

339 Peary, Danny. "Common Law Cabin/How Much Loving Does a Normal Couple Need?" *Guide*

for the Film Fanatic, p. 101. New York: Simon & Schuster, 1986.

The "Existential aspects" of the story lead Peary to conclude that had the film been made in a foreign language by a European director "it could pass as a masterpiece" worthy to share a double bill with *Knife in the Water*.

340 Rimmer, Robert. "Common Law Cabin." *The X-Rated Videotape Guide*, pp. 74–75. New York: Arlington House, 1984.

Rimmer notes that in this 1967 production Meyer had yet to perfect his "sex-and-violence bit" as much as in later films.

Darlene Grey in *Mondo Topless*—"A mere slip of a frail tipping the scales at only 112 pounds ... but get this ... her untoppable ... gravity-defying ... bra-busting Boobs have got to comprise nearly 23 lbs. of that total by themselves!"—Publicity.

341 Sabatier, J.M. "Combien de fois faut-il faire l'amour pour être un couple normal?" *Revue du Cinéma*, 288/289:68–69, Oct. 1974.

A favorable, rather bemused, review of the "totally absurd" *Common-Law Cabin* which was not distributed in France until six years after its release.

Good Morning and Goodbye! (1967)

CENSORSHIP—KENTUCKY

342 Simpson, Woody. "Movies." *Lexington Herald Leader*, UNKNOWN, Jan. 19, 1969.

The confiscation of *Good Morning and Goodbye!* and the arrest of the projectionist showing it at a downtown Lexington, Kentucky, theatre serve as the basis for Simpson's eloquent essay attacking censorship.

REVIEWS

343 Gearing, Nigel. "The Lust Seekers." *Monthly Film Bulletin*, 42 (496):111, May 1975.

British critic Gearing's retrospective review of Meyer's 1967 film *The Lust Seekers*, exhibited in America under the title *Good Morning and Goodbye!*, points to character stereotypes and dialogue clichés that serve to "ensure *both* a serviceable skin-flick and a satire of the whole genre."

344 "Goodmorning and Goodbye." *Filmfacts*, 9:34–35, 1968.

In addition to a plot synopsis and cast/credits list, excerpts from reviews in *Variety* and the *New York Times* are included. (1 illus.) See entries 345 and 349.

Common-Law Cabin (1967) and *Mudhoney* (1965): Following their first run, Meyer often paired "theme" films together on double bills for later drive-in exhibition. Similarly, *Motorpsycho!* (1965) and *Faster, Pussycat! Kill! Kill!* (1966) also played in tandem.

345   Murf. "Good Morning . . . and Goodbye." *Variety,* 249(5):14, Dec. 4, 1967.

Murf. cites the film's strong script and technical excellence calling Meyer an American *auteur* "largely undiscovered by aesthetes who fawn over much lesser product from foreign and domestic obscurities."

346   Pelegrine, Louis. "Good Morning and Goodbye." *Film Daily,* 131 (118):7, Dec. 27, 1967.

A film with good box office potential that combines realistic sex with strong drama.

347   Redelings, Lowell. "Good Morning . . . and Goodbye!" *Motion Picture Daily,* UNKNOWN, Dec. 7, 1967.

Redelings maintains that this engrossing and well-paced adult drama has achieved Meyer's purpose: "to make an uncompromising, factual, no-punches-pulled film about the intimate lives of rural townspeople."

348   Rimmer, Robert. "Good Morning and Goodbye." *The X-Rated Videotape Guide,* p. 93. New York: Arlington House, 1984.

Rimmer notes that Meyer has an

Babette Bardot, no relation to Brigitte, frolics in the Colorado River in a publicity shot for *Common-Law Cabin* (1967). Originally titled *How Much Loving Does a Normal Couple Need?*, Meyer hastily retitled it after several exhibitors complained it was too large to fit on their marquees.

affinity for depicting older men/younger women relationships. *Good Morning and Goodbye!* is incorrectly dated as 1977 rather than 1967.

349 Weiler, A.H. "'Good Morning and Goodbye!' Opens." *New York Times,* p. 53, Feb. 20, 1968.
The film is described as a "paean to pectoral development."

Finders Keepers, Lovers Weepers! (1968)

MISCELLANEOUS

350 Eichelbaum, Stanley. "Hollywood Forcing Nudie King to Greater Depths." *San Francisco Examiner,* p. 31, Nov. 11, 1968.

Absent from this *Common-Law Cabin* montage comprised of blonde Babette Bardot and brunette Adele Rein is buxom Alaina Capri. Ads for the film sought to exploit the supposedly identical body measurements of the trio—44-24-34.

Meyer insists that nudity is essential for a low-budget film to succeed in the current box office environment of sexually permissive movies. In fact, Meyer points to the increasingly graphic offerings of the major studios as providing the impetus for his ever more outrageous depictions of simulated sex. The huge success of his latest "nudie suspense thriller," *Finders Keepers, Lovers Weepers!*, is also commented upon. (1 illus.)

351 Fosse, Lloyd Elisabeth. "She Enjoys Acting with Clothes On." *Kankakee Daily Journal*, p. 5, July 18, 1973.

On a visit with her aunt who resides in Kankakee, Illinois, actress Lavelle Roby *(Finders Keepers, Lovers Weepers!, Beyond the Valley of the Dolls)* is interviewed concerning the dearth of job opportunities for blacks in movies.

Also discussed is her non-nude work for Meyer, whom she describes as most respectful in his treatment of her as both an actress and a woman. (4 illus.)

352 Petzold, Charles. "He Puts a Grin in Skin Movies." *Philadelphia Daily News*, p. 35, Apr. 28, 1969.

Meyer discusses the humor in his work and compares the content of his films in relation to those produced by his competitors, the major studios. Of historical note, Meyer's current feature *Finders Keepers, Lovers Weepers!* is cited as the first of his "nude wave" films to be exhibited in a family theatre instead of an "art house." (1 illus.)

353 "Russ Meyer Nude Pic into Philly's 'Class' First-Run." *Variety*, UNKNOWN, Mar. 7, 1969.

The booking of *Finders Keepers, Lovers Weepers!* into Philadelphia's first-run Randolph Theatre marks a

...for those
who measure success
only in the hours before
the morning light!

The *ULTIMATE* Film...by *Russ Meyer*

Good Morning
...and goodbye!

RECOMMENDED FOR ONLY THE MOST MATURE

Starring

•Alaina CAPRI • Stuart LANCASTER • HAJI •
Pat WRIGHT • Karen CIRAL • Don JOHNSON
Tom HOWLAND • Megan TIMOTHY
Toby ADLER • Sylvia TEDEMAR • Carol PETERS

an EVE PRODUCTION in EASTMANCOLOR screenplay John E. MORAN

Good Morning and Goodbye! (1967): "The characters in 'Good Morning and Goodbye!' are identifiable . . . perhaps even familiar . . . because their words and actions reflect the basic emotions of man—love, lust, hate, fear, jealousy, contentment . . . desire."—Publicity.

breakthrough for Meyer, whose films usually play in art houses. Meyer attributes a lot of his success to the fact that he travels extensively to promote his films.

354 Schier, Ernest. "Show World: You Spell Success with Dollar Signs." *Philadelphia Evening Bulletin*, p. 37, Apr. 22, 1969.

Meyer credits the current wave of sex and nudity in mainstream films with the heavy demand his *Finders Keepers,*

Lovers Weepers! has been enjoying from theatre chains who previously refused to exhibit his work. The film marks Meyer's initial entry into first-run theatres in Philadelphia. (1 illus.)

CENSORSHIP—LOUISIANA

355 Goldstein, Al. "Short Shit." *Screw,* 53:12, Mar. 8, 1970.

The Louisiana State Supreme Court by a four-to-two decision upheld a

Classic "bitch" Alaina Capri verbally and sexually taunts her impotent husband in an early
scene from *Good Morning and Goodbye!*

lower court ruling that the district attorney of Baton Rouge violated the law
when he ordered *Finders Keepers, Lovers
Weepers!* seized as obscene without a
prior adversary hearing. Goldstein wrote
this article under his pen-name "Al
Pseudonym."

CENSORSHIP — MISSOURI

356   "Judge Drops 'Obscene' Charge
in Film Seizure." *Boxoffice,* 95
(21):C-1, Sept. 8, 1969.
Obscenity charges are dropped
against a St. Louis theatre operator for
showing *Finders Keepers, Lovers Weepers!* after it was determined that the film
was confiscated without a prior adversary
hearing to determine if it was obscene.

REVIEWS

*357   Canby, Vincent. "Screen: By Russ
Meyer." *New York Times,* p. 21,
Sept. 6, 1969.
Using the "grunting love scenes"
in *Finders Keepers, Lovers Weepers!* as a
basis for discussion, Canby questions
whether the "changing patterns of sexual
behavior in conventional films" have not
made Meyer's "decently intended softcore pornographic films" a bit archaic.
Canby does, however, number among
the film's virtues "a lack of moral preten-
sion" and "a sort of low humor." Recommended. (1 illus.)

358   Eichelbaum, Stanley. "Suspense
Plot Laid Bare." *San Francisco Examiner,* p. 9, Nov. 9, 1968.
Eichelbaum's savage review attacks *Finders Keepers, Lovers Weepers!*
as "trash" and Meyer's direction as
"primitive." Meyer is further chided for
his seeming refusal to test his talent by
making legitimate films.

"The Catalyst" (Haji) prepares to revivify an impotent "Burt Boland" (Stuart Lancaster) in a mystical sequence from *Good Morning and Goodbye!*

359 Elliott, David. "Vintage Trash from Russ." *Chicago Daily News* (Red Streak Ed.), p. 14, Apr. 20, 1971.

Compared with the big-budget, studio-produced *Beyond the Valley of the Dolls,* Elliott finds this low-budget, independently produced film to be "a vigorous, glossy, well-trimmed piece of schlock entertainment" representative of Meyer's early films of "vintage vulgarity." (1 illus.)

360 Etchison, Michael. "Lover's Promises." *Los Angeles Herald-Examiner,* sec. C, p. 6, Oct. 30, 1968.

Though Meyer's technical expertise has improved from film to film, his plots continue to be so simplistic that the viewer feels as though something is missing. Meyer's "obsession with violence" is noted and blamed for making the sex in the film "boring after a while."

361 "Finders Keepers, Lovers Weepers." *Filmfacts,* 12(19):441–443, 1969.

Detailed credits and a plot synopsis are followed by excerpts from five newspaper and magazine reviews. (1 illus.)

362 "Finders Keepers, Lovers Weepers." *Cinema,* 8th Annual Awards Issue, p. 16, 1971.

The "thoughtful performances" of Gordon Wescourt and Anne Chapman are cited as helping to make this "Russ Meyer's most satisfying film."

363 Imeson, Jo. "Finders Keepers, Lovers Weepers." *Monthly Film Bulletin,* 48(575):243–244, Dec. 1981.

The film lacks "the fast-paced comic-strip gusto of Meyer's more developed work" due no doubt to its "more restricted plot line."

Finders Keepers, Lovers Weepers! (1968): The first of Meyer's films to be booked into a "class" first-run house—Philadelphia's Randolph Theatre, summer of 1969.

364 Knoblauch, Mary. "Meyer's 'Finders Keepers'." *Chicago Today,* sec. Family Today, p. 32, Apr. 20, 1971.

Knoblauch concludes that Meyer "could be one of the best directors of mystery-suspense films around" if he chose to "cast and direct performers for their acting ability" rather than for their bodies.

365 Mahoney, John. "'Finders Keepers' Good: Russ Meyer Is Producer-Director." *Hollywood Reporter,* 200(46):3–4, May 10, 1968.

A technically proficient, slick production "for the androgen auditoriums."

366 Monahan, Anthony. "The Movies: '...Lovers Weepers." *Chicago Sun-Times,* p. 54, Apr. 19, 1971.

Only just playing first-run in Chicago three years after it was released in 1968, *Finders Keepers, Lovers Weepers!* is termed "small budget and shows it." Rated two stars out of a possible four.

367 Murf. "Finders Keepers, Lovers Weepers." *Variety,* 250(13):26, May 15, 1968.

Murf.'s highly favorable review, calling the film Meyer's "best to date," is of special interest in that it also mentions the early career difficulties Meyer encountered trying to break into moviemaking.

Aquatic adulterers Anne Chapman and Gordon Wescourt make love in a pool scene from *Finders Keepers, Lovers Weepers!* A moralizing Meyer intercut footage of a stock car demolition derby into this scene to comment on the impending disastrous consequences of adultery.

368 "N.Y. Critics Focus on Fellini's Episode and Meyer's Enjoyable Pornography." *Variety,* 256(4):6, Sept. 10, 1969.

A short piece noting that the recent film openings in New York City feature the names of prominent directors like Fellini and Meyer over the marquee for box office drawing power. Reviews of *Finders Keepers, Lovers Weepers!* from two sources are cited.

369 Ogar, Richard. "Bright Knight of the Nudies." *Berkeley Barb,* 7(21), no. 170, p. 7, Nov. 15–21, 1968.

A negative review of *Finders Keepers, Lovers Weepers!* appearing in the underground tabloid *Berkeley Barb* that roundly criticizes Meyer's system of personal values as depicted in his films. (1 illus.)

370 Peary, Danny. "Finders Keepers . . . Lovers Weepers." *Guide for the Film Fanatic,* pp. 149–150. New York: Simon & Schuster, 1986.

Meyer's typical humor is replaced by a "cruel edge" that Peary feels will disappoint even the filmmaker's most diehard fans.

371 Rimmer, Robert. "Finders Keepers . . . Lovers Weepers." *The X-Rated Videotape Guide,* p. 90. New York: Arlington House, 1984.

A standard Meyer film that combines large-breasted women and violence. Rimmer incorrectly dates the film 1978 rather than 1968.

372 Thomas, Kevin. "'Finders Keepers' at Cinema Theater." *Los Angeles Times,* pt. IV, p. 9, Oct. 29, 1968.

Proceeding at the pace of a "Pearl White serial," *Finders* is a "kind of glorious trash" made by a man that

Thomas feels has "decided directorial ability." The critic also likens Meyer to a "Victorian melodramatist" who paradoxically has such a clean and healthy mind for a person who produces sexploitation films.

373 Wasserman, John L. "'Finders Keepers' Opens Here." *San Francisco Chronicle*, p. 33, Nov. 9, 1968.

Meyer's latest has the "dubious distinction" of being a "good sex-and-violence film." (1 illus.)

374 Wolf, William. "New Films." *Cue*, 38(37):88, Sept. 13, 1969.

Meyer's films always promise "beautiful busts" and "amusing ... dialogue," but the coupling of sex with violence makes *Finders Keepers, Lovers Weepers!* "brutal, ugly, and mean."

Vixen (1968)

PRODUCTION NOTES

375 "Movie Call Sheet." *Los Angeles Times*, pt. IV, p. 22, Sept. 7, 1972.

The screenplay for Russ Meyer Films sequel to *Vixen, Foxy,* will be written by Jerry Wish from an original story by Meyer.

*376 Peary, Danny. "From 'Vixen' to Vindication: Erica Gavin Interviewed." *Velvet Light Trap*, 16: 22–27, Fall 1976.

A bitter Erica Gavin talks about her post–Meyer career and on reflection blames the filmmaker for sexually exploiting and subsequently stereotyping her as the title character *Vixen* in the eyes of the motion picture industry. This lengthy interview conducted in January 1975 chronicles Gavin's nascent feminism and paints a highly unflattering view of Meyer's directorial abilities. The most positive comment Gavin can make regarding Meyer is "that he never once came on to me sexually." Must reading

for those interested in Erica Gavin's career and her personal behind-the-scenes perceptions of the making of *Vixen*. (6 illus.)

*377 Wolfe, Burton. "King of the Nudie Movies." *True*, pp. 43–47, 100–101, 104–105, Mar. 1969.

A great biographical piece by Wolfe that gives a highly accurate and fair assessment of Meyer and his films. Visiting Meyer on the location of *Vixen*, Wolfe describes the shooting of the film's lesbian lovemaking scene and its traumatic effect on actress Erica ("Vixen") Gavin. Meyer's fear that hardcore will destroy the market for his type of softcore entertainment leads Wolfe to conclude that "censorship ... has been the real secret of Russ Meyer's success." Highly recommended. (5 illus.)

PROMOTION

378 Kay, Virginia. ["Virginia Kay Byline."]. *Chicago Daily News* (Red Streak Ed.), p. 17, Feb. 13, 1969.

In Chicago promoting *Vixen*, Meyer identifies his chief competition as being the major studios who produce big-budget sex films like *Candy* and *The Killing of Sister George*.

379 Safran, Don. "Britain's Townsend Due." *Dallas Times Herald*, sec. E, p. 1, Apr. 20, 1969.

In Dallas promoting *Vixen*, Meyer declares that there was never any perversion in his films because he found it to be "un–American."

380 "'Vixen' Debut in N.Y." *Boxoffice*, 95(4):E-1, May 12, 1969.

In this short piece announcing the May 16th New York premiere of *Vixen*, Meyer is credited with initiating "a new trend in American film production and exhibition."

MISCELLANEOUS

381 Boyd, L.M. "The Grab Bag." *San Francisco Chronicle*, sec. Punch, p. 8, Sept. 28, 1980.

Vixen (1968): Meyer's first and only attempt to make an erotic film grossed $15 million on a $72,000 investment and spawned numerous lawsuits for obscenity. Attributing much of the film's success to Erica Gavin, *Vixen* represents the solidification of Meyer's cinematic view of woman as sexual predator.

In response to a reader's question, Boyd identifies *Vixen* as the longest running movie at a drive-in theatre: 54 straight weeks in Aurora, Illinois.

382 Branzburg, Paul. "Campus Competition." *Chicago Tribune,* sec. 11, p. 11, Nov. 7, 1971.

Vixen is featured in an article reporting on the "soaring national phenomenon" of commercial films being shown on college campuses by student groups and its financially negative impact on local movie exhibitors and their trade organizations.

383 Calloway, Earl. "Harrison Page, Black Actor Debuts in 'Vixen' Role." *Chicago Daily Defender,* p. 11, Feb. 18, 1969.

A biographical sketch of Harrison Page, the actor who portrays the black draft dodger "Niles" in *Vixen.*

384 Cassyd, Syd. "Backstage." *Boxoffice,* 96(19):W-2, Feb. 23, 1970.

Meyer announces at the Directors Guild Awards that *Vixen* has grossed so well that he is investing in a nineteen-story building on Hollywood Boulevard as part of a syndicate.

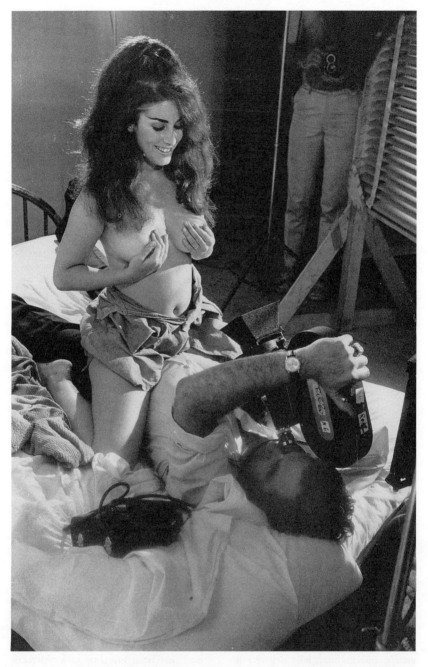

Typically involved in every phase of production, director/cameraman Meyer photographs an enthusiastic Erica Gavin in *Vixen*.

385   "Chi B.O. Big, 'Vixen' Nabbing Record Receipts." *Daily Variety,* 142(57):2, Feb. 26, 1969.

The "giant" $55,000 Chicago premiere of *Vixen* establishes a new house record at the Loop Theatre.

386   "Chicago." *Boxoffice,* 95(8):C-4, June 9, 1969.

In what will mark the first uncut showing of *Vixen* in Wisconsin, the management of the Rialto Theatre in Racine negotiate with Gilbreth Films for rights to the exclusive run of the film.

387   "Chicago." *Boxoffice,* 104(15): C-4, Jan. 21, 1974.

The incredible business *Vixen* is still doing in theatres that only a year ago would never have played it leads many exhibitors to explain that the film is distinguished from other adult features by its humor and outstanding photography.

388   Cross, Robert. "The 'Skin-Flicks' of Producer Russ Meyer." *Chicago Tribune,* sec. 1A, p. 8, Feb. 16, 1969.

Chicago critic Cross examines Meyer's career and notes the slowly increasing critical attention the filmmaker is receiving. Of interest are the observations of Oscar Brotman, owner of several showcase theatres in downtown Chicago including the Loop where *Vixen* is currently playing, on his efforts to placate local authorities who threatened to censor the film. (1 illus.)

389   Haas, Joseph. "The Year of the Vixen." *Chicago Daily News* (Red Streak Ed.), sec. Panorama, p. 13, Dec. 27–28, 1969.

Vixen's nearly one million dollar gross accumulated over a 42 consecutive week run at the 585 seat Loop Theatre raises the question why business for "quality pictures" is decreasing in downtown Chicago while "flesh-and-blood cheapies" are prospering. Opinions of several distributors and local industry insiders are offered to explain the phenomenon. (1 illus.)

390   Lavin, Cheryl. "The Fast Track: Runners." *Chicago Tribune,* sec. 9, p. 6, July 18, 1982.

The status of *Vixen* as the longest continuously running film in one theatre (57 weeks at the Starlight Drive-In in Elgin, Illinois) is noted as is Meyer's upcoming $2.7 million "hard R" rated film, *Blitzen, Vixen and Harry.*

391   Porter, Bob. "Meyer Faces Competition." *Dallas Times Herald,* sec. B, p. 5, Apr. 18, 1969.

Meyer views the competition *Vixen* is receiving from the major studio films as indicative of the new screen freedom. (1 illus.)

392   Prelutsky, Burt. "King Leer: Keeping America Safe for Skin Flicks Is Tough Work for Russ Meyer." *Los Angeles Times,* sec. WEST Magazine, p. 8, June 8, 1969.

Meyer's seminal influence in changing the sexual mores of mainstream motion pictures is examined. The anticommunist message in *Vixen* is also discussed as illustrative of Meyer's use of sex to make a personal statement.

393   "Russ Meyer Extends Mileage His Esoterica Erotica Pics." *Hollywood Reporter,* 205(42):3, Apr. 29, 1969.

In order to extend the playdates and exhibit in the more prestigious non-art house venues, Meyer plans to release his proposed next film, *Moonshine Massacre,* in both "R" and "X" rated versions. Subsequent to exhausting the art house market in first-run, Meyer then intends to re-edit the self-imposed X-rated film and submit it to the MPAA for an R-rating. A significant indication of the majors' newfound acceptance of nudity, Meyer notes, is the booking of *Vixen* into three first-class Loew's theatres in Los Angeles ... a first for Meyer.

394   Siskel, Gene. "It's All Fabulous." *Chicago Tribune,* sec. 2, p. 5, Mar. 17, 1970.

Meyer expresses his opinion that

skin flicks are not solely responsible for the decline of Chicago's Loop, pointing instead to fast food outlets and discount transistor radio shops which abound in the area.

*395 Siskel, Gene. "Next: 'Karate Rape in Harlem'." *Chicago Tribune*, sec. 6, pp. 3–4, Dec. 2, 1973.

Siskel blames the deterioration of quality films exhibited in the Loop on the trend initiated by the low-budget, high-grossing successes of three genre exploitation films: *Vixen, Sweet Sweetback's Baadasss Song,* and *Five Fingers of Death.* More importantly, Siskel's cogent discussion identifies the various economic, racial, and sexual elements both within and outside the movie world that have contributed to making the Loop what he terms as "the movie cesspool of Chicago." Siskel further attributes the incredible commercial success of *Vixen* and its spawn of imitators with the responsibility for earmarking Chicago as "a skin-flick hick town." This excellent article also offers comments from Oscar Brotman, owner of the Loop Theatre where *Vixen* played for 43 weeks, on the advertising strategy he employed for the film. Highly recommended. (3 illus.)

396 Storck, Dorothy. "Director Russ Meyer: He Sees Everything with the Naked Eye." *Chicago Today American*, sec. 1, p. 4, Feb. 15, 1969.

Prior to the opening of *Vixen* in Chicago, Oscar Brotman (owner of the Loop Theatre) plans to submit the film to the state attorney's office for review to determine if it can be prosecuted as obscene. Storck whimsically notes that although she has yet to see the film, a *Vixen* trailer at the Loop caused a crowd rush to get into the theatre. (1 illus.)

CENSORSHIP — FLORIDA

397 "After Five Weeks, Shut Down 'Vixen'." *Variety*, 256(11):8, Oct. 29, 1969.

Jacksonville, Florida police shut down Sheldon Mandell's Five Points Theatre on obscenity charges even though *Vixen* had shown there unharassed for five continuous weeks. The circuit court suit charges Mandell with "showing for public consumption an obscene, lewd, lascivious, filthy and indecent picture" that "sullies the reputation of the Canadian mounted police."

398 "Fla. Censorship Is Illegal, Federal Judge Rules." *Boxoffice*, 97 (16):4, Aug. 3, 1970.

In a split decision, three federal judges rule that the Florida obscenity law used by police to seize a print of *Vixen* at Sheldon Mandell's Five Points Theatre in Jacksonville is unconstitutional because it does not permit a prior court hearing to determine if the film was obscene by national standards.

399 "Florida Obscenity Law Before Supreme Court." *Boxoffice,* 98 (6): 4, Nov. 23, 1970.

The U.S. Supreme Court agrees to review the constitutionality of the Florida obscenity law which attorneys for *Vixen* persuaded a lower federal district court to be unconstitutional.

400 "Florida Obscenity Rules Target in New Film Suit." *Boxoffice,* 96 (5):SE-1, Nov. 17, 1969.

Attorneys for plaintiffs Meyer, Eve Productions, and Atlanta film distributor Jack Vaughn request that a three-judge federal court review the constitutionality of a section of Florida's obscenity law to determine if police seizure of a print of *Vixen* from Sheldon Mandell's Five Points Theatre in Jacksonville was legal.

401 "Halts 'RM's Vixen' After Receiving Court Summons." *Boxoffice,* 95(26):SE-1, Oct. 13, 1969.

Jacksonville police serve exhibitor Sheldon Mandell with a summons to appear in court to answer the charge that he violated a state statute against showing a lewd film by exhibiting *Vixen.* The film, which the summons charges is "an obscene, lewd, lascivious, filthy and

Considered by Meyer to be the most erotic scene he has yet filmed, brother "Judd" (Jon Evans) and sister "Vixen" (Erica Gavin) share more than a shower in the 1968 box office smash *Vixen*.

indecent picture...," had just begun its sixth lucrative week at the theatre.

402 Mouer, Dan. "Vixen Busted on Stone-Age Law." *Screw,* 51:10, Feb. 23, 1970.

Jacksonville, Florida, police seize *Vixen* on obscenity charges and arrest Sheldon Mandell, owner of the Five Points Theatre where the film was playing to packed houses. Mandell, who won a federal court suit to re-exhibit *Vixen,* voluntarily withdrew the popular film after receiving threatening phone calls and the "cold shoulder treatment" from friends and associates. An attorney representing the film's distributor who is challenging the Florida law maintains the obscenity statute is unconstitutional because it requires "film seizure prior to any hearings" and permits "arrests and seizures solely on a policeman's decision." Mouer argues against the absurdity of allowing the police to determine

obscenity and warns Florida that by "busting" *Vixen,* a "decent, non-exploitative ... sex film," they are letting the rest of the world pass them by.

403 Perkins, Otis. "Lawyers Attack Obscenity Law." *Florida Times-Union and Jacksonville Journal,* sec. D, p. 10, Jan. 18, 1970.

An attorney for the owner of the Jacksonville, Florida, Five Points Theatre where a print of *Vixen* was seized by police argues before a three-judge federal court that the state's vague obscenity law violates the First Amendment (freedom of speech) and "chills the legal rights and monetary interests of the persons against whom it is invoked."

404 Perkins, Otis. "'Vixen' Returns: Seizure Stayed." *Florida Times-Union,* sec. B, p. 1, Oct. 8, 1969.

Just days following the seizure of *Vixen* from the Five Points Theatre by

Jacksonville, Florida, vice squad officers, U.S. District Court Judge William A. McRae, Jr., issues a temporary restraining order which enjoins police from suppressing the film until a hearing is held to determine if it is obscene.

405 "Print Sprung, 'Vixen' Suing Fla. Sheriff; Sez Law Fractured." *Variety*, 257(8):5, Jan. 7, 1970.

Plaintiffs Meyer of Eve Productions and Atlanta distributor Jack Vaughn request a three-judge federal court to review the constitutionality of Florida's obscenity law which was used to seize a print of *Vixen* from the Five Points Theatre in Jacksonville on October 3, 1969.

406/7 "'Vixen' Closed as Lewd Film." *National Decency Reporter*, 6(9–10):14, Sept.-Oct. 1969.

Jacksonville, Florida, officers stop a performance of *Vixen* and charge the theatre's owner-manager with exhibiting a lewd movie that graphically depicts (according to the charge) "a physically attractive female engaging in sexual intercourse with a Canadian mountie."

CENSORSHIP — GEORGIA

408 "Nab 'Vixen' Print and 18-Year-Old House Mgr. in Macon Porno Protest." *Variety*, 253(10):12, Jan. 22, 1969.

Bibb County sheriff's officers halt the showing of *Vixen* at the Weis Drive-In near Macon, Georgia, and charge an 18-year-old house manager and a projectionist with the possession and exhibition of an obscene work.

409 "Police Halt Movie." *National Decency Reporter*, 6(1–2):15, Jan.-Feb. 1969.

Vixen is confiscated from the Weis Drive-In Theater in Macon, Georgia, and the manager and projectionist arrested on obscenity charges by police acting on citizens' complaints. The two were indicted by the Bibb County Grand Jury who urged strong legislation to curb the influx of smut into the county.

410 "'Vixen' Counter-Sues Officials; Legal Costs of Their Defense Now Issue." *Variety*, 254(6):22, Mar. 26, 1969.

An attorney for the Weis Drive-In files a countersuit in federal court against four local sheriff's officers who seized a print of *Vixen* in a middle Georgia theatre in January 1969. Speculation centered on whether the state of Georgia or the Bibb County Board of Commissioners were legally responsible for payment of legal fees engendered by the officers' defense.

411 "A Year of Litigation in Macon, Ga.; 'Vixen' Seems 'Free,' Though Ended." *Variety*, 257(9):38, Jan. 14, 1970.

One year after a print of *Vixen* was seized by county sheriff's officers as allegedly obscene, a Bibb County Superior Court judge dismisses the original indictments against Weis Drive-In employees and officials. The return of the film to the theatre prompted both sides to withdraw their appeals to the higher federal court. The owner of the Weis chain, however, voluntarily stated he would never again show *Vixen* in his theatres.

CENSORSHIP — GREAT BRITAIN

412 Middleman. "Russ Meyer and His Boobs." *Video Trade Weekly*, 58:41, Jan. 13, 1983.

The filmmaker is interviewed while in London to deliver The Guardian Lecture at the National Film Theatre's restrospective of his work. The main topic under discussion is censorship, especially of *Vixen* which the British Film Censorship Board shortened from 71 to 47 minutes. (3 illus.)

CENSORSHIP — ILLINOIS

413 Acton, Bill. "Jury Rules 'Vixen' Obscene." *Danville Commercial-News*, p. 19, Apr. 16, 1970.

A Danville, Illinois, jury convicts

the owner of the Illiana Drive-In Theater of exhibiting the film *Vixen* despite a defense appearance by noted film critic Arthur Knight who testified that *Vixen* was not obscene, had some redeeming social value, and did not violate prevailing community standards on obscenity as witnessed by the 10,000 persons who had viewed the film in its seven-week run in Danville. Attorneys for the plaintiff plan to appeal the case to the Supreme Court if necessary.

414 Ebert, Roger. "Film Notebook: Hitting the Little Guy." *Chicago Sun-Times*, p. 45, Feb. 14, 1969.

Ebert defends *Vixen* against prosecutorial rumors that threaten to postpone its Chicago opening.

CENSORSHIP — MICHIGAN

415 "Judge Took Trooper's Word Re 'Vixen'; Mgr., Boothman Freed in Niles, Mich." *Variety*, 255 (22):30, May 28, 1969.

Obscenity charges are dropped against the manager and projectionist of the Number 31 Drive-In Theatre in Niles, Michigan, after Chicago attorney Elmer Gertz persuades a district court judge that their arrests were unconstitutional without a prior adversary judicial hearing to determine if *Vixen* is obscene. The arrests and film confiscation stemmed from a warrant based upon the affidavit of a state trooper who personally considered the film obscene.

416 "Michigan Drops Its Charge of Obscenity Against 'Vixen'." *Daily Variety*, UNKNOWN, May 15, 1969.

The State's obscenity charge against *Vixen* is dropped without trial after the Niles 31 Drive-In pleads guilty to having allowed one minor into the theatre. The state prosecutor said he would not object to *Vixen* being shown to adult-only audiences indoors.

417 "Theatre Employes [sic] Freed from 'Obscene' Charges." *Boxoffice*, 95(9):ME-1, June 16, 1969.

Charges are dropped against the manager and projectionist of the Niles 31 Drive-In in St. Joseph, Michigan, after Elmer Gertz, Meyer's counsel, convinces a local judge that the seizure of the allegedly obscene *Vixen* was unconstitutional. The theatre was fined $500 for exhibiting the X-rated film to someone under the age of 18.

418 "'Vixen' Print Seized in Niles Airer Raid." *Boxoffice*, 95(6):ME-2, May 26, 1969.

The manager, projectionist, and owners of the Niles 31 Outdoor Theatre are arraigned in St. Joseph, Michigan, on obscenity charges stemming from the May 1, 1969, seizure of *Vixen* by Berrien County police.

CENSORSHIP — NORTH CAROLINA

419 "Criminal Obscenity Dangles; Nabbed Duo of Prints Returned." *Variety*, UNKNOWN, June 4, 1969.

North Carolina's obscenity case against *Vixen* and *Finders Keepers, Lovers Weepers!* is dismissed at the prosecutor's request because the defendants were successful in persuading the federal court to return the evidence (the prints) to the distributor. The action leaves the question of criminal obscenity in North Carolina open-ended.

420 "Movie Obscenity Conviction Appealed." *National Decency Reporter*, 7(5–6):3, May-June 1970.

The manager of the Center Theater in Monroe, North Carolina, gives notice of appeal to his attorney following a district court judge's ruling finding him guilty of showing the obscene film *Vixen*.

421 "Parts of NC Obscenity Law Judged Unconstitutional by Federal Panel." *Boxoffice*, 98(16):SE-1, Feb. 1, 1971.

Ruling in the case of a theatre owner in Monroe, North Carolina, charged with obscenity for showing *Vixen*, a panel of three federal judges determines that parts of North Carolina's law covering the exhibition of "obscene" motion pictures is unconstitutional because it violates the First Amendment right of free speech.

CENSORSHIP — OHIO

422 "Appeals Court Outlaws 'Vixen'." *National Decency Reporter,* 7(7–8):10, July-Aug. 1970.

The First District Court of Appeals of Ohio in a unanimous 3–0 decision upholds a lower court decision which concluded the film *Vixen* to be obscene. The suit was initiated by Charles Keating, Jr., president of the Citizens for Decent Literature and a member of the Presidential Commission on Pornography.

423 "Appellate Court Affirms Ban Against Film 'Vixen'." *Cincinnati Enquirer,* p. 11, July 21, 1970.

Affirming a lower court decision that found *Vixen* obscene, the First District Court of Appeals of Ohio grants a permanent injunction against the defendants (among them Russ Meyer) from exhibiting the film in Hamilton, Clermont, Butler, Warren, and Clinton counties.

424 Baldwin, Jay. "'Vixen' and Censorship." *Cincinnati Post & Times Star,* p. 14, Sept. 30, 1969.

Jay Baldwin's letter to the editor protesting the police closure of *Vixen* in Cincinnati questions the right of Charles H. Keating, Jr., of the Citizens for Decent Literature to impose his moral values on the rest of the community.

425 "Citizen Granted Smut Injunction." *Motion Picture Daily,* UNKNOWN, Nov. 21, 1969.

Hamilton County Common Pleas Court Judge Simon Leis grants an injunction to bar the exhibition of *Vixen* in Cincinnati to Charles H. Keating, Jr., founder of Citizens for Decent Literature, Inc. and President Nixon's only appointee to the Presidential Commission on Obscenity and Pornography. Leis applauded Keating's precedent-setting action, stating that it stopped "a filthy and lascivious film from poisoning the Cincinnati community."

426 "Court Asked to Rule Vixen Not Obscene: Injunction Sought to Prevent Further Seizure of Film." *Cincinnati Post & Times Star,* p. 42, Sept. 25, 1969.

An attorney for Malibu Inc., owner of the Guild Fine Arts Theatre, and Eve Productions, Inc. files suit in U.S. District Court asking that *Vixen* be found not obscene. An injunction is also sought against the city of Cincinnati and Charles H. Keating, Jr., enjoining them from any further seizure or interference with the showing of the film.

427 "Court Bans 'Vixen' in 5 Ohio Counties." *Boxoffice,* 97(16):ME-1, Aug. 3, 1970.

Upholding a lower court ruling, the Ohio First District Court of Appeals declares *Vixen* to be obscene and bans the film in the counties of Hamilton, Clermont, Warren, Butler, and Clinton.

428 "Court Won't Block Suit Against Movie 'Vixen'." *National Decency Reporter,* 8(5–7):15, May-July 1971.

Citing five recent Supreme Court rulings, a three-judge federal court panel dismisses an Eve Productions, Inc. and Malibu Inc. suit attempting to block the prosecution of *Vixen* in Cincinnati on an obscenity charge.

*429 de Grazia, Edward, and Newman, Roger K. "The Vixen." *Banned Films: Movies, Censorship and the First Amendment,* pp. 331–333. New York: R.R. Bowker, 1982.

The legal importance of two highly publicized, but unrelated, censorship cases regarding the exhibition of *Vixen* in Ohio and Florida is discussed. Most noteworthy are the legal issues surrounding the film in Ohio where de Grazia and Newman point out that in ruling against *Vixen* the Ohio Supreme Court legally failed to distinguish between conduct and free speech, i.e. that a filmed sexual act is different than the same act performed in a public place. By far the best summary of the legal proceedings against *Vixen* in Ohio and Florida. Highly recommended.

430 "Defense Motion Fails in 'Vixen' Movie Case." *Cincinnati Post,* p. 12, Mar. 27, 1971.

A defense argument that the police seizure of the film *Vixen* was illegal and unconstitutional on the grounds that no prior adversary hearing was conducted to determine if the film was in fact obscene is denied by Common Pleas Court Judge Frank M. Gusweiler.

431 "Disputed Film 'Vixen' Returned to Owners." *Cincinnati Post & Times Star,* p. 15, Sept. 29, 1969.

U.S. District Court Judge David S. Porter orders the city of Cincinnati to return confiscated copies of *Vixen* to Eve Productions, Inc. and theatre owners, Malibu Inc. and to desist from seizing any more prints until the question of obscenity can be determined by an adversary hearing.

*432 Eckberg, John. "The Show's Off; 'Vixen' Too Risky." *Cincinnati Enquirer,* sec. D, p. 1, Apr. 28, 1984.

Bowing to legal pressure from the Hamilton County Prosecutor's office, the University of Cincinnati Film Society cancels its plans to show *Vixen* as part of a campus film series. In failing to exhibit the film banned as obscene in Ohio since 1969, the legal question remains unanswered whether the community standards used to judge and/or define what is obscene can change over time. Recommended.

*433 "'Exploit Sex for the Sake of Money' an Issue in 5–2 Top Court Ruling." *Variety,* 263(12):7, 27, Aug. 4, 1971.

The majority and minority opinions of the Ohio State Supreme Court, which upheld a lower court's decision banning *Vixen* as obscene in certain Ohio counties, are given in an excellent summary of the case. In a 5–2 decision against *Vixen,* the majority held that

"purported acts of sexual intercourse solely for the profit of the producer and exhibitors can not constitute the communications of an idea or thought protected by the First and 14th Amendments." The two dissenting justices objected to the majority's emphasis on the profit motive behind the film's production and to the idea that the same laws apply to a film enactment of "offensively shocking conduct" and the actual conduct. Recommended.

434 Gordon, Richard L. "The Other Keating: Crusader in the Fight Against Pornography." *Cincinnati Magazine,* pp. 49–50, 55–58, June 1970.

Cincinnati lawyer and founder of the Citizens for Decent Literature, Inc., Charles H. Keating, Jr., is profiled in his role as a "crusader in the fight against pornography." Keating's thoughts on the subject are offered as are his criticisms of the press for its reportage of his successful prosecution of Meyer's *Vixen.* (1 illus.)

435 "High Court Upholds 'Vixen' Censorship." *Cincinnati Post & Times Star,* p. 35, July 21, 1971.

In a 5–2 decision upholding a lower court ruling the Ohio State Supreme Court rules that scenes in *Vixen* which seemingly depict "purported acts of sexual intercourse" can not be shown in Cincinnati.

436 "Judge Delays Ruling on 'Vixen'." *Cincinnati Post & Times Star,* p. 9, Sept. 26, 1969.

U.S. District Court Judge David S. Porter takes under advisement a motion filed by attorney Elmer Gertz representing Eve Productions, Inc. and Malibu, Inc. seeking to prevent the City of Cincinnati and Charles H. Keating, Jr., from interfering with the exhibition of *Vixen.* Gertz argued that the film had played in 40 states and 10 Ohio cities without legal incident and that its prosecution in Cincinnati represents a conspiracy between Keating and city Safety Director Henry Sandman "to violate the rights of his clients and the public."

437 Kemme, Steve. "Planned Showing of Movie 'Vixen' Causes Stir at UC." *Cincinnati Enquirer,* sec. D, pp. 1–2, Apr. 25, 1984.

Plans by the University of Cincinnati Film Society to show *Vixen,* banned as obscene by that city in 1969, raise controversy among members of the student body who object to it as "pornography." Liz Manion, co-president of the UC Film Society, citing the city police's lack of jurisdiction on campus, said any disruption of the film by authorities would be illegal. See entry **438**.

438 Kemme, Steve. "'Vixen' Film Is Still Too Blue, County Prosecutor Rules." *Cincinnati Enquirer,* sec. E, p. 1, Apr. 27, 1984.

Hamilton County Prosecutor Arthur M. Ney, Jr., notifies the University of Cincinnati Film Society that *Vixen* can still not be exhibited legally in the area and that those showing the film could be subject to arrest. UC officials, citing the autonomy of student groups, refused to prevent the organization from showing the controversial film.

439 Lackman, Libby. "Judge to Decide Whether to Stop Movie 'Vixen'." *Cincinnati Enquirer,* p. 16, Sept. 27, 1969.

In an article which recaps the already lengthy Cincinnati censorship proceedings against *Vixen,* U.S. District Court Judge David S. Porter is expected to decide if he will issue a temporary restraining order to prevent city officials from interfering with the exhibition of the allegedly obscene film at the Guild Fine Arts Theatre.

440 Moores, Lew. "UC Film Society Flirts with Trouble — Again." *Cincinnati Post,* sec. A, p. 2, Apr. 26, 1984.

The flap over the scheduled showing of *Vixen* by the University of Cincinnati Film Society is demonstrated by Moores to be only one instance of the trouble the student group has experienced over the years in its effort to exhibit controversial films on campus. A sympa-

thetic Moores argues that even obnoxious ideas deserve to be openly discussed and he applauds the administration of UC for not interfering with the selection of movies slated by the Film Society.

*441 "New Legal Weapon Tested!" *National Decency Reporter,* 6(11–12):4–6, Nov.-Dec. 1969.

This excellent, albeit obviously biased account of the legal action filed by Citizens for Decent Literature, Inc. founder Charles H. Keating, Jr., against the exhibition of *Vixen* in Cincinnati contains quotes from Common Pleas Court Judge Simon Leis' judgment against the film. The "incredible arguments" of defense witnesses to justify *Vixen* are offered as are the comments of the prosecution's only witness, L.A. psychiatrist and physician Dr. Melvin Anchell, who testified that films like *Vixen* are "responsible for the increase in perversion today." Highly recommended. (2 illus.)

442 "Ohio Judge Bans Film in 'Obscenity' Trial." *Boxoffice,* 96(7): ME-1, Dec. 1, 1969.

Common Pleas Court Judge Simon L. Leis rules *Vixen* obscene and on November 17, 1969, issues a permanent injunction against its ever being shown in Cincinnati. Judge Leis, however, did disallow claims made by defendant Charles H. Keating, Jr., who had requested an accounting of box office receipts with all monies being turned over to the state of Ohio.

443 Ornstein, Bill. "Russ Meyer Finds Sex Censorship Mostly Racial." *Hollywood Reporter,* 210(6):6, Mar. 3, 1970.

In discussing the censorship problems confronting *Vixen* in seven U.S. cities, the majority of which are "associated with or near the Mason-Dixon line," Meyer concludes that the film's "frank, racial exposition" is the primary reason it is being "harassed."

444 Palmer, George. "Vixen Is Screened for the Court." *Cincinnati Enquirer,* p. 12, Oct. 3, 1969.

Palmer is in the audience when *Vixen* is screened for the court to determine if it is obscene and reports that on artistic merit alone the film is "bum" characterized by well-endowed females with flat voices. Rather than shock over the film's content, most of the audience reacted with laughter directed at the "amateurish performances."

445   Rose, Lisa Cardillo. "Trouble May Be in Picture at UC Movie." *Cincinnati Post*, sec. B, p. 13, Apr. 25, 1984.

The scheduled showing of *Vixen* at the University of Cincinnati creates a controversy over whether the film is still X-rated or with the passage of time should now be rated "R." If the UC police determine the film to be X-rated, it could be confiscated and the projectionist arrested.

446   Rose, Lisa Cardillo, and Ivanovich, David. "'Vixen' Won't Be Shown." *Cincinnati Post*, sec. A, p. 12, Apr. 27, 1984.

The University of Cincinnati Film Society in a letter to Hamilton County Prosecutor Arthur M. Ney, Jr., promises "not to show *(Vixen)* now or at any other time." The decision to cancel was made when authorities informed the student group that the 15-year-old obscenity ruling against *Vixen* was still in effect.

447   "Russ Meyer's 'Vixen' Seized in Cincinnati." *Boxoffice*, 95(25): ME-4, Oct. 6, 1969.

Acting upon a Common Pleas Court suit filed by local attorney and founder of the Citizens for Decent Literature, Charles Keating, Jr., Cincinnati Safety Director Henry Sandman seizes *Vixen* from the Guild Fine Arts Theatre. In an injunction naming Keating and County Prosecutor Melvin Rueger as defendants, Eve Productions and Guild operator, Clarence Gall, seek to ban further seizures and interference with the film's showing in Cincinnati citing that *Vixen* has never been determined obscene in Ohio and has played without incident in 39 other states.

448   Schmidt, William. "There Are Other Dangers." *Cincinnati Post & Times Star*, p. 14, Sept. 30, 1969.

In a letter to the editor, Cincinnati resident Schmidt suggests Charles H. Keating, Jr., and "his fellow puritans" might better serve the community by channeling their censorship efforts toward ridding society of clear and present dangers (cigarette smoking, air/water pollution) rather than movies like *Vixen* that have not been proven harmful.

449   "Second Copy of 'Vixen' Confiscated." *Cincinnati Post & Times Star*, p. 52, Sept. 24, 1969.

Cincinnati vice squad officials seize a second copy of *Vixen* at the Guild Arts Theatre and charge manager Clarence F. Gall with possession of an obscene movie. Acting on a citizen's complaint filed by Charles H. Keating, Jr., lawyer and founder of the Citizens for Decent Literature, police had seized the first print September 22nd.

450   "Special Notice." *National Decency Reporter*, 6(9–10):15, Sept.-Oct. 1969.

The Legal Counsel staff of the Citizens for Decent Literature announce their willingness to cooperate with local district attorneys in their prosecution of *Vixen* and *I Am Curious (Yellow)* by providing them with counsel and legal material (briefs, rulings on adversary hearings, etc.).

451   Stein, Jerry. "The Guild Returns to Life." *Cincinnati Post & Times Star*, p. 33, Sept. 17, 1969.

The newly renovated 271-seat Guild Fine Arts Cinema in Cincinnati is scheduled to reopen on September 17 with *Vixen* as its inaugural feature. Peter Gall, owner of the theatre, is interviewed. (1 illus.)

452   "Theater Firm Indicted for Showing 'Vixen'." *Cincinnati Post*, p. 1, Nov. 13, 1970.

In charges stemming from two September 1969 showings of *Vixen* at the

Guild Fine Arts Cinema in Cincinnati, Malibu Inc. president Clarence F. Gall, corporate operator of the theatre, has been indicted by the Hamilton County Grand Jury on two counts of exhibition and possession of an obscene film.

453 Vitucci, Joseph A. "On Movie Censorship." *Cincinnati Post & Times Star*, p. 4, Oct. 4, 1969.

In yet another letter to the editor, a Cincinnati resident supports the seizure of *Vixen* and advises the small minority of people who need stuff like this for excitement to seek for it "in a dungeon" where it can not be inflicted on an entire community.

*454 "'Vixen' Obscene, Judge Leis Rules." *Cincinnati Enquirer*, p. 13, Nov. 18, 1969.

In ruling *Vixen* obscene, Cincinnati Common Pleas Court Judge Simon Leis derides the producers of such films as "a cancer on society" that threatens to destroy America unless legally restricted. Meyer is accused by Judge Leis of taking advantage of, and capitalizing on the lack of censorship to spread "this disease." The ruling serves as a permanent injunction against the film's exhibition in Cincinnati. Highly recommended.

455 "'Vixen' Promoters Fail in Court Bid." *Cincinnati Enquirer*, p. 15, Sept. 30, 1969.

U.S. District Court Judge David S. Porter refuses a petition filed by attorneys for Eve Productions, Inc. and Malibu, Inc. to remove the obscenity suit filed against *Vixen* from the Hamilton County, Pleas Court. Porter's ruling held that no federal or civil rights questions were involved in the case.

456 "'Vixen' Seized, Hearing Is Continued." *Cincinnati Post*, p. 1, Sept. 23, 1969.

Clarence Gall, owner of the Guild Fine Arts Theatre where a print of *Vixen* was confiscated by Cincinnati Vice Control officers, says another print of the film will be shown immediately at the theatre.

457 "'Vixen' Status Cloudy." *Cincinnati Post*, sec. B, p. 10, Apr. 26, 1984.

Following a screening of *Vixen* attended with University of Cincinnati police and the city vice squad, Hamilton County Prosecutor Arthur M. Ney, Jr., declined to comment on what course authorities plan to take if the film is shown at the University of Cincinnati.

458 Webb, Robert. "Local Film Ban Cited in Capitol Obscenity Hearing." *Cincinnati Enquirer*, p. 8, May 14, 1970.

The president of the General Federation of Women's Clubs, testifying before a public hearing of the Presidential Commission on Obscenity and Pornography, points to the Cincinnati court ban of *Vixen* as proof that the "contemporary community standards" rule to determine obscenity can be used to stamp out pornography.

459 Wilp, Mrs. John. "Praise for Mr. Keating." *Cincinnati Post & Times Star*, p. 14, Oct. 1, 1969.

In a letter to the editor supporting the actions of Charles H. Keating, Jr., a mother of five calls upon all "decent-minded-citizens" to back the lawyer in his efforts to "rid our communities of the flood of sexual films. . . ."

CENSORSHIP — OKLAHOMA

460 "Back Yard View of Winchester Film Displeasing to Rep. Kenneth Nance." *Boxoffice*, 95(10): SW-7, June 23, 1969.

Oklahoma state representative Kenneth Nance is among a number of church leaders, reporters, and neighbors invited to a residential backyard in Oklahoma City to view the R-rated *Vixen* playing at nearby Winchester Drive-In. Acting upon a complaint from one of his constituents that the "filthy" film is clearly visible from her backyard which adjoins the drive-in, Nance stated that if outdoor theatres were unwilling to regulate what they show, the legislature may have to compel them to erect screens to block the view of their films from residential areas and public streets.

CENSORSHIP—UTAH

461 "Not Guilty 'Vixen' Verdict." *Hollywood Reporter,* 211(28):11, June 11, 1970.
The not guilty verdict in municipal court on obscenity charges against the Cinema Theatre for showing *Vixen* clears the way for the film to be shown in Salt Lake City, Utah.

462 "'Vixen' Beats Obscenity Charge in Salt Lake." *Daily Variety,* 148 (4):2, June 11, 1970.
In a June 10 decision, Salt Lake City municipal Judge Maurice Jones returns a not guilty verdict on a charge of obscenity filed against the Cinema Theatre for showing *Vixen.*

CENSORSHIP—WISCONSIN

463 Gahagan, James. "Sue to Keep Milwaukee from Censoring 'Vixen'." *Daily Variety,* 145(2):6, Sept. 9, 1969.
Eve Productions and Gilbreth Film Company, an Illinois distribution concern, jointly file a federal court suit in Milwaukee against Waukesha District Attorney Roger Murphy, the Milwaukee Motion Picture Commission, and District Attorney Thomas Fink of Winnebago County seeking to prevent them from censoring *Vixen.*

464 "Milwaukee." *Boxoffice,* UN-KNOWN:NC-3, June 2, 1969.
After numerous protests in Milwaukee and Oshkosh over the exhibition of a highly censored version of *Vixen,* the film is withdrawn from theatres.

465 "Milwaukee Bans 'Vixen'." *National Decency Reporter,* 6(5–6): 14, Mar.-June 1969.
Acting in concert with the police chief of Milwaukee and that city's Motion Picture Commission, the Waukesha County District Attorney bans *Vixen* as obscene and pornographic. Claiming that "Milwaukee is one of the last censorship strongholds" in America, Meyer hires Chicago attorney Elmer Gertz to fight the ban.

466 "Moral Values Aplenty in 'Vixen' Says R. Meyer." *Variety,* 255(3): 24, June 4, 1969.
Reacting to the banning of *Vixen* in Waukesha County, Wisconsin, Meyer retains Chicago attorney Elmer Gertz to represent him in Milwaukee. In defending the film against charges of obscenity and pornography, Meyer pointed to the film's anti-communist and anti-racist themes.

467 "Russ Meyer to Fight Ban by Milwaukee of 'Vixen'." *Daily Variety,* 143(57):19, May 23, 1969.
An irate Meyer vows to fight the banning of *Vixen* in Milwaukee with his counsel Elmer Gertz to argue that the film contains strong socially redeeming arguments against communism and racial bigotry.

468 "'Vixen' Showing Awaits Federal Court Decision." *Boxoffice,* 95 (22):NC-2, Sept. 15, 1969.
Eve Productions and Gilbreth Film Co. file suit in federal court over the right to show *Vixen* at Milwaukee's Ruby Isle Theatre where the city district attorney opposed its exhibition. In an unusual move, the local district attorney is being represented by the Wisconsin Attorney General.

469 "'You Cut or We Grab' Threat Stops Manager; Then Meyer Yanks 'Vixen'." *Variety,* 255(3): 24, June 4, 1969.
Reacting to arrest threats from the Oshkosh, Wisconsin, district attorney, the manager of the Grand Theatre, in violation of his contract with the film's Midwest distributor, Jack Gilbreth, makes the D.A.'s ordered cuts in *Vixen* whereupon Gilbreth pulls the film.

REVIEWS

470 "Boy-Type and Girl-Type Film Critics Vary But Broadly as to New Sex Pix." *Variety,* 255(1):32, May 21, 1969.

In a *Variety* poll of critical opinion on numerous sex films which opened in New York City the previous week, *Vixen* is found to have "provoked a kind of 'no comment'." In the "Critics Roundup" concluding the article, *Vixen* was given "four amused unfavorables" by movie reviewers.

471 Breslaw, Jonathan. "Russ Meyer's *Vixen.*" *Motion Picture Daily,* UNKNOWN, May 19, 1969.

Breslaw's excellent review recommends that general exhibitors seriously consider booking the film since it contains "more genuine 'redeeming social significance'" than most sexploitation films. In fact, Breslaw concludes that this distinctive film "transcends the limitations of its genre."

472 Dettmer, Roger. "'Tawdry Teaser': 'Vixen' One Step from Pornography." *Chicago's American,* sec. 1, p. 18, Feb. 24, 1969.

Dettmer's bitterly negative review accuses *Vixen* of being "a dirty movie without the guts to be hard-core."

473 Durgnat, Raymond. "An Evening with Meyer and Masoch: Aspects of 'Vixen' and 'Venus in Furs'." *Film Comment,* 9(1):52–61, Jan./Feb. 1973.

A turgid, nearly unreadable article on the "diagonalist" style in *Vixen* written by a critic who obviously considers himself to be far above the material. (8 illus.)

*474 Ebert, Roger. "The Movies: Vixen." *Chicago-Sun Times,* p. 50, Feb. 24, 1969.

Calling *Vixen* "...the best film to date in that uniquely American genre, the skin-flick," Ebert was the first important film critic to understand Meyer's work represented "...a merciless put-on

of the whole genre." As for Meyer's position in this genre, Ebert writes, "In a field filled with cheap, dreary productions, Meyer is the best craftsman and the only artist." Rated 3 stars out of 4.

475 "Glandscape Artist." *Time,* 93 (24):103, June 13, 1969.

Vixen is a happily unpretentious sexploitation film that is "too juvenile to be considered a stag movie." Meyer is characterized as a softcore filmmaker who, challenged by the financial success of hardcore films like *I Am Curious (Yellow),* is being forced to reassess the future direction of his career.

476 Lesner, Sam. "'Vixen' Hits Bottom in Screen Freedom." *Chicago Daily News* (Red Streak Ed.), p. 24, Feb. 24, 1969.

Panning the film as "corrupt, degrading and disgusting," Lesner damns *Vixen* as "the most indecent abuse of the new freedom of the screen to date."

477 Mahoney, John. "'Vixen'—Meyer Produced, Directed, Edited." *Hollywood Reporter,* 203(14):3, 11, Oct. 28, 1968.

Terming *Vixen* as a "class delivery for its caliber," Mahoney's lukewarm review is long on plot synopsis, but short on criticism.

478 Malina, Martin. "Vixen Shows B.C. Wilds." *Montreal Star,* p. 17, Apr. 20, 1970.

Malina, who expressed his admiration for Meyer in an earlier *Montreal Star* article (see entry **79**), limits himself here to a synopsis of *Vixen.* The critic does, however, note that half the audience at the weekend showing he attended were couples under 30.

479 McGillivray, David. "Vixen." *Monthly Film Bulletin,* 38(449): 126–127, June 1971.

Hacked by British censors from its original 71 minutes down to 47 minutes, the abridged *Vixen* is difficult for McGillivray to review, but he can state "that the reports of Meyer's technical skills were not exaggerated." See entry **480** for

McGillivray's review of the "unexpurgated" version.

480 McGillivray, David. "Vixen." *Monthly Film Bulletin,* 48(568): 98, May 1981.

Reviewing the "unexpurgated version" of the film ten years after he reported on a censored 47-minute version (see entry **479**), McGillivray notes that *Vixen* "makes a fascinating yardstick to the changes wrought by the permissive society" in Britain. The film itself represents a parody of the "conventions of the sex film" whereas the eroticism conforms to softcore standards.

481 Meier, Jim. "More on 'Vixen'." *Cincinnati Post & Times Star,* p. 14, Oct. 1, 1969.

Meier, in a letter to the editor, agrees with reporter Jerry Stein's review (see entry **489**) that although *Vixen* fails as both a film and pornography, it contains enough "socially redeeming themes" to ensure that it can not be successfully prosecuted as obscene in Cincinnati.

482 Murf. "Vixen." *Variety,* 252(11): 6, Oct. 30, 1968.

Murf. comments on the "frankness" of the film's sex scenes and notes the production's "overall excellent technical polish."

483 Peary, Danny. "Russ Meyer's Vixen/Vixen." *Guide for the Film Fanatic,* pp. 367–368. New York: Simon & Schuster, 1986.

A "perfect film for swingers," Peary further describes *Vixen* as the landmark softcore sex film that helped open the doors for the exhibition of hardcore films like *Deep Throat* in mainstream theatres. Peary attributes much of the film's success to Erica Gavin's vivid portrayal of "Vixen" which (as her fan mail indicates) appealed equally to both male and female viewers.

484 Peterson, Clarence. "The Movies: Vixen." *Chicago Tribune,* sec. 2, p. 5, Apr. 1, 1970.

A non-critical review that cites *Vixen* as failing on the level of "adolescent fantasy" in that the character Vixen's promiscuity negates the essential element of that fantasy, that the girl turns into a wanton only for you. (1 illus.)

485 Rimmer, Robert. "Vixen." *The X-Rated Videotape Guide,* pp. 152–153. New York: Arlington House, 1984.

Though touching on a few well-known aspects of Meyer's career, Rimmer's comments on *Vixen* are confined to noting the film's incredible commercial success and to providing a brief plot synopsis.

486 Royko, Mike. "A Deep, Dark, Danger, Dad!" *Chicago Daily News* (Red Streak Ed.), p. 3, Feb. 20, 1969.

A *Chicago Daily News* reader expresses his moral outrage over the exhibition of the "stag film" *Vixen* at the Loop Theatre. Royko offers an ironic comment.

487 "Russ Meyer's Vixen." *Filmfacts,* 12(10):255–257, 1969.

A roundup of critical comment on *Vixen* featuring excerpts from entries **474** and **497**. Of ten reviews, five were favorable with the remaining five either mixed or negative. A plot synopsis and cast list are also included. (1 illus.)

488 Smith, Kent. "Vixen." *Adam Film World Guide,* 2(10):163, Mar. 1986.

Though Meyer's unabashed depiction of woman as a purely sexual animal sparked a major controversy in 1968, Smith asserts *Vixen* is in actuality "an all-out comedy." Rated 3 ½ stars out of 5, *Adam Film World Guide* considers the film to be classic adult fare. (1 illus.)

489 Stein, Jerry. "What Jerry Stein Thinks About 'Vixen'." *Cincinnati Post & Times Star,* p. 1, Sept. 23, 1969.

Cincinnati reporter Jerry Stein outlines four yardsticks used in determining if a film is obscene (nudity, language, depiction of sexual acts, sheer number of sex scenes) and determines that only the quantity of sex scenes in

Vixen could cause the film to be considered obscene. Stein's review criticizes the film's lack of tenderness which causes its sex scenes to be "heartless and grotesque."

490 Thomas, Kevin. "'Vixen' Screening Citywide." *Los Angeles Times,* pt. IV, p. 20, May 1, 1969.

Noting that Meyer's films are "sex fantasies projected from a notably healthy mind," Thomas deems *Vixen* to be Meyer's "best film to date." Harrison Page, who portrays the film's black draft dodger, is singled out as an "actor of unmistakable talent and intensity."

491 Thomas, Larry. "'Meyer's Vixen' Attracts Good Business in W. Va." *Boxoffice,* 97(4):74, May 11, 1970.

A film exhibitor in Summersville, West Virginia, writes that *Vixen* has excellent production values, a fine cast, and most importantly, that business was good at his theatre.

492 Thompson, Howard. "Screen: Sensationalism: Russ Meyer's 'Vixen' at Three Theaters." *New York Times,* p. 19, May 17, 1969.

Thompson confines his criticism to the acting inadequacies of the cast, except for Harrison Page, the black draft dodger "Niles," whom he cites as giving "the picture's one and only performance."

493 Turan, Kenneth. "'Vixen': Top of the 'Skin Flick' Heap." *Washington Post,* sec. D, p. 8, Aug. 13, 1969.

Turan views the sexual explicitness in *Vixen* as Meyer's commercial response to the increased explicitness in so-called "serious" films. Erica Gavin is singled out as the film's biggest asset with Turan finding her look of calculated lust to be "as striking in its own right as any of the more famous closeups of Garbo or Dietrich."

494 "Vixen." *Boxoffice,* sec. Bookinguide, p. 4161, Dec. 2, 1968.

The Bookinguide of *Boxoffice* which features reviews, synopses, and "exploitips" for exhibitors enthusiasti-

cally praises *Vixen* as a classy, technically competent film that promises "to be a runaway sensation in the sexploitation market." The suggested catchline for newspaper advertising asked: "Is She Woman ... Or Animal? ... 'Vixen' Will Jerk Your Emotions, Straddle Your Soul, Jar Your Senses!"

495 "Vixen." *Catholic Film Newsletter,* 34(11):44, June 15, 1969.

Meyer's "overall technical competence" fails to justify the film's graphic sexuality. Condemned by the National Catholic Office for Motion Pictures as containing material judged to be morally objectionable to all viewers.

496 "Vixen." *Playboy,* 16(8):28, Aug. 1969.

Playboy observes that the film is so far "the most wholesome dirty movie" of 1969.

497 Wasserman, John L. "'Vixen'— Another Presidio Special." *San Francisco Chronicle,* p. 45, Mar. 6, 1969.

In addition to the two constants in Meyer's films, nudity and lust, *Vixen* introduces the added "gimmicks" of racism and politics.

498 Winsten, Archer. "'Russ Meyer's Vixen' at 3 Theaters." *New York Post,* p. 53, May 17, 1969.

Winsten points out that Russ Meyer's *Vixen* is a landmark in the sex film industry for three reasons: it is opening at a respectable theatre, Meyer's name preceding the title reminds the audience that he is the "King of Skin Flicks," and lastly, relief from constant sex is offered by beautiful outdoor shots of British Columbia. While ultimately boring to anyone but a voyeur, Winsten concludes that the film's "frank approach" to sex "is almost wholesome."

499 Wolf, William. "Russ Meyer's Vixen." *Cue,* 38(20):72, May 17, 1969.

Wolf's non-critical review cites the film's elements of sex, "social significance," and "oodles of Erica-erotica."

Cherry, Harry & Raquel (1969): "A dusty Arizona border town and vast expanses of baked desert provide the magnificent scenic backdrop for fast cars, blazing guns, and super-ample women ... each and all hot." — Publicity.

Cherry, Harry & Raquel (1969)

PROMOTION

500 "Chicago." *Boxoffice*, 96(21): C-8, Mar. 9, 1970.
Jack Gilbreth, president of Gilbreth Films, plays host to Meyer and one of the stars of *Cherry, Harry & Raquel* in Chicago where the film is set to open at the Brotman and Sherman Loop Theatre on March 13.

501 "Oh! Russmeyer!" *Chicago Daily News* (Weekend Ed.), sec. Panorama, p. 3, Mar. 14–15, 1970.

In Chicago to promote *Cherry, Harry & Raquel*, Meyer describes the film as "sort of a parody of 'Coogan's Bluff,' 'The Stalking Moon,' and 'Bullitt'." (1 illus.)

502 "Sexy Voice Lures Patrons to Georgia Art Theatre." *Boxoffice*, 97(17):118, Aug. 10, 1970.
As part of a promotional scheme for the grand opening of a refurbished Columbus, Georgia, art theatre, newspaper teaser ads for *Cherry, Harry & Raquel* are run featuring "Raquel's" phone number. The theatre's manager reports that his phone lines have been jammed by callers anxious to hear the

taped promotional spot for the film read by a sexy female voice promising "torrid love scenes."

MISCELLANEOUS

503 Cassyd, Syd. "Backstage." *Box-office*, 95(25):W-2, Oct. 6, 1969.
A preview of Meyer's *Cherry, Harry & Raquel* fills the projection room at the Goldwyn studio with everyone from local and national critics to film suppliers and studio executives.

REVIEWS

504 Archibald, Lewis. "Cherry, Harry & Raquel." *Motion Picture Daily*, UNKNOWN, Apr. 24, 1970.
A carefully crafted melodrama filled with sex, violence, and phallic symbolism that nevertheless leaves Archibald with reservations that it is a "cop-out at one of the lower levels."

505 "Cherry, Harry & Raquel." *Independent Film Journal*, p. 1254, Apr. 29, 1970.
In what appears to be his last independent production since he has graduated to the majors with a contract at Fox, Meyer delivers the "swift sex melodrama" his fans have come to expect.

506 "Cherry, Harry & Raquel." *Box-office*, sec. Bookinguide, p. 4287, May 4, 1970.
Director-producer-photographer-editor-writer-actor Meyer is the whole show in a film that "graphically demonstrates how he made his reputation with sex pictures."

507 "Cherry, Harry & Raquel." *Film Information*, 1(1):4, Jan. 15, 1970.
A short blurb describing the film as "more of the same" from Meyer.

508 "Cherry, Harry & Raquel." *Film Bulletin*, 39(2):20, Jan. 26, 1970.
A "healthy" sexploitation film that ranks among Meyer's best work for

"directorial merit" and box office potential.

509 "Cherry, Harry and Raquel." *Catholic Film Newsletter*, 35(5): 20, Mar. 15, 1970.
The film's emphasis on blood, sex, nudity, vulgar language, and perversions "keep(s) Mr. Meyer's reputation intact." Rated "C" (condemned) by the National Catholic Office for Motion Pictures.

510 Cohen, Richard. "Cherry, Harry & Raquel." *Women's Wear Daily*, 120(78):20, Apr. 22, 1970.
Although the film is "rotten," it does reveal "a highly skilled professional filmmaker" who bears watching when he begins his tenure at 20th Century–Fox.

*511 Corliss, Richard. "Film: Cherry & Harry & Raquel!" *Village Voice*, 15(24):56, 59, June 11, 1970.
An insightful essay that compares and contrasts the themes, styles, and cinematic approaches of two pioneers in the sexploitation genre: Radley *(Camille 2000)* Metzger and Russ Meyer. *Cherry, Harry & Raquel* is termed Meyer's "most surreal, and occasionally inexplicable, film to date." Must reading.

512 "Film Fix." *Good Times*, 3(36): 17, Sept. 11, 1970.
A highly politicized review of *Cherry, Harry & Raquel* in the underground newspaper *Good Times* (formerly the *San Francisco Express Times*) which focuses on the film's exaggerated portrayal of American society where human action is motivated solely by "hedonistic drives." (1 illus.)

513 Flynn, Charles. "'Cherry, Harry and Raquel'." *Chicago Sun-Times*, p. 73, Mar. 18, 1970.
An excellent review which focuses on the underlying tension between sexual frustration and fulfillment in the film. While each aspect of the production is praised (with the exception of Meyer's "rather frivolous attitude toward plot"), Flynn unreservedly calls Meyer's photography "consistently excellent" and

Three central themes in Meyer's film formula coalesce in this scene from *Cherry, Harry & Raquel:* big bosoms (Linda Ashton), square jaws (Charles Napier), and lovemaking under natural and arduous conditions (the desert).

states that his color quality is better than that of any major Hollywood studio.

514 Goldstein, Al. "1970—the Best and Worst in Fuck Films." *Screw,* 98:10, Jan. 18, 1971.

Cherry, Harry & Raquel, scoring a "Peter-Meter" rating of 4 percent, is listed by *Screw* as among the worst sex films of 1970. Only *Barbara* with a rating of 3 percent scored lower than "Russ Meyer's piece of excrement." (1 illus.)

515 Goldstein, Al. "Russ Meyer Sucks." *Screw,* 60:21, Apr. 27, 1970.

Exercising his considerable powers of critical rhetoric to their fullest, Goldstein eviscerates *Cherry, Harry & Raquel* as "a waste of 71 precious minutes of my life" perpetrated by "a perfect example of the celluloid huckster," Russ Meyer, whose essence as a filmmaker is "the essence of mediocrity." Rated a negligi-

ble 4 percent on the *Screw* "Peter-Meter" which judges a film on the basis of its interest level, sexuality, and technical merit. (5 illus.)

516 Greenspun, Roger. "Russ Meyer's Film 'Cherry, Harry & Raquel' Opens." *New York Times,* p. 44, Apr. 23, 1970.

Greenspun's rave review notes that Meyer would probably make very good mainstream films, but the critic is pleased the filmmaker continues to explore the full "range of his special imagination" by making "extraordinary movies."

517 Haas, Joseph. "'Cherry' Stupid." *Chicago Daily News* (Red Streak Ed.), p. 21, Mar. 17, 1970.

A short and totally negative review attacks Meyer as a filmmaker beginning to believe the pretentious publicity depicting him as a "real moviemaker."

Haas says little about the film because of his refusal to allow his comments to be turned into publicity by "Meyer and his henchmen."

518 Herridge, Frances. "Cherry Invades 60 Houses." *New York Post*, p. 45, Apr. 23, 1970.

The film is dismissed as "one of the cruder and messier peep shows around."

519 King, Vance. "Cherry, Harry & Raquel." *Film and Television Daily*, 135(55):3, Sept. 18, 1969.

The film is distinguished from other "nudie" pictures by its strong plot and excellent technical achievements.

520 Knoblauch, Mary. "Playboy Edition in the Flesh?" *Chicago Today American*, sec. Family Today, p. 42, Mar. 18, 1970.

Finding *Cherry, Harry & Raquel* to be "too silly to get mad at," Knoblauch judges the film's desert photography to be "at least as interesting" as that in Michelangelo Antonioni's *Zabriskie Point.*

521 Mahoney, John. "Meyer's 'Cherry, Harry' Satiric Sexploitation Pic: Producer Also Wrote, Directed." *Hollywood Reporter*, 207(42):17–18, Sept. 19, 1969.

Mahoney notes that "something has to be wrong" when a movie has three endings. Includes partial credits list.

522 Peary, Danny. "Cherry, Harry and Raquel." *Guide for the Film Fanatic*, p. 87. New York: Simon & Schuster, 1986.

Judging the movie to be "one of Meyer's best," Peary praises the film's "sharp editing," its "Don Siegel–like action sequences," and the acting of lead Charles ("Harry") Napier.

523 Peterson, Lowell. "Cherry, Harry and Raquel." *UCLA Summer Bruin*, p. 6, Aug. 20, 1970.

Meyer's "vigorously moral" and comic attitude toward his material is highlighted by an "intense visual style" and "beautiful production values." (1 illus.)

524 Rimmer, Robert. "Cherry, Harry & Raquel." *The X-Rated Videotape Guide*, p. 73, New York: Arlington House, 1984.

Rimmer comments favorably on Meyer's editing technique of intercutting quick shots into longer action sequences to show what the character is actually thinking. He also notes that "Meyer's films have excellent color transference to tape." The film is incorrectly dated as 1979 rather than its release date of 1969.

525 Sabatier, J.M. "Les Stimulatrices." *Revue du Cinéma*, 301:122, Dec. 1975.

A bad review of the French release of *Cherry, Harry & Raquel* which condemns the film's images as being unconvincing and worn out. Sabatier feels the film is "very minor" in the Meyer canon.

526 Smith, Kent. "Cherry, Harry and Raquel." *Adam Film World Guide*, 2(10):47, Mar. 1986.

Meyer at his best. Rated 3½ out of 5 stars (between "good" and "excellent.") (1 illus.)

527 Thomas, Kevin. "Napier Plays Crooked Sheriff in 'Cherry'." *Los Angeles Times*, pt. IV, p. 14, Aug. 7, 1970.

Reviewed after the release of *Beyond the Valley of the Dolls*, Thomas views *Cherry* as a welcome return to Meyer's "old King Leer vein" of "expert photography" and "supersonic pacing." Charles Napier ("Harry") and Franklin Bolger ("Franklin") receive acting kudos. In short, "lots of fun."

528 Thomas, Larry. "Plenty of Skin, Action in Russ Meyer Flick." *Boxoffice*, 97(20):131, Aug. 31, 1970.

Cherry, Harry & Raquel is recommended to other distributors if they "can use it."

529 Whit. "Cherry, Harry & Raquel." *Variety*, 256(6):30, Sept. 27, 1969.

The film's production values are extolled with Meyer's direction described as "on the rugged side."

530 Williams, Ann Sheldon. "Cherry, Harry and Raquel." *Monthly Film Bulletin,* 38(446):46, Mar. 1971.

Williams criticizes the film as overplotted and melodramatic. The symbolic sex scenes as well are accused of exuding "an ineffable coyness." Still, Williams finds the desert locations spectacular and the film's car chase to be dramatic and exciting.

531 Wolf, William. "Cherry, Harry & Raquel." *Cue,* 39(17):88, Apr. 25, 1970.

Severe criticism is directed at the film's violence that extends beyond "normal sadism."

Beyond the Valley of the Dolls (1970)

PRODUCTION NOTES

532 Anderson, John. "Where He's At." *Chicago Daily News* (Red Streak Ed.), sec. 2, p. 13, Aug. 18, 1969.

A blurb announcing Meyer's signing of *Chicago Sun-Times* film critic, Roger Ebert, to write the screenplay for the 20th Century–Fox produced film *Beyond the Valley of the Dolls.*

533 Bacon, James. "Russ Meyer: King Leer at Work." *Los Angeles Herald-Examiner,* sec. B, p. 2, Jan. 20, 1970.

Bacon visits the set of *Beyond the Valley of the Dolls* and is disappointed to discover no nude scenes being filmed, but pleased to see his "favorite sex symbol" Edy Williams. (1 illus.)

534 Batdorff, Emerson. "All's Well in Silicone Valley." *Cleveland Plain Dealer,* sec. H, p. 1, Apr. 19, 1970.

Insiders at 20th Century–Fox jokingly refer to the stage where Meyer is shooting *Beyond the Valley of the Dolls* as "Silicone Valley." The investment acumen of Veronica Erickson, one of the film's players and also seen in Meyer's *Fanny Hill,* is also humorously treated.

535 Batdorff, Emerson. "Russ Meyer Doesn't Regret. . ." *Cleveland Plain Dealer,* sec. PD Action, p. 3, Mar. 6, 1970.

Interviewed during the editing of *Beyond the Valley of the Dolls,* Meyer discusses what the opportunity to work for a major studio means to him and describes the film as "a serious daytime soap opera with a lot of steam." The production and historical importance of *The Immoral Mr. Teas* are also discussed. (2 illus.)

*536 Berkowitz, Stan. "18—Count 'Em—18 Couplings and an X-Rating: Russ Meyer in Hollywood." *UCLA Daily Bruin,* 79(1): 19–20, Jan. 7, 1970.

During the shooting of *Beyond the Valley of the Dolls* Meyer gave UCLA film student Stan Berkowitz a lot of his time and the result is a fine piece that focuses on the actual production of the director's first major studio film. In addition to a concise and fairly accurate biographical sketch of the filmmaker, Berkowitz also profiles Erica *(Vixen)* Gavin, the star of the hit film that Meyer credits with bringing him to the attention of 20th Century–Fox. Highly recommended. (3 illus.)

*537 Boz. "Beyond the Valley of Russ Meyer: Manny Diez Interview." *Suburban Relapse,* 13:13–14, July 1985.

Manny Diez, assistant to the producer on *Beyond the Valley of the Dolls* and *The Seven Minutes,* fondly describes his warm association with Meyer during the two-year period they were at 20th Century–Fox together and offers vivid recollections of the filming of *BVD.* Diez, it should be noted, not only served as dialogue director on *BVD,* but also contributed to the film's screenplay although studio regulations prohibited his name appearing as such in the credits. Highly recommended. (3 illus.) See entry **10.**

538 Carnes, Del. "Backstage." *Denver Post,* p. 81, Sept. 24, 1969.

Beyond the Valley of the Dolls (1970): Meyer's personal favorite of his films, described by coscriptwriter Roger Ebert as "a camp sexploitation horror musical that ends with a quadruple ritual murder and a triple wedding." While it could not save a financially ailing 20th Century-Fox, it was a solid box office winner.

The signing of Meyer by 20th Century–Fox to direct *Beyond the Valley of the Dolls* marks his graduation from nudie films into the "big leagues" and also a recognition by the studio that he is "a director of quality."

539 Cuskelly, Richard. "Russ Meyer Abdicating Title 'King of the Nudie Movies'." *Los Angeles Herald-Examiner*, sec. G, p. 5, Apr. 12, 1970.

Prior to its general release, Meyer discusses *Beyond the Valley of the Dolls* and relates that studio head Richard D. Zanuck told him to deliver a film rated "R-minus," i.e. as close to an X as possible. (1 illus.)

540 Davis, Ivor. "Meyer: An Ultimate in Sexploitation." *Toronto Globe and Mail*, p. 25, Feb. 14, 1970.

"Rebel picturemaker" Meyer is profiled as the "savior of 20th Century-Fox" in a nice Canadian piece done on him during the production of *Beyond the Valley of the Dolls*. Pleased to be finally working for a major studio, Meyer feels his transition from independent filmmaker to Fox staffer is long overdue and a just reward for his artistic efforts. (1 illus.)

541 Ebert, Roger. "Critics Film-Making Itch." *Los Angeles Times*, pt. IV, p. 18, Sept. 1970.

One year after receiving the cable from 20th Century-Fox studio head Richard Zanuck okaying the first draft of *Beyond the Valley of the Dolls*, film critic Roger Ebert reminisces about his six-week experience in Hollywood writing the screenplay for the film.

*542 Ebert, Roger. "Russ Meyer: 10 Years After the 'Beyond'." *Film Comment*, 16(4):43–44, July/Aug. 1980.

A decade after the release of *Beyond the Valley of the Dolls*, Ebert, who collaborated with Meyer on the screenplay, fondly remembers the film's production and offers his contemporary critical perceptions of the movie as a whole. The piece also includes important information on Meyer's directorial style. Highly recommended. (1 illus.)

543 "Edy Williams to Play 'Ashley Famous' at 20th." *Hollywood Reporter*, 208(24):1, Nov. 4, 1969.

Meyer signs Edy Williams to play sex novel writer "Ashley Famous" in *Beyond the Valley of the Dolls*. (In the finished film the character's name was changed to "Ashley St. Ives").

544 "Eve Meyer, Hershon on 20th's 'Dolls'." *Hollywood Reporter*, 208 (20):1, Oct. 29, 1969.

Eve Meyer and Red Hershon are named associate producers on *Beyond the Valley of the Dolls*.

545 Freedland, Nat. "Russ Meyer: Beyond Nudies." *Entertainment World*, 2(4):10–14, Jan. 30, 1970.

Freedland, who a year earlier had interviewed Meyer on radio concerning the treatment of women and blacks in *Vixen*, now speaks with the director on the set of *Beyond the Valley of the Dolls* and notes how far the "thorough cinematic craftsman" has come since then. Meyer's "new respectability," validated by his association with Fox, is examined in the light of mainstream cinema's shift toward more sexual explicitness and Freedland notes that current films like *Rosemary's Baby* and *The Killing of Sister George* show more than Meyer's work even though his films tend to be long on sex and short on plot. (5 illus.)

546 Greenberg, Abe. "Russ Meyer at 20th Wins Favor & Dollars." *Hollywood Citizen News*, UNKNOWN, Feb. 28, 1970.

Meyer is portrayed as a self-made man who has proven false the predictions of Hollywood insiders that he could not make the grade at a major studio by emerging as "the toast of 20th Century-Fox stockholders."

547 Guild, Leo. "Meyer Lauds Film Editing." *Citizen News*, p. 60, Apr. 29, 1970.

Meyer points to the importance of editing to enhance an actor's performance and voices his optimism for the futures of many of the players in his unreleased *Beyond the Valley of the Dolls*. Guild predicts that if the film is a success Meyer "will be an important man in town." (1 illus.)

548 Haber, Joyce. "Some New Faces in Crowd at Warner's." *Los Angeles Times*, pt. IV, p. 17, Aug. 20, 1969.

Meyer is announced as the director of *Beyond the Valley of the Dolls* and *Chicago Sun-Times* film critic Roger Ebert is reported to have taken a five-week leave of absence to write the screenplay.

549 Heffernan, Harold. "Everybody's Equal in Film Orgy: There's No Bias in the Buff." *Detroit News,* sec. C, p. 6, Mar. 10, 1970.

At a time when Hollywood producers are being pressured by the Justice Department to create more jobs for minority groups, Heffernan visits the set of *Beyond the Valley of the Dolls* only to discover several racial minorities represented in the film's "tempestuous orgy scene."

550 "Hollywood Happenings." *Boxoffice,* 96(4):W-2, Nov. 10, 1969.

Meyer delivers the final draft of his and Ebert's original screenplay for *Beyond the Valley of the Dolls* to studio president Richard D. Zanuck and receives the green light to begin production on December 1.

551 "Irv Mansfield Out as Fox Producer." *Variety,* 255(7):3, July 2, 1969.

A *Variety* blurb announcing the unexpected ouster of Irving Mansfield, husband of Jacqueline Susann, as producer of 20th Century–Fox's *Beyond the Valley of the Dolls* ostensibly to allow him more time to put together a deal for the film edition of Susann's *The Love Machine* at Columbia.

552 "'Love Machine' on Fox First Refusal." *Variety,* 254(4):4, Mar. 12, 1969.

Negotiations commence between 20th Century–Fox and Jacqueline Susann for a film version of her new novel *The Love Machine.* Tentative plans by Fox for a summer start on *Beyond the Valley of the Dolls* with an "original screen story" by Susann are also announced.

553 "Meyer Delivers 1st 'Beyond Dolls' Draft." *Hollywood Reporter,* 207 (34):4, Sept. 9, 1969.

Meyer and coscriptwriter Roger Ebert deliver the first draft of *Beyond the Valley of the Dolls* to Fox president Richard D. Zanuck.

554 "Meyer Sets Erica Gavin as One 20th's 'Dolls'." *Hollywood Re-porter,* 208(36):13, Nov. 20, 1969.

Erica Gavin is signed by Meyer to appear in *Beyond the Valley of the Dolls* beginning production December 1 at the Westwood lot of 20th Century–Fox.

555 "Meyer Sets Nine Songs for 'Dolls'." *Hollywood Reporter,* 210(30):10, Apr. 6, 1970.

Meyer hires four tunesmiths to compose songs for *Beyond the Valley of the Dolls* currently in post-production at 20th Century–Fox.

556 "Meyer's 'Dolls' Opening." *Hollywood Reporter,* 212(18):6, Aug. 6, 1970.

Beyond the Valley of the Dolls opens this week in 55 theatres in the U.S. and Canada.

557 "Mister X." *Newsweek,* 75(3):83, Jan. 19, 1970.

During production of *Beyond the Valley of the Dolls* for 20th Century–Fox, Meyer reflects on his first-time ever association with a major studio and the Hollywood Establishment's view of him. (1 illus.)

558 "Motion Pictures Rated by the Code & Rating Administration." *Boxoffice,* 97(11):9, June 29, 1970.

The X-rating imposed on *Beyond the Valley of the Dolls* by the Code and Rating Administration pursuant to the Motion Picture Code and Rating Program is sustained by the Code and Ratings Appeals Board after hearing an appeal by the film's distributor, Joseph Brenner Associates, seeking to have *BVD* re-rated to an "R."

559 "Myers Goes 'Beyond'." *Hollywood Reporter,* 208(25):4, Nov. 5, 1969.

Cynthia Myers, former *Playboy* playmate, is cast by Meyer for a part in *Beyond the Valley of the Dolls* to begin filming December 1.

560 "Our Man in Beyond the Valley of the Dolls." *Show,* 1(5):69–72, May 1970.

Show photographer Bruce McBroom, hired by Meyer to add authenticity to a brief scene in *Beyond the Valley of the Dolls*, reports on what it was like to shoot still photos of several of the film's alluring females (Haji, Erica Gavin, Phyllis Davis, and Dolly Read). (9 illus.)

561 "Producer-Director Meyer Doing Ad Art on 'Dolls'." *Hollywood Reporter*, 209(49):3, Feb. 20, 1970.

One-time top cheesecake photographer Meyer will shoot his own advertising art for *Beyond the Valley of the Dolls*.

562 "Russ Meyer Credits 55 Actors in 'Valley'." *Hollywood Reporter*, 210(12):8, Mar. 11, 1970.

In the longest such cast list in recent 20th Century–Fox history, Meyer gives screen credit to 55 day and weekly actors appearing in *Beyond the Valley of the Dolls*.

563 "Russ Meyer Guides 20th's New 'Dolls'." *Hollywood Reporter*, 207(24):4, Aug. 25, 1969.

Richard D. Zanuck, executive vice-president of production at 20th Century–Fox, confirms that Meyer will direct *Beyond the Valley of the Dolls*.

564 "Russ Meyer Has 'Just Under' $1 Mil. to Spend on 'Dolls'." *Daily Variety*, 145(64):3, Dec. 4, 1969.

Despite being saddled with $972,000 in overhead from a scrapped version of *Beyond the Valley of the Dolls*, a cost conscious Meyer vows to bring the film in under the additional $1 million budgeted for production by paying his no-name cast, with the exception of Fox contract player Edy Williams, no more than $500 each per week.

565 "Russ Meyer Spotlighted in Newsweek Magazine." *Boxoffice*, 96 (14):8, Jan. 19, 1970.

A short notice alerting the Industry to Meyer's *Newsweek* coverage which dubs the filmmaker "Mr. X." See entry **557**.

566 "Russ Meyer to Do Sequel on 'Valley' for 20th–Fox." *Boxoffice*, p. 8, Aug. 18, 1969.

A trade paper announcement of Meyer's signing by Fox president Richard D. Zanuck to cowrite, produce, and direct *Beyond the Valley of the Dolls*.

567 Thomas, Kevin. "King of the Nudies Takes on Biggest Film Caper Yet." *Los Angeles Times*, sec. Calendar, p. 18, Nov. 30, 1969.

Prior to the filming of *Beyond the Valley of the Dolls* for 20th Century–Fox, Meyer discusses with critic Kevin Thomas his feelings about being hired by the major studio to direct after years of independently producing his own unique type of sex films. Meyer recalls laughing heartily and feeling as though he "had pulled off the biggest caper in the world." Also of value are extensive quotes by Meyer concerning the script writing process for *Beyond the Valley of the Dolls* as well as budget and casting considerations. (1 illus.)

568 "22 Actors Signed for Meyer's 'Beyond' Party." *Hollywood Reporter*, 209(16):15, Jan. 6, 1970.

Meyer signs 22 actors for the party sequence in *Beyond the Valley of the Dolls* to be shot on a 10-day schedule.

569 "Two Dolls Aides Named." *Daily Variety*, 145(39):3, Oct. 29, 1969.

Meyer sets Red Hershon and Eve Meyer as associate producers for his 20th Century–Fox production of *Beyond the Valley of the Dolls*.

570 "'Valley' Rolling." *Hollywood Reporter*, 208(44):10, Dec. 3, 1969.

Production starts Dec. 2, 1969, on *Beyond the Valley of the Dolls*, a 20th Century–Fox production slated for a 55-day shooting schedule.

PROMOTION

571 "Beyond the Valley of the Dolls." *Films and Filming*, 17(5):54–55, Feb. 1971.

A photo preview of *Beyond the Valley of the Dolls* notes that the film represents Meyer's first feature for a "major production company" after a decade of being known in the U.S. as the "king of the nudie films."

572 "Chicago." *Boxoffice,* 97(14):C-10, July 20, 1970.

Meyer takes new bride Edy Williams on a promotional trip to Chicago for *Beyond the Valley of the Dolls.*

573 "The Dolls of 'Beyond the Valley'." *Playboy,* 17(7):121–129, July 1970.

Former Playmates turned actresses Dolly Read (May 1966) and Cynthia Myers (Dec. 1969) are showcased in a lavish *Playboy* pictorial publicizing *Beyond the Valley of the Dolls.* (30 illus.)

574 Mahar, Ted. "Nudie Film Producer Russ Meyer Grinds Out Success After Success." *Sunday Oregonian,* sec. 4, p. 22, Aug. 16, 1970.

Meyer and wife Edy Williams, while promoting *Beyond the Valley of the Dolls* in Portland, touch upon the strong moral streak of punishment and retribution which runs throughout his films. Meyer also explains why 20th Century–Fox elected to use Jacqueline Susann's title, but not her screen treatment for *BVD.* (1 illus.)

575 Marks, Arnold. "Entertainment." *Oregon Journal,* sec. 1, p. 8, Aug. 14, 1970.

Days before *Beyond the Valley of the Dolls* is to open in Portland, Meyer and wife Edy Williams visit to promote the film. Williams, in a biographical footnote, discusses her beauty contest experiences and her desire to act. For Meyer's part, he is content to rest and mention his upcoming film *The Seven Minutes.* (2 illus.)

576 "Meyers [sic] with Meyer Pubbing 'Beyond ... Dolls'." *Hollywood Reporter,* 210(6):4, Mar. 3, 1970.

Playboy playmate Cynthia Myers, "Casey Anderson" in *Beyond the Valley of the Dolls,* is set by 20th Century–Fox to accompany Meyer on a five-city personal appearance tour to promote the film.

577 "Russ Meyer Movie-Making Syndrome." *Chicago Metro News,* p. 16, Apr. 26, 1975.

A biographical piece in a weekly black newspaper traces Meyer's life and filmmaking activities up through the box office success of *Beyond the Valley of the Dolls.*

MISCELLANEOUS

578 "'Beyond the Valley of the Dolls' Album Now in Release." *Boxoffice,* 97(16):114, Aug. 3, 1970.

Twentieth Century–Fox releases the soundtrack album for *Beyond the Valley of the Dolls,* its "satirical social commentary on today's morals and manners." Among the numbers are several by the Strawberry Alarm Clock including "A Girl from the City" and "I'm Comin' Home."

579 "'Beyond the Valley of the Dolls' Premieres Friday at the Roosevelt." *Chicago Daily Defender,* 15(87):13, July 8, 1970.

A short account of Meyer's transition from "nudie" films to major studio recognition provides the background for a short piece in a black newspaper announcing the debut of *Beyond the Valley of the Dolls* at the Roosevelt. (1 illus.)

580 "Beyond the Valley of the Nudies." *Chicago Daily News* (Red Streak Ed.), sec. Panorama, p. 3, Apr. 3–4, 1971.

A conversation with Meyer during the interim period following the financial, but not critical, success of *Beyond the Valley of the Dolls,* and prior to the release of *The Seven Minutes,* in which the filmmaker proclaims the death of the nudie film and his intention to move into "the last real preserve of the independent producer," the horror film. (1 illus.)

581 Calloway, Earl. "Russ Meyer Begins New Era in Motion Pictures." *Chicago Daily Defender,* pp. 12–13, July 15, 1970.

Meyer discusses *Beyond the Valley of the Dolls* and his impressions and feelings concerning his first-time ever association with a major studio, 20th Century–Fox. (1 illus.)

582 Cameron, Sue. "Church Head Sees Disease Caused by Porno Features." *Hollywood Reporter,* 212(16):1, Aug. 4, 1970.

Incensed by the "screen pollution" represented by films like *Beyond the Valley of the Dolls* and *Myra Breckenridge,* Dr. Clifton E. Moore, director of the Radio-Television-Film Commission for the Council of Churches, demands the resignation of Motion Picture Association of America president Jack Valenti. In place of the ineffective MPAA ratings code, Dr. Moore suggests the establishment of a "Blue Ribbon" Citizens Committee to henceforth rate movies. Dr. Moore also recommends that pressure be brought to bear on 20th Century–Fox president Richard D. Zanuck to compel him to "cancel his contract with Russ Meyer."

583 Cargin, Peter. "Russ Meyer & the Great American Dream Boat." *Time Out,* 7(2):26–27, Feb. 21, 1971.

Cargin quickly traces the rise of Meyer's career up to *Beyond the Valley of the Dolls* and notes that the filmmaker did not forget to use actors and actresses from his earlier independent films in this his first major studio production. Following a short synopsis of *BVD,* Cargin concludes that "Meyer is laughing all the way to the bank." (5 illus.)

584 "Dick Zanuck Counterattacks Monash for Valenti Blast." *Daily Variety,* 148(16):1, 11, June 29, 1970.

Richard Zanuck defends Jack Valenti against charges made by producer Paul Monash that question Valenti's moral leadership of the Motion Picture Association of America. Monash's sharp remarks were generated by Valenti's enjoyment of the X-rated Fox film *Myra Breckenridge.* See entries **590, 594, 603.**

585 "'Dolls' World Premiered at Pantages June 17." *Boxoffice,* 97(10): W-1, June 22, 1970.

The invitational world premiere of *BVD* is held June 17 at Hollywood's Pantages Theatre with attendant festivities including the Strawberry Alarm Clock performing numbers from the film.

586 "'Dolls,' 'Myra' Doing Well at Boxoffice." *Daily Variety,* 148 (63):3, Sept. 2, 1970.

Twentieth Century–Fox projects that its two X-rated features *BVD* and *Myra Breckenridge* will have a combined domestic gross of between \$14 and \$15 million. The studio also notes that *BVD* "shows unusual strength" in locations where Meyer appears to promote it.

587 "Double-Date for Dolls." *Hollywood Reporter,* 211(39):1, June 23, 1970.

In addition to its previously announced engagement at New York's Penthouse Theatre on Broadway, *BVD* also opens at the Cinema Rendezvous Theatre on June 24.

588 Harmon, Charlotte. "Nudity vs. Art—: It's Hard to Tell the Difference." *Back Stage,* p. 24, Feb. 27, 1970.

Meyer's hiring by 20th Century–Fox to direct *BVD* convinces Harmon that she was correct in maintaining there is now little difference in content between skin films exhibited in nudie houses and the "general run of movies."

589 "Meyer's Happy 'Valley'." *Hollywood Reporter,* 217(43):4, Sept. 8, 1971.

With *Beyond the Valley of the Dolls* already having grossed \$8 million, 20th Century–Fox sends Meyer a check for \$32,000, his first under a 10 percent participation agreement with the studio.

590 "Monash Urges Valenti Resign for Scant 'Moral Leadership'." *Daily Variety,* 148(15):1, 17, June 26, 1970.

Producer Paul Monash blasts Jack Valenti, president of the Motion Picture Association of America, for his commendation of 20th Century–Fox for making X-rated films like *Myra Breckenridge* and *Beyond the Valley of the Dolls* that are designed to appeal to various audience segments. For Monash, films like *Beyond the Valley of the Dolls* might "squeeze out some profits, but they will be drops of blood sucked from the corpse" of the industry. The producer of such films as *Butch Cassidy and the Sundance Kid* concludes that if Valenti refuses to take a major position against Hollywood's "purveyors of filth" he should resign. See entries **584, 594, 603.**

591   Muir, Florabel. "Hollywood: Beyond the Valley." *New York Daily News*, p. 58, Apr. 20, 1970.

Muir reports on the plot of *Beyond the Valley of the Dolls* and Meyer explains how he came to be signed by 20th Century–Fox to direct his first major studio film. (2 illus.)

592   Ornstein, Bill. "Zanuck Commissions Meyer for Three Pics; Options." *Hollywood Reporter*, 211 (13):1, 9, May 21, 1970.

Based upon his acceptance of the first cut of *Beyond the Valley of the Dolls* as final, studio head Richard D. Zanuck commissions Meyer to produce and direct three more pictures for 20th Century–Fox with options for two other undisclosed features. Proposed films include *The Seven Minutes;* Peter George's novel, *The Final Steal;* and Edward Albee's play *Everything in the Garden.*

593   "Populist at the Movies." *Time*, 95(13):59, 61, Mar. 3, 1970.

The now-famous *Chicago Sun-Times* film critic Roger Ebert is profiled in an early *Time* article as the common man's critic who "prefers 'movies' to 'films'." Ebert's script collaboration with Meyer on *Beyond the Valley of the Dolls,* which the critic describes as "a camp sexploitation horror musical that ends with a quadruple ritual murder and a triple wedding," is also noted. (1 illus.)

594   "Richard Zanuck Replies to Monash on 'Dolls,' 'Myra'." *Hollywood Reporter,* 211(40):1, June 29, 1970.

Calling producer Paul Monash's criticism of MPAA's president Jack Valenti "publicity-motivated," Richard Zanuck defends Valenti's integrity. See entries **584, 590, 603.**

595   "Russ Meyer: Combat Photog to Nudie King." *Chicago Defender,* sec. Accent, pp. 11, 13, May 24, 1975.

The article traces Meyer's career from his early boyhood interest in photography up through his war and postwar professional experiences, finally culminating in his signing by 20th Century–Fox to direct *Beyond the Valley of the Dolls.*

596   Safran, Don. "Historic Feud." *Dallas Times Herald,* sec. A, p. 20, Sept. 16, 1969.

Safran conjectures that 20th Century–Fox must have offered Meyer "some incredible inducement" other than money to persuade the filmmaker to relinquish his usual total artistic control in order to direct *Beyond the Valley of the Dolls.*

597   Scott, Vernon. "Ask Russ Meyer: Arty or Nudie—the Thin Blue Line." *Detroit News,* sec. A, p. 11, Jan. 20, 1970.

Scott notes that the thin blue line between the art film and the nudie flick bordering on pornography disappeared when 20th Century–Fox hired Meyer to produce and direct *Beyond the Valley of the Dolls.* (1 illus.)

598   "Skinflick Exposure Won Russ Meyer 'Dolls'." *Daily Variety,* 144 (53):10, Aug. 20, 1969.

Based on his flair for producing financially successful nudie films, Meyer joins the Hollywood mainstream after being signed by 20th Century–Fox to direct *Beyond the Valley of the Dolls.*

599   Tarbox, Aubrey. "Sexcessful Indie Russ Meyer to Fox: It's 'Evolu-

tion' and Not 'Revolution'." *Variety*, 256(2):7, Aug. 27, 1969.

Meyer's move from independent production to major studio recognition with his hiring by 20th Century–Fox to direct *Beyond the Valley of the Dolls* is seen by film insiders as an industry precedent signalling an industry trend towards more graphic depictions of sex. Seen in this light, one film executive noted that Meyer's employment by Fox is "less revolutionary than evolutionary."

600 Thomas, Bob. "King of Nudies Takes on 'Dolls' Sequel." *San Francisco Examiner*, p. 12, Sept. 27, 1969.

Industry eyebrows are raised when independent sex film producer Meyer is hired by 20th Century–Fox to direct the sequel to its $20 million grossing film *Valley of the Dolls*. (1 illus.)

601 Von Hoffman, Nicholas. "Dirty Movies Are His Bag." *Washington Post*, sec. C, pp. 1, 5, Nov. 5, 1969.

Von Hoffman's commentary on Meyer presents him as a guy who "wants to make good movies" as witnessed by his "fumbling attempts" to deal with complex social issues in *Vixen*. Though Meyer has since been signed by 20th Century–Fox to direct a "with it" and "now" film called *Beyond the Valley of the Dolls*, Von Hoffman wonders if someone coming from the "American Legion smoker school of sex" can successfully make the transition. The meeting between Meyer and the studio wardrobe department which concludes the article illustrates how uneasy with supposedly contemporary society both parties are.

602 Weiler, A.H. "Meyer to Make 3 More Films for Fox." *New York Times*, p. 34, Feb. 17, 1970.

Richard D. Zanuck, president of 20th Century–Fox, announces that based upon his pleasure with *Beyond the Valley of the Dolls*, he has signed Meyer to make three more films for the studio. Unlike Meyer's previous independently produced sexploitation epics, the Fox

films (Irving Wallace's *The Seven Minutes;* Edward Albee's *Everything in the Garden;* and Peter George's *The Final Steal*) will be adaptations of works by well known authors.

603 "Zanuck Lauds Valenti After Monash Attack." *Boxoffice*, 97(12):7, July 6, 1970.

The text of Richard D. Zanuck's statement defending Jack Valenti against producer Paul Monash's criticism of his moral leadership of the MPAA is offered. See entries **584, 590, 594**.

CENSORSHIP — CALIFORNIA

604 "Court Allows 20th–Fox Right to Release Meyer's 'Dolls'." *Boxoffice*, 97(10):6, June 22, 1970.

Superior Court Judge Richard Schauer denies a motion for an injunction restraining 20th Century–Fox from releasing *Beyond the Valley of the Dolls* on the grounds it would damage Jacqueline Susann's reputation as a writer.

605 "Court Clears Meyer's 'Valley'." *Motion Picture Exhibitor*, 83(12):4, June 24, 1970.

Superior Court Judge Richard Schauer denies a motion filed by Jacqueline Susann seeking to block the release of *Beyond the Valley of the Dolls* on grounds that it would damage her reputation as a writer.

606 "Court Orders Fox to Pay Mansfield $2 Million in Suit." *Hollywood Reporter*, 237(28):1, 10, Aug. 4, 1975.

After deliberating more than 11 hours, a Los Angeles Superior Court jury rules that 20th Century–Fox should pay $2 million in damages to Irving Mansfield, the widower of Jacqueline Susann, for failing to adequately dissociate the alleged non-sequel *Beyond the Valley of the Dolls* from the author's *Valley of the Dolls*.

607 "Fox Pays Susann Estate $1,425,000." *Variety*, 280(8):3, Oct. 1, 1975.

A brief blurb on the financial settlement 20th Century–Fox negotiated with the Jacqueline Susann estate for the alleged damage to the writer's reputation and earnings caused by *Beyond the Valley of the Dolls*.

608 Haber, Joyce. "'Dolls' Lawsuit Being Pressed." *Los Angeles Times*, pt. IV, p. 20, June 22, 1970.

Despite claiming her reputation as an author would be damaged by the release of *Beyond the Valley of the Dolls* the Superior Court of California refuses to grant Jacqueline Susann's petition for an injunction restraining 20th Century–Fox from releasing the film. Susann, however, vows the negative ruling will not deter her from further legal action against the studio.

609 Haber, Joyce. "Double Trouble in Valley of the Dolls." *Los Angeles Times*, pt. IV, p. 8, Jan. 28, 1971.

Irving Mansfield, husband of novelist Jacqueline Susann, expresses outrage over the stupidity of 20th Century–Fox for playing *Valley of the Dolls* and *Beyond the Valley of the Dolls* on a double bill after having denied any relationship existed between the original film and Meyer's new production. Mansfield has brought suit against the studio for using the original title in the non-sequel. (1 illus.)

610 Ogren, Peter. "Naked City." *Screw*, 70:23, July 6, 1970.

Ogren's weekly *Screw* review of current "sex films" playing in New York City reports on Jacqueline Susann's unsuccessful legal attempt to block Meyer's use of her novel's title in his *Beyond the Valley of the Dolls*. Meyer's upcoming marriage to the film's star, Edy Williams, is also noted. (2 illus.)

611 Seaman, Barbara. "Beyond the Valley." *Lovely Me: The Life of Jacqueline Susann*, pp. 399–416. New York: William Morrow, 1987.

Chapter Thirty of Seaman's biography of pop novelist Jacqueline Susann contains an interesting, if cursory, account of the legal controversy surrounding the use of the *Valley of the Dolls* title in Meyer's 1970 box office smash *Beyond the Valley of the Dolls*.

612 "650 Protest Smut in Pix at L.A. Rally." *Daily Variety*, 150(35):1, 6, Jan. 26, 1971.

Prior to a smut "protest luncheon" in Los Angeles, Charles Keating, Jr., of the Citizens for Decent Literature, Inc. declares to reporters that Meyer and Fox studio head Zanuck "ought to be arrested and jailed for making 'Beyond the Valley of the Dolls'."

613 "Susann Suit Loses, Judge Greenlights Release of 'Dolls'." *Daily Variety*, 148(7):1, 9, June 16, 1970.

After viewing both *Valley of the Dolls* and *Beyond the Valley of the Dolls*, Los Angeles Superior Court Judge Richard Schauer denies Jacqueline Susann's injunction against the release of Meyer's film based on her contention that it would damage her reputation as a writer. The decision clears the way for the film's June 17 world premiere at Hollywood's Pantages Theatre.

614 "Susann's Widower Awarded $2 Mil; Fox Will Appeal." *Variety*, 279:22, Aug. 6, 1975.

Jacqueline Susann's widower, Irv Mansfield, is awarded a $2 million settlement in a suit filed in 1970 by the late author charging that 20th Century–Fox illegally used her title *Valley of the Dolls* in its alleged non-sequel *Beyond the Valley of the Dolls*.

615 Warga, Wayne. "Jackie Susann Is a Pure Pop Doll." *Los Angeles Times*, sec. Calendar, pp. 1, 16, July 26, 1970.

Jacqueline Susann, described by Warga as a "masterfully entrenched piece of pop American culture," is profiled in a personality piece that mentions her $10 million lawsuit against Fox for allegedly damaging her literary reputation with the release of *Beyond the Valley of the Dolls.* Warga incorrectly notes that *Beyond the Valley of the Dolls* is failing at the box office when in reality it scored a major commercial hit. (1 illus.)

CENSORSHIP—MARYLAND

616 "Baltimore." *Boxoffice,* 97(13): E-8, July 13, 1970.

The Baltimore premiere of *Beyond the Valley of the Dolls* set for July 1, 1970, is temporarily held up until the deletions ordered by the Maryland State Board of Motion Pictures Censors are made. The Board approved the censored version and it will be released to major theatres there soon.

CENSORSHIP—NEW JERSEY

617 "Grand Jury Indicts Theater Manager." *National Decency Reporter,* 7(11–12):15, Nov.-Dec. 1970.

The grand jury of Burlington County indicts the manager of the Maple Shade Drive-In in Mount Holly, New Jersey, for allegedly contributing to the delinquency of a minor by showing two X-rated films, *Beyond the Valley of the Dolls* and *The Daughter,* to audiences containing minors. The indictment also charges that since the films were plainly visible to passing motorists (including minors) they represented a "nuisance to all."

CENSORSHIP—UTAH

618 "District Court Lifts Ban on 'Beyond Valley Dolls'." *Boxoffice,* 97(19):W-5, Aug. 24, 1970.

A U.S. District Court judge signs an order allowing exhibition of *Beyond the Valley of the Dolls* in the Utah cities of Salt Lake City, Provo, and Ogden based upon a suit filed by National General Corp. and managers of theatres where the film had been closed. An attorney for NGC argued that a fair trial in

Utah would be impossible due to a highly publicized statement made by an official who concluded that "Only a pervert would see that show."

619 "'Dolls' Ruling Brings Tirade in Salt Lake." *Boxoffice,* 97(18): W-8, Aug. 17, 1970.

The city commission of Salt Lake City reacts angrily to the ruling of a city judge pointing out that there was "insufficient evidence" to indicate that *Beyond the Valley of the Dolls* was "obscene and should be seized." One particularly angry commissioner suggested that police photograph patrons entering the theatre so as "to complete ... (their) ... file on 'perverts'."

620 "Utah Official Asks Test in 'Doll' Litigation." *Boxoffice,* 97(25):W-8, Oct. 5, 1970.

The Utah attorney general petitions the U.S. District Court in Salt Lake City for permission to intervene in an obscenity case resulting from the city of Provo's closure of *Beyond the Valley of the Dolls* after a two-week run at the Uptown Theatre. The attorney general seeks to involve the State to expeditiously determine matters of obscenity.

REVIEWS

621 Alpert, Hollis. "Beyond Belief." *Saturday Review,* 53:40, July 11, 1970.

An incredulous Hollis Alpert roundly criticizes the "debasement" and "materialistic corruption" of the executive level at 20th Century–Fox for releasing a "major skinflick" like *Beyond the Valley of the Dolls.* The noted critic is further disturbed by what he perceives as the film's "distinct hostility toward the female underlying ... (its) ... shots of bulbous bosoms" and suggests Meyer is perhaps the unhappy victim of a neurosis which could be more successfully treated by psychiatry than by filmmaking.

622 Arlecchino, Hank. "Eddra Holly and Russ." *Screw,* 71:18, July 13, 1970.

Arlecchino terms *Beyond the Valley of the Dolls* a "brilliant" and "insanely funny parody of the exploitation film" which Meyer's "madness" drives "into the realm of bizarre pop art." Dan Mouer's companion review in the same issue of *Screw* diametrically opposes Arlecchino's assessment. (1 illus.) See entry *662*.

623 Arnold, Gary. "Russ Meyer May Be Saviour At Fox." *Austin American*, p. 19, July 21, 1970.
Beyond the Valley of the Dolls is panned as the "most wretched of wretched movies" and it is questioned if former nudie film director Meyer can be "the financial saviour" of 20th Century–Fox.

624 Berkowitz, Stan. "The Perils of Self Parody." *UCLA Summer Bruin*, pp. 5–7, July 2, 1970.
Berkowitz compares the elements of self-parody in *Finders Keepers, Lovers Weepers!*, and *Beyond the Valley of the Dolls* and notes that Meyer's intensely serious direction of Ebert's absurdly satirical script is responsible for *BVD*'s "charm as a self parody." (4 illus.)

625 "'Beyond Dolls' About Nothing and for the Very Same People." *Hollywood Reporter*, 211(39):5, June 23, 1970.
While grudgingly admitting that much of the film is funny and that its box office prospects are superior, the anonymous reviewer describes *Beyond the Valley of the Dolls* as "a contemptible achievement . . . a movie made for everyone to feel superior to."

626 "Beyond the Valley of the Dolls." *Independent Film Journal*, UNKNOWN, July 8, 1970.
Meyer's first big-budget studio film marks a new low for the independent director whose former high speed, amusing style seems "cramped by the studio sets." While some may agree that the film is a put-on, the unnamed reviewer finds little amusing in decapitations and gunshot murders.

627 "Beyond the Valley of the Dolls." *Catholic Film Newsletter*, 35(13): 57, July 15, 1970.
Rated "C" (condemned) by the National Catholic Office for Motion Pictures, *Beyond the Valley of the Dolls* is severely criticized on both artistic and moral grounds.

628 "Beyond the Valley of the Dolls." *Mass Media Ministries Bi-Weekly Newsletter*, 12(10):7, Sept. 21, 1970.
A morbid exercise in "brash voyeurism and sexual vulgarity."

629 Bray, Lew. "Beyond the Valley of the Dolls." *Boxoffice*, 98(7):179, Nov. 30, 1970.
Commenting in the "Exploiter Has His Say About Pictures" section of *Boxoffice*, an exhibitor in Mercedes, Texas, terms *Beyond the Valley of the Dolls* "sick, sick, sick."

*630 Canby, Vincent. "Getting Beyond Myra and the Valley of the Junk." *New York Times*, sec. 2, p. 1, July 5, 1970.
Canby offers a capsule assessment of Meyer's past career and states the "clever" and "self-satisfied" *Beyond the Valley of the Dolls* may succeed on the level of popular culture as "both junk and cult." *Myra Breckenridge* is also reviewed. A thoughtful essay by an influential American film critic. Highly recommended.

*631 Canby, Vincent. "Screen: 'Beyond the Valley of the Dolls': Russ Meyer Presents a View of Show Biz: Film Seems to Parody His Earlier Efforts." *New York Times*, p. 19, June 27, 1970.
A humorous review characterizing *Beyond the Valley of the Dolls* as a conscious attempt by Meyer to parody his earlier films which Canby summarizes as "unconscious robust parodies of conventional Hollywood presentations of sex, violence, breast sizes and sin." While early in his career Meyer unselfconsciously gave the audience what it wanted,

Canby asserts that by moving into the realm of self-parody, he succeeds in making fun not only of himself, but also his audience. Recommended. (1 illus.)

*632 Champlin, Charles. "Breakthrough or Breakdown in Film Standards?" *Los Angeles Times,* sec. Calendar, pp. 1, 22–23, July 5, 1970.
Champlin eloquently argues that the two X-rated films currently in release, *Myra Breckenridge* and *Beyond the Valley of the Dolls,* can be viewed as either a breakthrough or breakdown of major studio film standards. Both films represent an obvious attempt by Fox to appeal solely to prurient interest sans any redemptive social value and thereby create discussion among some of the need for stronger film censorship. While recognizing censorship as a greater danger than any it seeks to correct, Champlin concludes that an irresponsible and financially strapped Fox has possibly set the wheels of censorship into motion. Highly recommended.

633 Cocks, Jay. "Beyond and Below." *Time,* 96:70, July 27, 1970.
Cocks concludes that the film is a "big camp" with the kind of sexual innuendo that "might impress a lickerish Boy Scout."

634 Cohen, Richard. "Beyond the Valley of the Dolls." *Women's Wear Daily,* 120(125):12, June 29, 1970.
Beyond the Valley of the Dolls, writes Cohen, is a "minor landmark in films" representing as it does the first instance of a skinflick crossing the barrier separating the genre from "fully realized" movies. Meyer and Ebert are credited with making "a hell-of-a-movie" that variously puts on a plethora of movie and lifestyle clichés in a "terrifically funny" manner.

635 Collins, William. "'Beyond the Valley of the Dolls' Is a Travesty." *Philadelphia Inquirer,* p. 11, July 16, 1970.

Despite having the bankroll of 20th Century–Fox behind him, Meyer's reputation as a "callous ... pornographer" remains intact with what Collins calls the "stale camp" of *Beyond the Valley of the Dolls.* (1 illus.)

636 Cook, Bruce. "Usual Sexploitation." *The National Observer,* p. 20, July 20, 1970.
Meyer's big-budget major studio-backed attempt to recreate his usual exploitation fare in a more attractive package for general audiences fails, with the result that *BVD* "is about as erotically stimulating as a dose of saltpeter."

*637 Corliss, Richard. "Film: Beyond the Valley of the Dolls." *Village Voice,* 15(28):54, July 9, 1970.
For long-time Meyer enthusiast Corliss, *Beyond the Valley of the Dolls* is "sensational and hysterical" despite its "unusually strained and restrained" first hour. Attributing the film's slow start to Meyer's unease with his new studio environment and the unfamiliar types of characters he is portraying in *BVD,* Corliss feels the film's "surreal climax" of murder and mayhem more than compensates for its "laborious preparation." Unreservedly proclaiming that "Meyer is sex and violence," the critic cites *BVD* as "the most satisfying expression of his manic and unsettling genius." Recommended.

638 Cragin, Donald. "'Beyond the Valley of the Dolls' at Gary Theater." *Boston Herald Traveler,* p. 25, July 7, 1970.
Cragin's negative review classes the film as "gutter-gore and sub-gutter camp." Commenting on Meyer's transition from low-budget independently produced sexploitation films to his current status at 20th Century–Fox, Cragin observes "you can take a director out of the gutter, but you can't take the gutter out of the director."

*639 Crist, Judith. "Mal de Merde, or Myra in the Mire." *New York,* 3(28):54–55, July 13, 1970.

In a wonderfully biting and funny criticism of two X-rated "Twentieth Stenchery–Fox" films, *Myra Brecken-ridge* and *Beyond the Valley of the Dolls,* Crist damns the studio for releasing "this pair of excrescences." *BVD* is termed dull and stupidly coarse with Meyer himself berated for having left the world of cheapie skinflicks where his photography and choice of women were exquisite. Highly recommended. (1 illus.)

640   Cuskelly, Richard. "'Beyond the Valley'—a Funny Parody." *Los Angeles Herald-Examiner,* sec. B, p. 5, June 18, 1970.

Based upon the type of picture Meyer promised to deliver to 20th Cen-tury–Fox ("the wildest, the craziest, the farthest out Musical-Horror-Sex-Comedy ever released"), Cuskelly assesses *Beyond the Valley of the Dolls* to be an un-qualified success. In his opinion, no one but Meyer would or could have made such a devastatingly funny film parody based on the theme of good girls being corrupted by the evils of Hollywood. Cuskelly's one criticism, the film's "over-use of violence and sadism." (1 illus.)

641   Dazat, Olivier. "Hollywood Vix-ens." *Cinématographe,* 104:54, Nov. 1984.

Beyond the Valley of the Dolls, a masterpiece of camp, derides the world of show business and in its x-ray of U.S. manners is essentially the work of a moralist whom Dazat calls "a curious yankee Rohmer." (2 illus.)

642   Elliott, David. "'Beyond Valley' Is Disaster Area." *Chicago Daily News* (Red Streak Ed.), sec. 3, p. 22, July 13, 1970.

A devastatingly bad review that criticizes Meyer's inability to make a bet-ter film given the expanded resources afforded him by a major studio. Elliott dismisses the film as "the absolute ground zero of mental inebriation. . . ." (1 illus.)

643   Fairbanks, Harold. "'Beyond Dolls'—How to Make Worse Out

of Bad." *The Advocate,* 4(10):13, 15, July 8–21, 1970.

A blistering review featured in the gay tabloid *The Advocate* which takes strong exception to the film's "snig-gering" portrayal of homosexuality. Scriptwriter Roger Ebert is especially taken to task by Fairbanks who accuses his fellow critic of having had his ideas of homosexuality formed by the 1956 film *Tea and Sympathy. Beyond the Valley of the Dolls,* Fairbanks concludes, is Ebert's "revenge for all the bad movies he reviewed in his tenure as a critic."

644   Foley, Mike. "Russ Meyer Beyond the Buck." *Cincinnati Enquirer,* p. 8, July 4, 1970.

Beyond the Valley of the Dolls is panned as being "as bad as it can be" and both Meyer and 20th Century–Fox are criticized for being interested only in the "almighty buck."

645   Gilmour, Clyde. "Already a Rival for Myra." *The Toronto Telegram,* p. 45, July 6, 1970.

After viewing *Beyond the Valley of the Dolls,* reviewer Gilmour questions his choice of *Myra Breckenridge* as the worst movie he has ever seen. Twentieth Century–Fox, responsible for both films, is condemned for offering the public "gift-wrapped garbage."

646   Goodwin, Michael. "Beyond the Valley of the Dolls." *Rolling Stone,* 66:50, Sept. 17, 1970.

A perplexed Goodwin likes the film, but can not figure out why when it is "so absurdly terrible." He does, however, comment favorably on Meyer's directorial choice to film the absurd script almost perfectly straight. (1 illus.)

*647   Greg. "Beyond the Valley of the Dolls." *Motion Picture Exhibitor,* p. 7, July 8, 1970.

Beyond the Valley of the Dolls, a "purposely commercial film" lacking in social significance, is, however, excellent entertainment. Greg. also observes that the New York critics who questioned whether Meyer was trying to be serious or camp have obviously not seen his past work which makes "such speculation . . . superfluous." Highly recommended.

648 Gumberts, William. "'Beyond the Valley' Not Far Enough." *Evansville Press*, p. 4, Aug. 15, 1970.

Gumberts likens the film to an unexpurgated version of a daytime television soap opera and concludes that *Beyond the Valley of the Dolls* "is so ludicrous that it borders on high camp comedy."

649 Harmetz, Richard S. "Film Review: 'Out of Towners' & 'Beyond Valley of the Dolls'." *Los Angeles Free Press*, 7(26):45, June 26–July 2, 1970.

While all facets of the production are panned, Harmetz is particularly critical of the film's lack of sexual content which he feels does not justify its X-rating. He concludes the rating was imposed by altruistic censors who wished "to spare juveniles an unimaginably boring evening."

650 Hartl, John. "'Dolls' Redefines Bad Taste." *Seattle Times*, sec. C, p. 4, Aug. 13, 1970.

Perhaps the "wildest deliberately awful movie ever made," Hartl admits the film can be fun if the viewer accepts it as "trash, without pretensions or redeeming social value."

651 Herridge, Frances. "Russ Meyer's Dolls." *New York Post*, p. 20, June 27, 1970.

Condemning the film as a piece of "unrelieved trash," Herridge wishes Meyer would return to the cheaply amusing sexploitation films he independently produced prior to being signed and (in her opinion) ruined by 20th Century–Fox.

652 Jones, Will. "Director Loses Sense of Humor." *Minneapolis Tribune*, p. 22, Aug. 6, 1970.

Jones, in a companion piece to his comments on *Beyond the Valley of the Dolls*, states that his disappointment

with the film is based on his past respect for Meyer as a filmmaker of humorous movies like *Eve and the Handyman*. That humor was evidently lost somewhere between Meyer's early days as an independent and his present association with a major studio. See entry **653**.

653 Jones, Will. "Warning of Bad Movie Ignored." *Minneapolis Tribune*, p. 22, Aug. 6, 1970.

Despite warnings from insiders at 20th Century–Fox, Jacqueline Susann, and several reviewers, a curious Jones was still not prepared for a film "so relentlessly . . . (and) . . . indescribably bad" as *Beyond the Valley of the Dolls*. See entry **652**.

654 Kass, Carole. "Beyond the Valley of the Dolls." *Richmond Times-Dispatch*, sec. D, p. 12, July 2, 1970.

A film made purposely to be obscene which Kass derides as "hard core pornography."

655 Kauffmann, Stanley. "Myra Breckenridge and Other Disasters." *The New Republic*, 163(3): 22, 34–35, July 18, 1970.

By trying to simultaneously appeal to the "cognoscenti" with camp and to the "yobs" with straight excitement, *Beyond the Valley of the Dolls* ends up as "utter garbage" with its violent murder sequence going "past trash into obscenity." *Cherry, Harry & Raquel* is also cited as "reeking" of hatred against women by he-men who "hate their sexual need of them."

656 Kay, Terry. "Beyond the Valley of the Dolls." *Atlanta Journal*, sec. A, p. 21, July 14, 1970.

A "vulgar, tasteless and completely repulsive film" that Kay believes to be a commentary on a society that has gone beyond merely being sick to definitely diseased. While not an advocate of censorship, Kay maintains that if directors like Meyer are "willing to sacrifice integrity" then "censorship should follow." (1 illus.)

657 Knoblauch, Mary. "He Made 'B.V.D.' Too Long." *Chicago Today*, sec. Family Today, p. 31, July 13, 1970.

After being impressed with Meyer's previous low-budget, independently produced sex spoofs, Knoblauch is disappointed with the director's first big-budget, studio-produced "trash epic." Criticisms center around Ebert's "talky" script which interferes with Meyer's "action-oriented" directorial style.

658 Kupcinet, Irv. "Kup's Column." *Chicago Sun-Times*, p. 62, July 15, 1970.

A Chicago wag quips that *Beyond the Valley of the Dolls* should have been rated "X-it."

659 Mahar, Ted. "Soap Opera Spoof Pulls Out All Stops." *The Oregonian*, sec. 1, p. 13, Aug. 31, 1970.

Mahar's enthusiastic review places the film in a long tradition of movies portraying Hollywood as a morally corrupt town which taints everyone it touches. Citing Meyer's fear that the film would not be recognized as a put-on, Mahar asserts the fact some critics have failed to do so only proves that it is "a really good spoof." (1 illus.)

660 Mahéo, Michel. "Hollywood Vixens." *Cinéma*, 311:50, Nov. 1984.

Released 14 years late in France, *Beyond the Valley of the Dolls* is somewhat dated, but still has an "iconoclastic charm."

661 Merrick, Hélène. "Hollywood Vixens: les renardes attaquent!" *Starfix*, 20:16, Nov. 1984.

Hollywood Vixens, the French title for *Beyond the Valley of the Dolls,* is identified by Merrick as the pride of Russ Meyer and the shame of 20th Century–Fox. For Merrick, the film is more evocative of *Caligula* or *Satyricon* than the "antiseptic soap operas" on television. (1 illus.)

*662 Mouer, Dan. "Muck & Meyer: Beyond the Valley of the Dolts." *Screw,* 71:21, July 13, 1970.

In a bitterly scathing and damning review, *Screw* film critic Dan Mouer systematically condemns every aspect of *Beyond the Valley of the Dolls.* In his most telling comment on the film and the talents involved, Mouer states that he would feel "Christlike" if he could but "influence people to run out and take the head of Russ Meyer and the producer from 20th Century, and hang them from Times Square..." Rated 11 percent on the *Screw* "Peter-Meter." Highly recommended. (3 illus.) See entry **622.**

663 Murf. "Beyond the Valley of the Dolls." *Variety,* 259(6):20, 22, June 24, 1970.

While conceding *Beyond the Valley of the Dolls* to be "exploitable in certain markets," Murf. sees little in Meyer's first major studio-produced film to praise except the technical credits. Although costing 20 to 30 times more than one of his independently produced sex films, Murf. concludes Meyer got less for his money with *BVD.*

664 Niogret, Hubert. "Hollywood Vixens (Beyond the Valley of the Dolls)." *Positif,* 286:74–75, Dec. 1984.

A bitter indictment of the world of California show business, *Beyond the Valley of the Dolls* stands as "the exceptional parenthesis" to Meyer's independent film career.

665 Ogren, Peter. "Naked City." *Screw,* 72:23, July 20, 1970.

Ogren agrees with *Screw* colleague Dan Mouer's low assessment of *Beyond the Valley of the Dolls,* calling it "the worst movie of the decade" and characterizing Meyer as "just plain sick." (1 illus.) See entry **662.**

666 Ogren, Peter. "Naked City." *Screw,* 73:23, July 27, 1970.

While "blood-and-guts fans will love" the film, *Beyond the Valley of the Dolls* "isn't even a *good* bad movie."

*667 Peary, Danny. "Beyond the Valley of the Dolls." *Cult Movies,* pp. 24–27. New York: Dell Pub. Co., 1981.

Peary contends that for those who had admired Meyer's earlier independent work (himself included), *Beyond the Valley of the Dolls* proved to be a revelation that "we'd overestimated his talents." Describing the film as "a multimillion-dollar spoof of movies that are already self-parodies," the critic condemns Meyer for being "conservative and lazy" rather than trying to expand upon his past sexploitation themes. In his most damning comment, Peary accuses Meyer of realizing midway through the production how bad the film was which prompted his hurried decision to make the dialogue and plot situations so outrageous that they would provide him with "an out" if the film did not succeed. Peary concludes *BVD* "signalled the demise of Meyer" as a filmmaker critics had to seriously consider. Recommended. (6 illus.)

668 Peary, Danny. "Beyond the Valley of the Dolls." *Guide for the Film Fanatic,* p. 50. New York: Simon & Schuster, 1986.

Meyer's first studio picture is a "lazy and conservative" exercise that spoofs a genre, the Hollywood soap opera, which is itself already a self-parody. Ebert's script is termed "smug and vulgar" and filled with scenes of violence against women which he decried as a critic. For a fuller discussion of this film, (from which this review is condensed) see entry 667.

669 Rice, Susan. "Homily Grits." *Media & Methods,* 7(1):10, 14, 16, 18, 20, Sept. 1970.

Rice terms the film "boring bisexualism." Note: the short review appears on p. 16 only.

670 Rimmer, Robert. "Beyond the Valley of the Dolls." *The X-Rated Videotape Guide,* pp. 63–64. New York: Arlington House, 1984.

Rimmer is impressed by the "very fast, sophisticated cutting" of the film's first hour and informs video viewers that while *Beyond the Valley of the Dolls* contains some nudity and a lot of sex, it is not explicit.

671 Royko, Mike. "'Beyond the Valley of the Dolls': His Parody Didn't Make It." *Los Angeles Times,* pt. IV, p. 9, July 27, 1970.

Royko, a newspaper colleague of Roger Ebert, humorously savages *Beyond the Valley of the Dolls* and concludes that the "decent" and "talented" screenwriter's parody of dirty and violent movies failed because for a dirty movie to be any good it must be written by "a dirty old man."

672 Sabatier, J.M. "Orgissimo." *Revue du Cinéma.* 294:124, Mar. 1975.

Sabatier asserts that *Beyond the Valley of the Dolls* will enthusiastically please lovers of humor and the unusual, but "cruelly deceive erotomaniacs." The "tragic universe" in *BVD* is described as "half way between Faulkner and the photo-novel" while Meyer is identified as a "marginal world unto himself," but a world which is necessary to understand "Hollywood Babylon."

673 Segal, Lewis. "Beyond the Valley of the Dolls." *Show,* 1(11):41, Aug. 20, 1970.

A "perfect" film that combines "directorial zeal and unerring bad taste" with a screenplay that "preserves virtually every film cliché of the 1960's." (1 illus.)

674 Silber, Irwin. "Adventures in the Skin Trade." *Guardian: Independent Radical Weekly,* 22(40):17, July 18, 1970.

Silber offers an interesting Marxist perspective on Meyer's hiring by 20th Century–Fox and by and large comments favorably on *Beyond the Valley of the Dolls.* (1 illus.)

*675 Simon, John. "Meyer's Blue Heaven." *The New Leader,* 53 (15):19–21, July 20, 1970.
Simon considers *Beyond the Valley of the Dolls* to be "true pornography" in that despite its "fleeting nudity" and numerous "disembodied scene(s) of sexual activity" the film's "idea of sex is totally divorced from reality" and it therefore "incites to masturbation" rather than "leads to intercourse." A thought-provoking article well worth reading. Highly recommended.

676 Stein, Jerry. "Russ Meyer's Gaudy Extravagances." *Cincinnati Post & Times Star,* p. 29, July 8, 1970.
Beyond the Valley of the Dolls is assessed as a near self-parody succeeding because of its "baroque extravagance."

677 Suhrheinrich, Jeanne. "Front Row Center: At the Majestic and West Side." *Evansville Courier,* p. 15, Aug. 15, 1970.
Suhrheinrich's "capsule" review of *Beyond the Valley of the Dolls:* "Yawnsville."

678 Swinney, Ed. "Dolls Should Have Stayed in the Valley." *Houston Post,* sec. 3, p. 20, July 9, 1970.
Promising that Meyer's fans will not be disappointed by this "erotic soap opera," Swinney terms the film a farce.

679 Taylor, John Russell. "Telling It Like It Is." *London Times,* p. 9, Feb. 12, 1971.
Meyer's mock-serious handling of the soap opera elements in *Beyond the Valley of the Dolls* is "deliciously ludicrous in small doses," though ultimately too much to take as a whole.

680 Taylor, Robert. "Meyer's Dolls: Beyond Belief." *Oakland Tribune,* p. 43, Aug. 6. 1970.
Though Taylor declares the film to be a celebration of the "new pornography, violence," Meyer explains the picture's bloody climax as a convenient and exciting script device employed to resolve a plot involving 12 major characters. (1 illus.)

681 Wall, James M. "Beyond the Valley of the Dolls." *Film Information,* 1(8/9):4–5, Aug./Sept. 1970.
The unlikely combination of Meyer and 20th Century–Fox has resulted in a satiric film with a "tedious plot."

682 Wallington, Mike. "Beyond the Valley of the Dolls." *Monthly Film Bulletin,* 38(446):44–45, Mar. 1971.
Though criticizing the film as "corny" and as "visually . . . appealing as a Christmas wrapper," Wallington finds the film to be "perversely enjoyable" if the viewer is prepared to laugh both with and at it.

683 Williams, Alton. "Beyond the Valley of the Dolls." *Richmond News Leader,* UNKNOWN, July 2, 1970.
Worthy of a double X-rating for its excessive sex and brutal violence, Williams dismisses the film as "sexploitation trash."

684 Wolf, William. "Beyond the Valley of the Dolls." *Cue,* 39(27):64, July 4, 1970.
Wolf adds the film to his "year's-worst list."

*685 Yanni, Nick. "Beyond the Valley of the Dolls." *Motion Picture Herald,* 240(17):481, July 15, 1970.
Unlike many reviewers, Yanni recognizes *BVD* for what it is: a "grossly exaggerated" put-on that consciously strives to be camp in depicting sex and violence. Although the film is rated "X," Yanni observes that it is so not because of its sex scenes, but because of Meyer's reputation. Citing the film's breakneck pace and "soap-operaish plot," Yanni concludes that *BVD* could end the current wave of sex and violence films by "simply revealing it all for what little it really is." Highly recommended.

686 Zimmerman, Paul D. "X-Rated Mind." *Newsweek,* 76(1):85, July 6, 1970.

Zimmerman describes *Beyond the Valley of the Dolls* as "the most lavishly tasteless masturbation fantasy since Hugh Hefner started retailing his topless hedonism." Despite *BVD*'s celebration of "sexuality in all its polymorphous forms," Zimmerman charges Meyer with remaining consistent with his "1950s puritanism ... (by having) all crotches keep their backs to the camera."

The Seven Minutes (1971)

PRODUCTION NOTES

687 Archerd, Army. "Just for Variety." *Daily Variety*, 146(59):2, Mar. 2, 1970.
Novelist Irving Wallace reacts positively to news from 20th Century–Fox that Meyer will replace Richard Fleischer as director for *The Seven Minutes* now reduced in budget from $6 million to $1.8 million.

688 Archerd, Army. "Just for Variety." *Daily Variety*, 149(4):2, Sept. 11, 1970.
In an attempt to ensure that *The Seven Minutes* will receive the all-important R-rating, Meyer has already shown the script to the Motion Picture Association of America.

689 Cuskelly, Richard. "Censorship-Themed 'The Seven Minutes' New Meyer Project." *Los Angeles Herald-Examiner*, sec. F, p. 5, Nov. 15, 1970.
Cuskelly's report on *The Seven Minutes*, Meyer's follow-up film to his box office smash *BVD*, presents the director with an opportunity to air his views on the political motivation he feels underlies most film censorship. (1 illus.)

690 Haber, Joyce. "Kim Darby Passes Her 'Tiger' Test." *Los Angeles Times*, pt. IV, p. 13, Jan. 11, 1971.
Irving Wallace visits the set of *The Seven Minutes* and comments that Meyer is apparently following his novel

and does not seem to be making a skin-flick.

691 Haber, Joyce. "'Portnoy' Moves Off the Lot." *Los Angeles Times*, pt. IV, p. 22, Oct. 7, 1970.
Meyer is briefly questioned concerning his casting of *The Seven Minutes*. (1 illus.)

692 Leverence, John, and Grogg, Sam, Jr. "Irving Wallace — the Interview: The Author of *The Word*." *Journal of Popular Culture*, 7(1):185–208, Summer 1973.
In a lengthy interview, Irving Wallace briefly touches upon Meyer's filmization of his novel *The Seven Minutes*. Wallace states that the filmmaker approached the complex and sensitive problem of pornography and censorship "like a bull in a china shop" trying unsuccessfully to combine seriousness with camp. Meyer's biggest error, however, was in trying to stick too closely to the book despite Wallace's allegedly numerous attempts to persuade him to change the script. (1 illus.)

693 Manners, Dorothy. "Courtroom Expert to Assist Meyer." *Los Angeles Herald-Examiner*, sec. C, p. 4, Jan. 7, 1971.
Burt Katz, deputy assistant district attorney on the Charles Manson trial, spends four days at Meyer's request on the set of *The Seven Minutes* instructing actors on the "'now' courtroom techniques."

694 "Obscenity Is Theme of Upcoming Film." *Variety*, 254(12):5, May 7, 1969.
Twentieth Century–Fox announces a "deal" for the film edition of Irving Wallace's novel *The Seven Minutes* to be produced and directed by Richard Fleischer.

695 "Richard Lewis Screenplay Bow on '7 Minutes'." *Hollywood Reporter*, 210(10):4, Mar. 9, 1970.
Meyer signs newcomer Richard Warren Lewis to write the screenplay for *The Seven Minutes*.

696	"Russ Meyer from Sexploitation to 'Seven Minutes'." *Movies Now,* 1(1):46–47, Summer 1971.

In an interview conducted during the editing of *The Seven Minutes,* Meyer describes the film as his first serious attempt to appeal to a broad cross-section of moviegoers. Meyer also comments on the Motion Picture Association of America's X-rating and its deleterious effect on promotion and potential exhibitors. (3 illus.)

697	"Russ Meyer Makes Three-Pic Pact; Sets Three Films." *Hollywood Reporter,* 209(45):1, 9, Feb. 16, 1970.

Eve Productions signs a three-picture deal with 20th Century–Fox to make *The Seven Minutes, The Final Steal,* and *Everything in the Garden.*

698	"'Seven Minutes' Rolls." *Hollywood Reporter,* 213(17):8, Oct. 15, 1970.

Meyer's second, and final, film for Fox begins production on October 14, 1970, with a 50-day shooting schedule planned.

699	"Three for 'Minutes'." *Hollywood Reporter,* 213(17):4, Oct. 15, 1970.

Tom Selleck, Olan Soulé, and Jan Shutan are signed by Meyer for parts in *The Seven Minutes.*

700	"3 More 20th Pix for Russ Meyer." *Daily Variety,* 146(49):3, Feb. 16, 1970.

Eve Productions and 20th Century–Fox sign an exclusive deal which sets Meyer to produce three more films for the studio: *The Seven Minutes, The Final Steal,* and *Everything in the Garden.* Production is set to begin on *The Seven Minutes* in July 1970, with the other two films scheduled for completion within 18 months after *Minutes* is finished.

701	"20th–Fox Rolls Three Pics This Week, Two Here." *Hollywood Reporter,* 213(14):4, Oct. 12, 1970.

Twentieth Century–Fox president Richard D. Zanuck announces the October 14, 1970, production start of *The Seven Minutes* to be filmed at the studio and nearby locations.

702	"20th Will Roll 3 Pix in 3 Days." *Daily Variety,* 149(25):2, Oct. 12, 1970.

The Seven Minutes is among two other 20th Century–Fox films which studio head Richard D. Zanuck reports will begin production this week.

PROMOTION

703	Goldberg, Joe. "The Immoral Mr. Tease: I Call on Russ Meyer." *Coast,* 12(11):38–40, Nov. 1971.

In an interview arranged by 20th Century–Fox to promote *The Seven Minutes,* Meyer discusses his upcoming debate on censorship with Ohio porno crusader Charles Keating, Jr. Goldberg, who characterizes the filmmaker as one of the most "courteous" and "considerate" men in Hollywood, hopes *The Seven Minutes* ends Meyer's stint as a social crusader like Stanley Kramer, and that his next scheduled film, *Choice Cuts,* marks a return to straight, non-message entertainment. (2 illus.)

704	Kay, Terry. "Russ Meyer Unnoticed in Company of His Wife." *Atlanta Journal,* sec. A, p. 16, July 12, 1971.

In Atlanta promoting *The Seven Minutes,* Meyer, accompanied by provocatively attired wife Edy Williams, expresses his opinion that the sex film is on the way out and that his future film projects will be in the horror and mystery genre. An enthusiastic Kay describes Williams as "sex in motion . . . even when she's standing still."

705	Marks, Arnold. "Nudie Film Maker 'Grows Up'." *Oregon Journal,* sec. 1, p. 11, Aug. 18, 1971.

A pre-publicity piece on *The Seven Minutes* features biographical information on former Portland schoolgirl Edy Williams and notes that for the first time in Meyer's career he has experienced actors in key roles. (1 illus.)

706 Osterhaus, Carolyn. "'Vixen' Director Has R-Rated Film." *Cincinnati Post & Times Star*, p. 22, June 28, 1971.

In Cincinnati for a preview showing of *The Seven Minutes* at the Ambassador Theater, Meyer states that the $2.4 million film will give him "full respectability" with the Hollywood Establishment.

MISCELLANEOUS

707 Archerd, Army. "Just for Variety." *Daily Variety*, 154(54):2, Feb. 17, 1972.

Author Irving Wallace notes that although Meyer's name preceded *The Seven Minutes* on theatre marquees when it was first released, it is now billed as "Irving Wallace's *Seven Minutes.*"

708 "Fox Signs Meyer for Three Pictures." *Oakland Tribune*, p. 44, Feb. 25, 1970.

Twentieth Century–Fox and Russ Meyer's Eve Productions sign an exclusive three-picture deal under which the filmmaker will produce and direct Wallace's *The Seven Minutes*, Edward Albee's *Everything in the Garden*, and *The Final Steal* by Peter George.

709 "Meyer Readies a Treat for Smut Crusader." *Daily Variety*, 150 (36):3, Jan. 27, 1971.

Responding to a *Daily Variety* article in which Charles Keating, Jr. states that he "ought to be arrested and jailed" for making *BVD* (see entry **612**), Meyer promises that his next film, *The Seven Minutes*, will not only expose "political opportunists" like Keating, but will also world premiere in the porno crusader's hometown of Cincinnati.

REVIEWS

710 Buckley, Peter. "The Seven Minutes." *Films and Filming*, 18(7): 57, 60, Apr. 1972.

British critic Buckley affectionately calls the film "pure hokum" that is "almost always fun to watch." Meyer, "the Mack Sennett of the '70's," begs comparison with that filmmaker in their mutual ability to overblow a cliché to the point of hilarity and to demonstrate a precision-like craftsmanship in producing films "with an efficiency unrivalled among their contemporaries."

711 Cooper, Arthur. "Stick-in-the-Mud." *Newsweek*, 73(6):72, Aug. 9, 1971.

The Seven Minutes is denounced as banal and cliché-ridden, with Meyer criticized as a "sexual stick-in-the-mud" who still plays the "skin game" by the "rules of the 1960s."

*712 Corliss, Richard. "Film: From Cult Hero to Company Man." *Village Voice*, 16(31):55, Aug. 5, 1971.

In one of the few good reviews of *The Seven Minutes*, Corliss states that not only is it "a well-wrought, highly entertaining" production, but that it also proves to industry executives that Meyer is capable of turning out a film in the "well made" studio tradition. Despite the praise, however, Corliss laments the intersection of the careers of Meyer and Wallace at a point "where both are seeking the respect of their undeserving peers." Had they met during the four-year period which produced Meyer's best films (*Good Morning and Goodbye!* [1967] through *Beyond the Valley of the Dolls* [1970]), Corliss believes the pairing would have resulted in the stuff "a sexploitation aesthete's dreams are made of." Corliss seems to hint that the price of Meyer's transformation from cult hero to company man was the sacrifice of a uniquely personal film style. Recommended.

713 Dawson, Jan. "The Seven Minutes." *Monthly Film Bulletin*, 38(455):247–248, Dec. 1971.

While the film is "curiously watchable," it is not "high art."

714 Ell, David. "'B-Movies' Meyer Now at Saucy Satirical Best in 'Seven Minutes'." *Salt Lake Tribune*, sec. A, p. 15, July 21, 1971.

Meyer is applauded for having "injected an extraordinary amount of vital energy" into Irving Wallace's talky book.

715 Fairbanks, Harold. "Russ Meyer's Latest: 'Seven Minutes' Lasts Two Godawful Hours." *The Advocate*, 65:18, Aug. 4–17, 1971.

Despite the ominous note of criticism in the title, Meyer receives high praise for his successful screen adaptation of Irving Wallace's 600-page novel dealing with attempts by organized censors to ban an allegedly pornographic book.

716 Goldstein, Al. "Cream of the Crap: The Worst Films of 1971." *Screw*, 150:19, Jan. 17, 1972.

In addition to co-winning the *Screw* "1971 Smegma in Film Award," *The Seven Minutes* also has the dubious honor of serving as "a tombstone for the dead talents of Russ Meyer." (3 illus.)

717 Goldstein, Al. "An Oscar for Meyer's Weenie." *Screw*, 124:23, July 19, 1971.

Goldstein's darkly amusing review of *The Seven Minutes* notes that Meyer is unique in his ability to make a two million dollar studio-produced film look like a cheap sexploitation epic that would be at home on 42nd Street. Based on the infamous *Screw* ratings system, the "Peter-Meter," which allocates combined percentage points up to 100 for a film's "interest," its "sexuality—explicit & implicit," and its "technical" virtues, *The Seven Minutes* scored a dismal 24 percent. (1 illus.)

718 Greenspun, Roger. "'The 7 Minutes': Court Is Focus of Russ Meyer's Latest." *New York Times*, p. 14, July 24, 1971.

Greenspun insists that the verbose complexities of the courtroom are not amenable "to that reduction to monumental simplicities that is near the center of Meyer's dramaturgy."

*719 Korda, Michael. "Russ Meyer—Better at Caricature Than Skin Flicks." *Glamour*, 66(3): 143, Nov. 1971.

In an excellent critique of *The Seven Minutes*, Korda identifies Meyer as a "brilliant caricaturist" of the American dream at its worst. However, Korda asserts that Meyer's "essential Puritanism" robs the film's characters of any real emotion and thereby reduces them to the status of "a group of sexually animated wax dummies." Highly recommended.

720 Marks, Arnold. "Four-Letter Words Spoil 7 Minutes for Reviewer." *Oregon Journal*, sec. 1, p. 5, Aug. 21, 1971.

Though the film is Meyer's "most polished" effort to date, the story line is weakened by his extreme use of four-letter words and pictorial sex.

721 McElfresh, Tom. "'The Seven Minutes' Trash." *Cincinnati Enquirer*, p. 8, July 2, 1971.

McElfresh suggests that a comparison between the "brilliant" *Carnal Knowledge* and Meyer's "trash" film *The Seven Minutes* answers the question of whether a competent director's handling of nudity and sexual slang can enhance the value of a film. Dismissing the film as pure insensitive sensationalism, McElfresh likens Meyer's directorial style to a "meat cleaver."

722 Peterson, Lowell. "'Seven Minutes' That Shook the World." *UCLA Daily Bruin*, p. 5, Sept. 9, 1971.

Meyer's rapid-fire editing technique in *The Seven Minutes* elicits Peterson to compare him favorably with the great Russian director and film theorist Sergei Eisenstein, and the noted American action director Sam Fuller. *The Seven Minutes* is termed "an absolute must-see." (2 illus.)

723 Rice, Susan. "Estival Festival." *Media & Methods*, 8(1):8, 10, 12, 14, 17–18, Sept. 1971.

Reviewed under the heading "The

Cinema of the Ridiculous," Rice's 17-word review characterizes Meyer as a "Porno King" who in *The Seven Minutes* directs "a cast of breasts."

724 "The Seven Minutes." *Cinema,* 8th Annual Awards Issue, p. 20, 1971.
A one-line review describes the film as "stupidly amusing."

725 "The Seven Minutes." *Show,* 2(8):59, Oct. 1971.
An uncited reviewer titles Meyer "the king of thoroughly enjoyable rotten movies" and assesses the overplotted film as "not art, but who cares?" (1 illus.)

726 "Seven Minutes." *Filmfacts,* 14: 296–298, 1971.
A detailed plot synopsis is followed by a "critique" section that summarizes the views of several notable newspaper and magazine-based film critics. Critical consensus on *The Seven Minutes* ranged from 2 favorable, 0 mixed, to 12 negative. Review includes cast and credits. (2 illus.)

727 "The Seven Minutes." *Catholic Film Newsletter,* 36(13):72, July 15, 1971.
The pairing of Irving Wallace and Meyer ("two of America's most profoundly banal creative talents") has resulted in an unfunny, dirty film which combines "the depth of a Hollywood press release" with "the titillation of an arcade peep show." Condemned by the National Catholic Office for Motion Pictures.

728 "The Seven Minutes." *Playboy,* 18(10):52, Oct. 1971.
The film is summarized as "a losing battle of mind over mattress."

729 "The Seven Minutes." *Motion Picture Herald,* 241(1):580, Sept. 8, 1971.
Called the "camp entertainment of the year," the uncited reviewer inaccurately predicted big box office for this film. Reviewer's rating—"Good."

730 Thomas, Kevin. "'Seven' Attacks Censorship." *Los Angeles Times,* pt. IV, p. 10, Sept. 8, 1971.

Thomas finds that in Meyer's earnestness to make a serious film about the evils of censorship he has replaced action with talk. While the film fascinates as a work of Pop Art, Thomas asserts that scriptwriter Richard Warren Lewis' verbiage makes the film tedious despite the comic strip effect produced by Meyer's rapid-fire editing. (1 illus.)

731 Wall, James M. "The Seven Minutes." *Film Information,* 2(8/9): 5, Aug./Sept. 1971.
Wall assesses the film as a "low-camp," inoffensive attack on "puritan hypocrisy" that makes no "real effort" to confront the issue of censorship.

732 Wasserman, John L. "'Literary' Work: A Sex Expert's 'Seven Minutes'." *San Francisco Chronicle,* p. 46, Aug. 26, 1971.
Wasserman's review dismisses the film as "a miserable piece of simple minded buffoonery." Meyer's direction and script are described as "pathetic." (1 illus.)

733 Wolf, William. "The Seven Minutes." *Cue,* 40(29):64, July 17, 1971.
Meyer's "cloddish" directorial style makes the filmization of Irving Wallace's novel look "like (a) soap opera in black sox."

Blacksnake! (1973)

PRODUCTION NOTES

734 "Chicago." *Boxoffice,* 102(10–11): C-1, Dec. 18, 1972.
Back from a five-day West Coast trip, Jack Gilbreth, president of Gilbreth Films, reports that he saw a complete print of *Blacksnake!* that still requires some editing before it can be shown to exhibitors.

735 "Dick Stafford Forms Distribution Company." *Daily Variety,* 159(21):22, Apr. 3, 1973.

Blacksnake! (1973): Meyer fails in his attempt to jump on the black exploitation bandwagon, but the film is memorable due to a short trailer for *Foxy* featuring third wife Edy Williams waterskiing nude!

Dick Stafford, former western division manager for Cinema V, announces the formation of a new distribution company, Cardinal Films, which is slated to release *Blacksnake!*

736   Gilkes, Al. "Barbadians Have Big Roles in Local Movie." *Advocate-News*, p. 6, Apr. 22, 1972.
A day spent on the set of *Blacksnake!* pleasantly convinces black columnist Gilkes that several local actors of color are prominently featured in the production.

737   Gilkes, Al. "Meet Milton—Our Own Film Star." *Advocate-News*, p. 6, May 13, 1972.
Barbados-born actor Milton McCollin, "Joshua" in *Blacksnake!*, is featured in a personality piece which calls him the island's "first ever film star in the true sense of the word." (1 illus.)

Behind the scenes with Meyer and crew on *Blacksnake!*, the first movie to be shot entirely on the island of Barbados.

738 McLean, Donald. "Meet Russ Meyer." *Bay Area Reporter,* 3 (10):10–12, May 16, 1973.

Interviewed in San Francisco during a promotional tour for *Blacksnake!*, Meyer discusses the production problems which arose from the drug overdose of the film's leading lady three days before the start of shooting. Meyer's recasting of the role with Anouska Hempel rather than with actress-wife Edy Williams, in turn caused marital problems assuaged only by the filmmaker's promise to star her in his next film, *Foxy.* Appended as a "Footnote" to the interview is McLean's review of *Blacksnake!* which he found to be a typical Russ Meyer work sporting "boobs, baskets and blood" highlighted by excellent photography and an "atrocious" script. (3 illus.)

739 "Shooting of 'Black Snake' Under Way." *Advocate-News,* p. 1, Apr. 18, 1972.

The opening interior and exterior scenes of *Blacksnake!* featuring British actors David Warbeck and Charles Walker are shot at "Abbotsford," the English-style manor house of a local Barbadian. (1 illus.)

740 "Shooting of U.S. Movie Begins Today." *Advocate-News,* p. 1, Apr. 17, 1972.

A six- to seven-week shooting schedule for *Blacksnake!* begins April 17, 1972, on Barbados. According to Meyer and co-producer James Ryan, the island was chosen for the tale of a 19th century slave uprising because of its historic 17th century plantation, Nicholas Abbey.

741 "Urging Rebellion in 'Black Snake'." *Sunday Advocate-News,* sec. Advocate Magazine, p. 1, Apr. 30, 1972.

While scenes from several films have been shot in Barbados, *Blacksnake!* represents the first full length movie to feature local Barbadian actors in major roles that will be filmed in its entirety on the island. (1 illus.)

PROMOTION

742 Bladen, Barbara. "The Marquee." *San Mateo Times,* p. 7, May 15, 1973.

Bladen quotes Meyer extensively on his new film *Blacksnake!* The filmmaker promises his next effort, *Supervixens,* will correct the inadvertent blow he struck for Women's Liberation with *Vixen.* (1 illus.)

743 Bykofsky, Stuart D. "I'm Not a Pornographer, Says Wealthy 'King Leer'." *Philadelphia Daily News,* UNKNOWN, Apr. 6, 1973.

While in Philadelphia to promote *Blacksnake!,* Meyer denies that he is a pornographer and offers an example of what the term "film pornography" means to him. Meyer describes his R-rated film as "an outrageous put-on." (1 illus.)

744 "Film Maker Says Critics Overlook His Humor." *El Paso Times,* sec. A, p. 10, Apr. 18, 1973.

Meyer charges critics who find his films too sexy and violent with overlooking the humor in them. Edy Williams, who accompanied Meyer to El Paso to help promote *Blacksnake!,* describes her initial feelings over her nude appearance in the film's three-minute trailer for *Viva Foxy!,* the filmmaker's next project. Meyer also mentions El Paso as a possible site for a movie he is planning based on "the first Pony Express rider."

745 Gilkes, Al. "'Black Snake' Preview Wednesday." *Advocate-News,* p. 8, Mar. 10, 1973.

Meyer will be flying in from Hollywood to host a special morning preview of *Blacksnake!* for the press and cast members prior to the film's official premiere later in the day.

746 Lewis, Bill. "Skin Flick to Premiere at LR; 'Camp' Meyer Says." *Arkansas Gazette,* sec. B, p. 20, Mar. 28, 1973.

In Little Rock for the March 28th world premiere of *Blacksnake!,* Meyer discusses the film's plot and its trailer sequence for *Viva Foxy!* which he insists marks the first time one film has been used to promote another. (1 illus.)

747 Miller, Jeanne. "'There's Only One Kind of Film Success'." *San Francisco Examiner,* p. 36, May 9, 1973.

Meyer explains that the sex in *Blacksnake!* is de-emphasized in favor of increased violence because it was imperative the film receive an R-rating in order to make it eligible for exhibition in the financially lucrative drive-in market. Meyer further maintains that ultimately the only criterion of success for a film is how much money it makes. (1 illus.)

748 Quarm, Joan. "Russ Meyer Is Rare Honest Man." *El Paso Herald-Post,* sec. C, p. 4, Apr. 18, 1973.

With Edy Williams in El Paso to promote *Blacksnake!,* Meyer impresses Quarm as an honest man when he admits to the reporter that he makes erotic films that young people like and critics do not for the purpose of making money.

749 Rayns, Tony. "Russ Meyer." *Time Out,* 106:43–44, Feb. 25–Mar. 2, 1972.

Meyer is quoted extensively concerning his involvement on *The Seven Minutes* and *Blacksnake!* Though disappointed with the critical and commercial reception of *The Seven Minutes,* Meyer feels that with *Blacksnake!* he is returning to the "parody/satire" genre where he is most comfortable. (5 illus.)

750 Villanch, Bruce. "The Russ and Edy Show . . . of Duck & Sex Films & Herman." *Chicago Today American,* sec. Now, pp. 29, 66, Apr. 6, 1973.

At a publicity luncheon in Chicago, Meyer and wife Edy Williams discuss her nude appearance in a three-minute trailer for *Viva Foxy!* tacked on to the end of the filmmaker's current release *Blacksnake!* Meyer also explains the reasoning behind his decision to de-emphasize sex in favor of violence in *Blacksnake!* (2 illus.)

MISCELLANEOUS

751 "Black Snake Show March 14." *Sunday Advocate-News,* p. 11, Mar. 4, 1973.

The world premiere of *Blacksnake!* will be on Wednesday, March 14, 1973, at the Roodal's Drive-In and the Empire Theatre in Bridgetown, Barbados.

752 "'Blacksnake' Tops Records." *Advocate-News,* p. 6, Mar. 22, 1973.

According to first week reports, *Blacksnake!* has outgrossed any picture to date shown in Barbados. Theatre owners say the film will run indefinitely depending on public interest.

753 Cassyd, Syd. "Russ Meyer Entry Set for December Release." *Box-office,* 101(18):W-1, Aug. 14, 1972.

A report on Meyer's $400,000 independently produced R-rated film *Blacksnake!* which recently finished filming in Barbados and is being edited for a Christmas release.

754 "Chicago." *Boxoffice,* 102(5): C-4-5, Nov. 13, 1972.

Queries of exhibitors anxious for a screening of *Blacksnake!* have deluged the office of Gilbreth Film Co. according to a firm representative. Special interest has been shown in the R-rated film because unlike Meyer's X-rated product it can be played in a full range of theatres.

755 Cuskelly, Richard. "Ancient Film Tradition: The Sneak Preview." *Los Angeles Herald-Examiner,* sec. B, p. 2, Apr. 16, 1973.

The occasion of a sneak preview of *Blacksnake!* affords Meyer the opportunity to discuss with Cuskelly the film and his return to independent production. The filmmaker also notes that since it is impossible for him to compete with financially successful hardcore films like *Deep Throat* he will now produce only R-rated movies.

756 "Four Premieres Set on USC Film Conference." *Los Angeles Times,* pt. II, p. 8, Mar. 31, 1973.

Blacksnake! premieres on the opening evening of the University of Southern California's Film Conference with Meyer as an invited guest at the screening.

757 Greene, Bob. "Russ Meyer Moves Beyond Sex—Now It's 'Race Relations'." *Chicago Sun-Times,* sec. 2, p. 59, Feb. 8, 1973.

Meyer's shift away from sexploitation into the genre of black exploitation films with the release of *Blacksnake!* is briefly discussed. (1 illus.)

758 "Morgan: Too Much Violence in Film." *Advocate-News,* p. 1, Mar. 15, 1973.

After viewing the morning sneak preview of *Blacksnake!,* Barbados' Minister of Tourism, Information and Public Relations, Peter Morgan, withdraws his patronage from the film on the grounds that the violence in *Blacksnake!* is "nauseating." At a press conference after the preview, Meyer defended the film's violence stating that it accurately portrays man's inhumanity to man and is com-

Sultry, but "skinny," British actress Anouska Hempel poses with a "blacksnake" from the 1973 box office loser of the same name. Afterwards, Meyer vowed in casting never to let acting ability take precedence over anatomical considerations, relying instead on his skill as an editor to compensate for any acting deficiencies.

mercially exploitable. The film was passed uncut by Barbados' Film Censors. (1 illus.)

759 Pennington, Ron. "'Blacksnake' Stirs Press in Barbados, Draws Public Favor." *Hollywood Reporter,* 225(50):7, Apr. 18, 1973.
Although Peter Morgan, the Minister of Tourism for Barbados, has with-

drawn his patronage from *Blacksnake!* due to its excessive violence, Meyer insists his parody on a slave rebellion has outgrossed any other film ever to play the island. Meyer also discusses the economic advantages of filming outside the States and voices his dismay over the reluctance of some Southern booking agents to contract the film due to its integration of blacks and whites. According to Meyer, the two-minute preview of *Viva Foxy!* tacked on to the end of *Blacksnake!* has resulted in three offers to completely finance the proposed $400,000 film to star wife Edy Williams.

760 "Sam Lord's Party for 'Black Snake' Team." *Advocate-News,* p. 6, Apr. 24, 1972.

Sam Lord's Castle, a popular Barbados vacation spot, is the scene of a cocktail party hosted by the hotel to introduce the cast and crew of *Blacksnake!* to representatives of the island's mass media.

REVIEWS

761 Anderson, George. "Russ Meyer's Sweet Suzy at Fulton Mini." *Pittsburgh Post-Gazette,* p. 20, July 7, 1973.

Sweet Suzy, one of the year's worst films, lacks everything ("wit, action, sex") an audience could want. All it does have is "gore by the bucket."

762 Bayley, Lawson. "Violence on the Cinema Screen Is Nothing New." *Advocate-News,* p. 4, Mar. 25, 1973.

While most Barbadians have criticized *Blacksnake!* as being too violent, Bayley asserts that the violence is historical and that the film has no responsibility to promote the scenic beauty of the island as some have maintained. The film can be criticized for using contemporary language in a historical period piece.

763 Best, Robert A.L. "'Blacksnake' Tells Us Nothing!" *Advocate-News,* p. 4, Mar. 16, 1973.

A disappointed Best dismisses *Blacksnake!* as "a study in sadism" and notes that the willingness of the Barbados minister of Tourism, Peter Morgan, to lend his patronage to the film betrays a national tendency to place "almost implicit faith . . . in 'people from away'." Mr. Morgan, citing the film's brutality, immediately withdrew his patronage after attending a special morning screening prior to its evening premiere.

764 Blackette, Harcourt, et al. "Blacksnake Tells Story About Our Past." *Advocate-News,* p. 4, Mar. 29, 1973.

In a rebuttal to Robert A.L. Best's article (see entry **763**), four Barbadians quote scripture to support their view that *Blacksnake!* is a "very good" movie. An editorial reply rebuking their foolishness notes that Meyer would be surprised to learn that his film belongs in the same category as *The Ten Commandments.*

765 Blank, Edward. "'Sweet Suzy' a Clinker." *Pittsburgh Press,* p. 8, July 7, 1973.

Blank labels *Sweet Suzy (Blacksnake!)* as Meyer's worst film, lacking in both humor and sensuality, and warns if others like it follow "King Leer" will lose his crown.

766 Bykofsky, Stuart D. "Is Meyer Mellowing in Tame Blacksnake?" *Philadelphia Daily News,* p. 38, Apr. 6, 1973.

In this "R-rated potboiler," Meyer seemingly forsakes sex and violence with the exception of a scene where a slave is crucified. The acting of Milton McCollin ("Joshua") and Bernard Boston (the homosexual captain of the guard) is praised.

767 Davis, M.S. "Blacksnake." *Audience,* 8(5):8, Nov. 1975.

The film is described as a "tenth-rate *Mandingo.*"

768 Disappointed. "Down with Blacksnake." *Advocate-News,* p. 4, Mar. 22, 1973.

The denunciation of *Blacksnake!* by Peter Morgan, Minister of Tourism, is strongly supported by "Disappointed" in a letter to the editor. The movie, which "must be nauseating to all but sick minds," is also criticized for being historically inaccurate.

769 Elliott, David. "'Blacksnake': Meyer's Best?" *Chicago Daily*

News (Red Streak Ed.), p. 33, Apr. 2, 1973.

Elliott characterizes Meyer's film as "muck," but notes *Blacksnake!* has a "hammy-hypnotic charm" that perhaps makes it his best effort to date. (1 illus.)

770 Howard, Alan R. "Sweet Suzy." *Hollywood Reporter,* 227(3):3-4, July 3, 1973.

The film might possibly be "acceptable camp" were its rampant sadism not so offensive to the audience. Howard notes that the film's low budget forced Meyer to replace his usual quick editing with "static long shots and close-ups."

771 Knoblauch, Mary. "'Blacksnake,' 'Vault'." *Chicago Today,* sec. Family Today, p. 47, Apr. 4, 1973.

The film is criticized for failing to amuse because it contains "too much torture and blood and far too little sex."

772 La Tour, Peaches. "What's Beyond the Valley of the Dolls." *Advocate-News,* p. 4, Mar. 26, 1973.

A sarcastic letter to the editor praises the subtle use of sex, violence, and symbolism in "Slacksnake."

773 Miller, Jeanne. "Obscenity Not of Sex But of Violence." *San Francisco Examiner,* p. 31, May 10, 1973.

A dreadful film which unashamedly panders "to the perverse persuasions of the sado-masochistic set." With *Blacksnake!,* Meyer proves himself "a total master of the obscenity of violence."

774 Milne, T. "Slaves." *Monthly Film Bulletin,* 45(530):54, Mar. 1978.

British critic Milne's retrospective review of *Slaves* (U.S. title *Blacksnake!*) notes that even though the film was made prior to *Mandingo* (1975) and *Roots* (1977) it still represents an effective "parody" of "slave trade" pictures. Milne concludes that although *Slaves* should have been more humorous, the racial violence in its final scenes "lends a genuinely subversive quality" to the production.

775 Murf. "Sweet Suzy." *Variety,* 271(9):18, July 11, 1973.

Sweet Suzy, also known as *Blacksnake!,* is dismissed as "a choppy period meller, low on sex and high on violence."

*776 Murray, Glyne. "'Blacksnake' Let Us Down." *Sunday-Advocate News,* p. 4, Mar. 18, 1973.

Blacksnake! not only fails as a "valid social commentary" on slavery, but despite solid acting by native Barbadians is "devoid of artistic merit." Meyer is also condemned for failing to make a serious attempt to portray "man's inhumanity to man," opting instead to exploit sexual sadomasochism and to cash in on the current wave of cheap "Black Movies." Recommended.

777 Proud Barbarian. "Historical Picture." *Advocate-News,* p. 4, Mar. 24, 1973.

"Proud Barbarian," in a letter to the *Advocate-News,* criticizes Peter Morgan, Minister of Tourism in Barbados, for his negative comments concerning the violence in *Blacksnake!* and states Meyer deserves "full praise" for accurately depicting the island's historical past.

778 Shear, David. "Russ Meyer's 'Blacksnake' Opens at the Goldman." *Philadelphia Evening Bulletin,* p. 26, Apr. 6, 1973.

Shear damns the film as a badly acted mess, "a farce with dramatic pretensions."

779 Sick Sadist. "Show for Sick Minds." *Advocate-News,* p. 4, Mar. 26, 1973.

"Sick Sadist" writes a thinly veiled letter of sarcasm to the editor of the *Advocate-News* applauding Meyer's controlled use of violence in producing "a film so rich in artistic merit and stimulating historical splendour...."

780 Stein, Jerry. "Films Starring Flesh." *Cincinnati Post & Times Star,* p. 10, Mar. 24, 1973.

Promoting *Blacksnake!* in Cincinnati, Meyer maintains that his main purpose as a filmmaker is to entertain the audience by spoofing sex and violence. (1 illus.)

781 Tuchman, Mitch. "Russ Meyer and the Body Politic." *Boston Phoenix,* sec. B, pp. 2, 4, 6, Nov. 27, 1973.

Calling *Sweet Suzy* (formerly titled *Blacksnake!*) "the most innovative, most impressive American political film in years," Tuchman discusses in detail the social significance of the film's ending which Meyer has since been compelled to radically alter at the insistence of local exhibitors and his own regional subdistributors who complained the finale was confusing to audiences. (1 illus.)

782 Ven. "Milton's Acting Was First Class." *Advocate-News,* p. 4, Mar. 26, 1973.

A letter to the editor praises the acting of Barbadian Milton McCollin as "Joshua" in *Blacksnake!*

783 Wasserman, John L. "Meyer's Latest: 'Blacksnake'—Whips N' Things." *San Francisco Chronicle,* p. 51, May 11, 1973.

In a blisteringly negative review, Wasserman notes that Meyer's "new gimmick" is to produce an R-rated film (his first) which contains no complete nudity or outsized bosoms. The absence of these Meyer hallmarks prompts Wasserman to liken the viewing of *Blacksnake!* to "watching a television show with the picture off."

784 White, Carol. "The Movies: Blacksnake." *Chicago Sun-Times,* sec. 2, p. 31, Apr. 2, 1973.

The film's "inattention to historical detail" astounds White more than its "abysmal performances" and "inept direction." White ironically notes that by distributing the violence in *Blacksnake!* equally among blacks and whites Meyer "appeals to racists of every creed and color." Rated ½ star out of 4.

785 Wilson, Barbara L. "Meyer Gets His Kicks from 'Blacksnake'." *Philadelphia Inquirer,* sec. B, p. 5, Apr. 5, 1973.

Wilson describes the film as a "tongue-in-cheek" put-on composed of three parts—historical melodrama, Barbados travelogue, and trailer for Meyer's next production, *Viva Foxy!* Meyer also touches on the hostility between himself and ex-employer 20th Century–Fox.

Supervixens (1975)

PRODUCTION NOTES

786 "Film Crew Here." *Palo Verde Valley Times,* p. 2, Mar. 28, 1974.

Meyer and crew are identified as being in Palo Verde Valley to film scenes for *Supervixens,* to "be released in October with either a "PG" or "R" rating." (1 illus.)

787 Hyduke, Jeanette. "R-Rated Movie Has Small Cast That Doubles as Crew." *Que Pasa?,* p. 5, Apr. 13–19, 1974.

Filming begins in Quartzsite, Arizona, on *Supervixens* which Meyer maintains will be R-rated due to its language. (1 illus.)

788 Nieland, Christine. "Russ Is Back in the Valley of the Vixens." *Chicago Daily News* (Red Streak Ed.), sec. Panorama, p. 4, Oct. 19–20, 1974.

During a stop in Chicago to shoot a G-rated trailer for *Supervixens,* Meyer discusses his firm resolve in the wake of box office disappointments *(The Seven Minutes, Blacksnake!)* and a failed project *(Foxy)* to return to the formula filmmaking that established him as "King of the Nudies." (2 illus.)

789 "Photo Preview & Interview: Russ Meyer's 'The Supervixens'." *Bright Lights,* 1(2):17–20, Spring 1975.

In a good interview with the British film magazine *Bright Lights,* Meyer describes the writing process which spawned *Supervixens* and credits the actors' contributions to the final screenplay. (5 illus.)

Supervixens (1975): The return to formula with big bosoms and square jaws: "Russ Meyer comes bolting out of the burning Sonora desert, with the vengeance of a mad Visigoth lusting to regain his throne." — Publicity.

790   "Pitts Stars in 'Vixens'." *Hollywood Reporter,* 235(39):24, Mar. 28, 1975.

Screen newcomer Charles Pitts has been set for the starring role in the RM Films Inc. release *Supervixens* to premiere April 2, 1975, in Dallas.

791   "Russ Meyer Tells Press He's Returning to 'What He Can Do Best'." *Boxoffice,* C-5, Dec. 16, 1974.
Excerpts from entry **788**.

PROMOTION

792   Anders, John. "A Frank Visit with Russ Meyer." *Dallas Morn-*

ing News, sec. C, p. 1, Apr. 13, 1975.

In a short career article written during the time Meyer was in Dallas for the premiere of *Supervixens,* Anders characterizes the filmmaker as "a sort of spaced out, corrupted Fellini." (1 illus.)

793   Batdorff, Emerson. "Father of the Nudies." *Cleveland Plain Dealer,* sec. A, p. 16, July 2, 1975.

Meyer, in Cleveland on a prepublicity campaign for *Supervixens,* expresses his opinion that screen nudity is more popular than ever.

794   Broeske, Pat H. "After Two Flops, the 'Nudie King' Is Back in the Ring." *Southeast Daily News,*

sec. Weekend Leisure Guide, pp. 1, 6, Sept. 20, 1974.

While still in the process of editing the film, Meyer vows *Supervixens* will mark his return to his past tried-and-true formula of lots of "big breasts and square-jawed men." Rebounding from years of professional and personal setbacks, Meyer is heartened that American International Pictures (AIP) head Sam Arkoff declared the work to be "the most erotic and sensual film he has ever seen" and has agreed to release it through AIP in December. (3 illus.)

795 Brooks, Elston. "'King of the Nudies' Making Another One." *Fort Worth Star-Telegram*, sec. B, p. 6, Apr. 3, 1975.

A straightforward career article written while Meyer and Shari Eubank were in Fort Worth doing pre-publicity for *Supervixens*. (1 illus.)

796 Dennis, John. "The Devil Returns." *Atlanta Gazette*, 1(23): 13, Feb. 5, 1975.

The "devil," Russ Meyer, is interviewed in Atlanta during post-production on *Supervixens*, his cinematic return to "big tits and square jaws."

797 Dietrich, Jean. "Russ Meyer Approaches Moviemaking as Mostly a Question of 'X-cellence'." *Louisville Courier-Journal*, sec. B, p. 4, June 11, 1975.

A short biographical article which appeared while Meyer was in Louisville to promote *Supervixens*. In addition to discussing public reaction to his films, Meyer mentioned that his maternal grandmother, Lydia Damrell, was born in the city. (1 illus.)

798 Fitzpatrick, Tom. "Porn King Grins as Dollars Roll In." *Chicago Sun-Times*, p. 79, Apr. 28, 1975.

In Chicago for the opening of *Supervixens*, Meyer reminisces about the women in his life and relates an amusing anecdote about Roger Ebert's first day on the job as scriptwriter for *Beyond the Valley of the Dolls*. (1 illus.)

799 Gray, Farnum. "Skin Flick King Recalls Career Low." *Atlanta Journal*, sec. F, p. 11, Jan. 12, 1975.

In Atlanta to promote *Supervixens*, Meyer expresses his bitter disappointment over the commercial failure of the 20th Century–Fox release *The Seven Minutes*. Other topics discussed are the influence of Horatio Alger's novels for boys on his life and films and a reflective Meyer's thoughts on the reasons for his three divorces.

800 Harb, Susan. "Mister X: He Put Porn in Mainstream." *Raleigh Times*, sec. ACT II, pp. 1, 3, 5, June 28, 1975.

Though Meyer considers *Last Tango in Paris* (1973) to be "the best X-rated movie ever made" and director Bernardo Bertolluci to be superior to him as a filmmaker, he ranks *Beyond the Valley of the Dolls* and *Supervixens* as the second and third best sex films ever produced. In Raleigh, North Carolina, to promote *Supervixens*, Meyer characterized his movies as "pure escapism," sexy spoofs he feels do not "turn anyone on sexually." (2 illus.)

801 Hartl, John. "Russ Meyer, the Immortal Mr. Tease." *Seattle Times*, sec. F, p. 7, June 30, 1975.

Pitching *Supervixens* in Seattle, a thoughtful Meyer touches on several aspects of his career including the refusal of 20th Century–Fox to reissue *Beyond the Valley of the Dolls* despite his guarantee of 2,000 playdates. The generally good reviews *Supervixens* has received combined with the lack of public outrage at the film also cause Meyer to wonder if "I'm not doing something wrong." (1 illus.)

802 Hogner, Steve. "Russ Meyer: The Amiable Bear of Erotic Cinema." *Austin American-Statesman*, p. 28, May 5, 1975.

Describing Meyer as "sensitive, articulate, (and) deeply fascinating," Hogner maintains that the filmmaker shatters the "dirty old man" image many would "expect the acknowledged 'king of the nudies'" to personify. In Austin to promote *Supervixens,* Meyer described his association with 20th Century–Fox and mentioned his recent eligibility for membership in the Academy of Motion Picture Arts and Sciences. (3 illus.)

803 Jones, Will. "After Last Night." *Minneapolis Tribune,* sec. B, pp. 1–2, May 29, 1975.

Meyer visits Minneapolis to push the May 30, 1975, city opening of *Supervixens* and discusses the film ("a parody of all my other parodies") with *Tribune* columnist Will Jones. As in past interviews, the director acknowledges the difficulties in finding the outrageously abundant women for his films and notes that two actresses from his stock company, Haji and Uschi Digard, serve as recruiters to approach showgirls backstage who are traditionally wary of men offering movie roles.

804 Lane, Marilyn. "'I Really Want to Turn the World On If I Can'." *Quad-City Times,* p. 8, May 2, 1975.

Shari ("SuperAngel") Eubank accompanies Meyer to the Quad-City area to promote *Supervixens* and in addition to complimenting the director on his professionalism also discusses her dramatic training while a graduate student at Illinois Wesleyan University. Meyer notes that his desire as a genre filmmaker is "to turn on the world if I can." (5 illus.)

805 "Los Angeles." *Boxoffice,* 107(7): W-4, May 26, 1975.

Meyer grants free admission to *Supervixens* to the first 450 blue-collar workers who present their union cards at the "Hard Hat" premiere of the film at the Holly Cinema in Hollywood.

806 Mahar, Ted. "Russ Meyer Goes Back to 'Formula'." *The Oregonian,* sec. A, p. 12, May 17, 1975.

Interviewed in Portland during a promotional tour for *Supervixens,* Meyer characterizes the film as a return to his tried and true formula of "big bosoms and square jaws." Earlier at a symposium at the University of Oregon, Meyer identified the primary reason for the strict code of moral conduct he enforces on the set is to ensure that he does not go over budget. Mahar assesses Meyer as "an important figure in American culture" whose films "were significant in broadening the standards of what a community would tolerate in its theaters." (1 illus.)

807 Marks, Arnold. "'Teas' Producer Turns to Sex Satire." *Oregon Journal,* p. 13, May 17, 1975.

In Portland to promote *Supervixens,* Meyer reminisced about the 1959 movie *The Immoral Mr. Teas* that established him as a name in the "jeopardy" movie field. Of historical interest is the brief mention of two industrial films Meyer made in Oregon in 1946; *Fresh and Good Looking* for Crown-Zellerbach, a logging and paper producer, and another for the Western Pine Association still shown in 1975 on Portland late-night television. (1 illus.)

808 "Milwaukee." *Boxoffice,* 107(6): NC-2, May 19, 1975.

Meyer and Shari Eubank tout *Supervixens* in Milwaukee where he tells the local press that the "ultimate test" of a film's worth is "the number of butts that cover the seats in a theatre."

809 Noth, Dominique Paul. "'King Leer' of '60s Returns to Sex Films." *Milwaukee Journal,* sec. Green Sheet, pp. 1–2, May 6, 1975.

Meyer, accompanied by Shari Eubank at a promotional stop in Milwaukee, tells Noth that he audience-tested *Supervixens* on five college campuses to gauge youthful reaction. After being called a male chauvinist by several coeds, Meyer inserted male nudity into the film. The life, career, and body image of the film's star, Shari Eubank, are also examined. (2 illus.)

810 Phelan, Charlotte. "Meyer Says Public Demands Films of His X-Rated 'Genre'." *Houston Post,* sec. B, p. 12, May 22, 1975.

Promoting *Supervixens* in Houston where it opens on May 23 at the Bellaire Theatre, Meyer notes that although he has created his own genre, the public will reject his films (as they did with *The Seven Minutes* and *Blacksnake!*) unless they feature his "kind of content." (1 illus.)

811 Porter, Bob. "Father Figure: That 'Supervixens' Man." *Dallas Times Herald,* sec. E, p. 6, Apr. 3, 1975.

In Dallas for the world premiere of *Supervixens,* Meyer credited his humor as responsible for the longevity of his career and current cult status. While Porter dislikes the violence in the film, he is impressed by the acting talent and physical appeal of Shari Eubank. (1 illus.)

812 Ritter, Jess. "Going Out." *Kansas City Star,* p. 19, May 1, 1975.

After taking a financial bath on two consecutive "message" pictures *(The Seven Minutes* and *Blacksnake!),* Meyer vows to produce only "Quality X" movies featuring what he does best—"big bosoms and square jaws." Meyer, accompanied by Shari Eubank, stopped briefly in Kansas City, Missouri, to promote the May 7 opening of *Supervixens* there.

813 "Russ Meyer Completes 'Super Vixens' Film." *Boxoffice,* 106(25): 7, Mar. 31, 1975.

Only recently completing *Supervixens,* Meyer outlines a four month promotional program that includes a first screening of the film at the Rotterdam Film Festival on February 28, press receptions in London and Munich, a six-university U.S. tour to test student reaction to the film, and an April 1 world premiere at the UA Cinema in Dallas.

814 "Russ Meyer, Shari Eubank Visit in Kansas City." *Boxoffice,* 107 (5):NC-6, May 12, 1975.

Meyer and Shari ("SuperAngel") Eubank promote *Supervixens* in Kansas City, Missouri where it opens on May 7, 1975.

815 "Seattle." *Boxoffice,* 107 (14):W-5, July 14, 1975.

Meyer visits Seattle for a round of pre-opening interviews to publicize *Supervixens* and to appear before the Seattle Film Society which was given a preview of the film.

816 Segers, Frank. "Russ Meyer on Screen Sex; Soft Is Beautiful, Hard Is FBI; Never Saw a Feminist Stunner." *Variety,* 279(10):6, 36, July 16, 1975.

Meyer, during a promotional trip to New York to publicize the August 8th opening of his $300,000 feature *Supervixens,* explains his reluctance to take the seemingly logical next step from softcore into hardcore pornography and also addresses feminist charges that his films sexually exploit women.

817 Stanley, John. "To Hell with Relevancy and Off with the Blouses..." *San Francisco Chronicle,* sec. Datebook, p. 21, Aug. 3, 1975.

In light of his two box office disappointments, *The Seven Minutes* and *Blacksnake!,* Meyer states that he has learned that audiences expect a certain type of film from him and he must deliver it to be successful. (3 illus.)

818 "Supervixens in Northwest." *Voice News,* 4(8):UNKNOWN, Aug. 1975.

Uschi Digard is briefly featured in a promotional item on *Supervixens* which also incorporates much of the film's press release provided by RM Films International. (3 illus.) See entries **819** and **829.**

819 "Supervixens in Northwest Now." *Voice News,* 4(7):14 ff., July 1975.

Biographical information is offered on Meyer in the *Voice News,* "the largest Northwest publication for singles of all ages," which also features several promotional photos from *Supervixens.* The article also contains a brief biography of Christy ("SuperLorna") Hartburg. (8 illus.) See entries **818** and **829.**

820 "'Supervixens' Star to Festival."

Meyer slates the hayloft scene in *Supervixens* featuring Uschi Digard and Charles Pitts.

Hollywood Reporter, 236(20):47, May 12, 1975.

Shari Eubank will act as Meyer's official representative at the Cannes Film Festival where *Supervixens* will be shown in out-of-competition screenings.

821   Winslow, Valerie. "What's a Nice Guy Like This. . .?" *Bellevue American,* sec. D, p. 4, July 3, 1975.

In a career piece written around the time of the release of *Supervixens,* Meyer expresses mock fear over the favorable reviews the film has been receiving and wonders aloud if he is not doing "something wrong." (1 illus.)

MISCELLANEOUS

822   Grant, Hank. "Rambling Reporter." *Hollywood Reporter,* 236(22):2, May 14, 1975.

Supervixens star Shari Eubank insists that her relationship with Meyer is "strictly professional."

823   Hunter, Frank. "That King Leer of Porn, Russ Meyer, Returning to the World of Sin & Skin." *St. Louis Globe Democrat,* sec. C, p. 9, June 21–22, 1975.

Meyer discusses his return to formula filmmaking with *Supervixens* and the code of moral conduct he expects his actors and actresses to adhere to during production. (1 illus.)

824   Lewis, Robert. "'The Walt Disney of Pornography': Russ Meyer, 'Super Vixens' at U of I." *Champaign-Urbana Courier,* p. 6, Mar. 9, 1975.

Supervixens receives its American public premiere at the University of Illinois where Meyer insists that sex and violence are movie staples. Meyer also discusses a proposed $2.2 million follow-up to *Beyond the Valley of the Dolls* entitled *Up the Valley of the Beyond* to be scripted by Roger Ebert and to star John Carradine and Ringo Starr.

825 Overbey, David. "Cannes Festival Moves to Curb Lang by Choosing French Films." *Hollywood Reporter,* 275(13):93, Jan. 18, 1983.

A brief news item on the multiple city screenings of *Supervixens* in France and the man, Jean-Pierre Jackson of Sinfonia Films, responsible for the director's cult status there which has prompted the Cinémathèque Française to honor Meyer with a full retrospective. Details are also given on the unique arrangement between Jackson and Meyer to distribute his films in France.

826 Preston, Marilyn. "Meyer: Up to His Old Chicks Again." *Chicago Tribune,* sec. 6, p. 16, Apr. 27, 1975.

The current financial success of Meyer's independently produced film *Supervixens* is contrasted with his past frustrations at 20th Century–Fox and the subsequent box office failure of his own independently produced film *Blacksnake!* (2 illus.)

827 "Russ Meyer's Way with Flesh Reappears in 'Supervixens'." *Boxoffice,* 107(5):C-8, May 12, 1975.

A rehash of entry **826.**

828 "'Supervixens' Takes Off in Key City Openings." *Boxoffice,* 107 (5):13, May 12, 1975.

The film does big box office in its openings in Kansas City, Chicago, and Dallas.

829 Tewkesbury, Don. "Photo Helps Singles Paper Sales Soar." *Seattle Post-Intelligencer,* sec. B, p. 4, July 13, 1975.

Sales of Seattle's *Voice News,* the Northwest's largest singles newspaper, skyrocket from a regular monthly circulation of 2,000 to a record high 12,000 when an uncensored photo of *Supervixens* poster girl Christy Hartburg appears on its cover. Though primarily an article on the newspaper's editor, it does feature a telling photo of the censored Seattle billboard for the film which graphically illustrates how various communities have chosen to alter Meyer's ads. (2 illus.) See entries **818–819.**

CENSORSHIP — CANADA

830 Base, Ron. "Meyer Mammary Films Smothered the World." *Toronto Sun,* p. 19, Jan. 14, 1976.

While in Toronto to cut scenes from *Supervixens* deemed objectionable by the Ontario Board of Censors, Meyer discusses among other topics his failed marriage to actress Edy Williams whom he describes as "a thoroughly unpleasant person" who despite early mutual feelings of love, ultimately married him to "further her own career." (2 illus.)

831 Goddard, Peter. "Porno King Russ Meyer a Winner." *Toronto Star,* sec. G, p. 24, Jan. 14, 1976.

Meyer is interviewed concerning various aspects of his career while in Toronto to make edits in *Supervixens* ordered by the Ontario Board of Censors prior to its approval for Canadian release. (1 illus.)

CENSORSHIP — GREAT BRITAIN

*832 Greenleaf, Richard, and Rayns, Tony. "Ferman's Pound of Flesh." *Time Out,* 359:10–11, 13, Feb. 4–10, 1977.

James Ferman, a leading member of the British Board of Film Censors, is lambasted for his censorship of cinematic sex and violence which Greenleaf contends reflects the critic's own arbitrary value judgments. Rayns agrees, arguing that the extensive cuts ordered in *Supervixens* boil down to a matter of taste— Ferman's versus Meyer's and his audience's. The deletion of the bathroom murder scene in *Supervixens* as well as the sexual elements in its climax, Rayns contends, makes the film meaningless by robbing it of its humor and suspense. Highly recommended. (5 illus.)

833 "Outrageous Exploits of an Incorrigible Chest Nut." *Manchester Guardian,* p. 7, Dec. 18, 1982.

In England for a retrospective of his work at the National Film Theatre, Meyer discusses the cuts British censors ordered in *Supervixens* and explains how censorship can be useful in promoting interest in a film. (1 illus.)

CENSORSHIP — INDIANA

834   Donovan, Joseph. "Meyer's Film Not Porno, But Satire." *Indiana Daily Student,* 112(157):4, Dec. 5, 1979.
A disappointed Indiana University graduate student complains via letter to the editor of the *Indiana Daily Student* about the Union Board's cancellation of *Supervixens,* arguing that Meyer is a critically acclaimed director who produces "trenchant satires of pornography." See entry **836.**

835   Geduld, Harry M. "Geduld: Fair Chance for Meyer." *Indiana Daily Student,* 112(159):4, Dec. 7, 1979.
Indiana University professor of Comparative Literature and Film Harry M. Geduld responds to the Union Board's cancellation of *Supervixens,* maintaining that while aesthetic and moral opinion over Meyer's work is sharply divided, the First Amendment guarantees adults the right to make up their own minds concerning such matters. See entry **836.**

836   Merenbloom, Bruce. "Films: Union Board's New Lineup Needs Approval, 'Emmanuelle' Included." *Indiana Daily Student,* 112(153):3, Nov. 29, 1979.
After strong opposition to its inclusion on a film schedule is voiced by Board members, *Supervixens* is dropped by the Indiana University Union Board. While *Supervixens* was termed "inhumane" and "an affront to every woman and sensitive man on this campus," *Emmanuelle* remains scheduled because it was judged "artistic, rather than exploitive."

CENSORSHIP — MARYLAND

837   "Roadside View of 'Supervixens' Brings Arrest." *Variety,* 280(9):8, Oct. 8, 1975.
The owner of Baltimore's Valley Drive-In is charged with a misdemeanor after a motorist complains that he saw parts of the X-rated film *Supervixens* while driving past the theatre. The county law passed in 1974 bans the exhibition of X-rated films at drive-ins where the screen can be seen by non-patrons. A similar law in Jacksonville, Florida, was struck down in June 1975 by the U.S. Supreme Court.

CENSORSHIP — NORTH CAROLINA

838   "Buxom Beauty in Bikini Banned from Billboards." *Boxoffice,* 107 (14):SE-1, July 14, 1975.
T. Carl Bogle, president of a Raleigh, North Carolina, sign company, orders eight *Supervixens* billboards featuring amply endowed Christy Hartburg pasted over because they were not in "good taste for outdoor advertising." Mr. Bogle insists that his company installed the billboards while he was out of town.

839   "Eye-Catcher." *Raleigh Times,* sec. A, p. 1, July 2, 1975.
A humorous photo catches a distracted Raleigh, North Carolina, worker pasting up the billboard advertisement for *Supervixens* which prominently features the deep cleavage of Christy Hartburg, one of the film's stars. (1 illus.)

840   "NC Feminist Duo Defaces 'Supervixens' Billboards." *Boxoffice,* 107(18):SE-3, Aug. 11, 1975.
Two unidentified females in Charlotte, North Carolina, react to the "sexist" depiction of women in the advertising for *Supervixens* by spray painting "This offends women" over four of the twenty billboards featuring the deep cleavage of Christy Hartburg. While the feminists explained the sign painting as a "political act," the local sign company owner characterized the actions as

Though she was featured in the oft-censored ads for *Supervixens,* ironically Christy Hartburg does not appear nude in the film.

vandalism and vowed the defaced signs would be replaced.

841 "Sexy Billboard Is Coverup Victim." *Raleigh Times,* sec. A, p. 1, July 3, 1975.

One day after the billboard advertisement for *Supervixens* featuring Christy Hartburg's portrait was put up, Carl Bogle, president of a North Carolina billboard agency ordered it covered up. Mr. Bogle based the action on his belief that the billboard "was not in good taste for outdoor advertising." Recommended as a "humorous" example of how advertising censorship can operate. (1 illus.)

CENSORSHIP — WASHINGTON

842 Watson, Emmett. "The Pulse-Intelligencer." *Seattle Post-Intelligencer,* sec. B, p. 1, July 11, 1975.

Watson has good news and bad news for Seattle area residents: the *Supervixens* billboard sports a "top heavy wench," but unfortunately city officials have convinced the sign company to add a large triangle to cover Christy Hartburg's "awesome décolletage." Ironically, the triangle has already had to be replaced several times.

REVIEWS

843 "Acting Out the Lust for a Throne." *Chicago Defender,* 70 (250):sec. Accent, p. 12, Apr. 26, 1975.

Supervixens is characterized as the "epitome of twenty years of guttearing filmmaking" by Meyer, the "rural Fellini." (1 illus.)

844 Anders, John. "'X' Marks the Spot for 'Supervixens'." *Dallas Morning News,* sec. A, p. 17, Apr. 2, 1975.

While expressing a grudging admiration for Meyer's ability to shock and stupefy an audience, Anders finds the stylized violence in *Supervixens* so startling that it justifies the film's X-rating. (1 illus.)

845 Andrews, Gage. "Supervixens: Violence Equals Sex?" *The Chicago Maroon,* p. 6, May 2, 1975.

Gage strongly criticizes the excessive violence in the film which he found totally overshadowed its sexuality. (1 illus.)

846 Andrews, Nigel. "Hungary Plain, Hollywood Coloured." *The Financial Times,* p. 3, Apr. 15, 1977.

In *Supervixens,* notes British critic Andrews, Meyer captures a "50's Hollywood innocence" which portrays erotica through innuendo and cleavage rather than through hardcore sexual depiction. The film's photography, editing, and dialogue combine to make *Supervixens* "a kind of runaway comic strip." (1 illus.)

847 Batdorff, Emerson. "'Supervixens' Is a Mad Sex Fantasy." *Cleveland Plain Dealer,* sec. B, p. 7, July 28, 1975.

The film's humor makes it "more than just another haunch-and-bosom show."

848 Borker, Pierre. "Supervixens." *Cinéma,* 288:83, Dec. 1982.

An aimless, negative review that points to the cartoon element in *Supervixens* and Meyer's other work. (1 illus.)

849 Brien, Alan. "Laughter in the Dark." *London Sunday Times,* p. 37, Apr. 3, 1977.

British critic Brien notes that the only difference between *Supervixens* and other film porn is in its open fear of women and its determination "to humiliate, and indeed, assassinate them in sickening detail." (1 illus.)

850 Charlton, A. Leigh. "Super Camp Meets Super Raunch in 'Super Vixens'." *UCLA Daily Bruin,* pp. 17–18, May 23, 1975.

The film's violence and weak script are criticized in a review that also features discussions with two of the film's stars, Uschi Digard and Charles Pitts, who present, respectively, positive and negative views of their work experience with Meyer. Digard defends the film's sex and violence as Meyer's personal fantasy while Pitts portrays Meyer as an insensitive director for whom he would not work again. (1 illus.)

851 Coursen, David. "'King of Nudies' Says: I Get Off on Violence." *Oregon Daily Emerald,* pp. 7–8, May 22, 1975.

Coursen, reporting for the student newspaper of the University of Oregon, portrays Meyer as a filmmaker who though insisting he is only interested in the commercial success and entertainment value of his product, still betrays obvious pride in his "auteur" status and the fact that four of his films are in the permanent collection of the Museum of Modern Art. *Supervixens* is also discussed with Coursen pointing out the film contains homages to both Alfred Hitchcock and Sam Fuller. (1 illus.)

852 Cuskelly, Richard. "Russ Meyer and His Supervixens." *Los Angeles Herald-Examiner,* sec. B, pp. 1–2, May 14, 1975.

Cuskelly discusses Meyer's association with 20th Century–Fox and reviews *Supervixens,* the filmmaker's financially successful return to his formula of "big-bosomed ladies and square-jawed guys." Calling Meyer "a near genius at providing multi-million dollar production values" on a low budget, Cuskelly cites the film as one of his "outrageous best." (1 illus.)

853 Delcourt, Guy. "Supervixens: l'érotisme fantastique de Russ Meyer en video." *Video-Actualité*, pp. 37–39, Sommaire 1983.

The French video release of *Supervixens* is heralded by Delcourt's glowing review of the film where "eroticism, violence, humor, and the fantastic (are all) blended into an extravagant plot." Meyer's technical maturity and use of "incisive montage" are also noted. (8 illus.)

854 Donnelly, Tom. "Making a Success of Violence." *Washington Post*, sec. C, pp. 1–2, June 28, 1975.

Reacting against Donnelly's criticism of the excess violence in *Supervixens,* Meyer explains his views on cinema violence and its popularity at the box office. (3 illus.)

855 Eder, Richard. "Of Walt Disney, Russ Meyer and King Lear." *New York Times*, sec. II, p. 13, Aug. 10, 1975.

Eder roundly criticizes 1975's crop of summer movies (including *Supervixens*) calling them "industrial films" produced "for the children industry, the horror industry, the sex industry. . . ." (1 illus.)

*856 Emerson, Ken. "Russ Meyer's Supervixens." *Boston Phoenix,* 4(31):sec. 2, p. 3, Aug. 5, 1975.

An offbeat review which interprets *Supervixens* as a film containing latent homo-erotic themes which was made "for men who hate women and love each other." Emerson's thesis is based upon the relationship between the characters "Clint" (an "archetypal gay porn figure"), his lover "SuperAngel," and sadistic cop "Harry Sledge" whose homosexual jealousy threatens to destroy them both. Recommended.

857 Flynn, Charles. "Outrageous Meyer Outdoes Himself." *Chicago Sun-Times,* p. 92. Apr. 30, 1975.

Flynn's rave review of *Supervixens* welcomes Meyer back into the sexploitation field after a three-film absence and calls him "the only genuine folk artist working in movies today." Rated three stars out of four.

858 Gardner, R.H. "'Supervixen' Carries Meyer Look to New Peaks of Nausea." *Baltimore Sun,* sec. B, p. 1, July 14, 1975.

Meant to be funny, the sex and violence in the film "defies laughter."

859 Garvin, Glenn. "Supervixens." *Delta Democrat-Times,* p. 31, Feb. 8, 1976.

Long-time fan Glenn Garvin notes that Meyer could probably be recognized as "one of the greats" if he chose to forsake sexploitation films for mainstream movies. *Supervixens* is rated 4 stars out of 5 ("Good") with only the infamous bathroom murder scene drawing negative criticism.

860 Goldstein, Al. "Star Drek." *Screw,* 341:23, Sept. 15, 1975.

Finding the simulated sexuality in *Supervixens* to be "quaintly obsolete," *Screw* editor Al Goldstein calls Meyer "a true craftsman" in terms of cinematic technique, but judges his "philosophical perceptions" to be "campy rather than valid" in the current adult film world of explicit sexuality. Goldstein is also "embarrassed" by the fact that the "gruesome" bathroom murder in *Supervixens,* "the most violent scene ever shot in film history," happened to appear in an X-rated movie. (1 illus.)

861 Hartl, John. "X-Rated Nostalgia and a Tired 'Lepke'." *Seattle Times,* sec. B. p. 1, July 3, 1975.

In light of the hardcore product now flooding the adult film market, Meyer's "slapstick" *Supervixens* strikes

Hartl as reminiscent of the more healthy and happy era of the 1960s skinflick.

862 Henderson, Mike. "Theater of Absurd." *Seattle Post-Intelligencer,* sec. B, p. 2, July 7, 1975.

In a review likening *Supervixens* to a "two-hour theater of the absurd," Henderson explores the motivation behind Meyer's depiction of violence in light of his professed admiration for its use in the films of Sam Peckinpah and Donald Siegel.

863 Hogner, Steve. "Meyer's 'Supervixens' Beyond Criticism." *Austin American-Statesman,* p. 16, May 12, 1975.

In a perceptive review of *Supervixens,* Meyer is characterized as being "beyond criticism" in the cinematic world of "comic eroticism" he has created. Hogner expresses regret, however, over what he perceives to be the waste of Meyer's gift for black humor and parody "in a minor genre on the absolute and almost forgettable periphery of film." The critic concludes by speculating that Meyer could perhaps be a "film giant" if he were to experiment in and "direct his energies to another area of film such as social farce sans sex." (1 illus.)

864 Jameson, R.T. "Supervixens." *Movietone News,* 42:34, 36, July 1975.

The film's "concentrated viciousness" upsets Jameson who quotes Meyer as saying "(I) . . . got some stuff out of my system" during its production.

*865 Kehr, Dave. "Meyer's Sex Cartoons." *Reader: Chicago's Free Weekly,* 4(31):11, May 9, 1975.

In an application of structural analysis to *Supervixens,* Kehr places Meyer squarely in the tradition of the Hollywood cartoon and compares him to other "American surrealists" like animators Chuck Jones and Tex Avery. Much like the Warner Bros. and MGM cartoons of the forties and fifties, Kehr points to Meyer's "genuine comic vision"

that "overrides the commonplaces of psychology and corporeality." Highly recommended. (1 illus.)

866 Kehr, Dave. "Russ Meyer: Back to Porn and Parody." *Reader: Chicago's Free Weekly,* 4(5):4, 12, Oct. 25, 1974.

Meyer discusses his upcoming film *Supervixens* and points to the importance of editing and parody to enliven the usually dull and static sex film genre. Kehr finds Meyer's films thematically reminiscent of Preston Sturges' "anthropological slapstick" and stylistically akin to Sergei Eisenstein. (3 illus.)

867 Kelly, Kevin. "Dark Horror in Bathtub: [Violence Hits New Low]." *Boston Globe,* p. 17, July 31, 1975.

A "boringly unfunny" attempt at satire that never recovers from the horror of the bathroom murder scene which Kelly calls "the most blatantly outrageous footage of sex and violence I've ever seen."

868 Klain, S. "Supervixens." *Independent Film Journal,* 76(7):6, Sept. 3, 1975.

Although technically "first-rate," the film's humor is undercut by its "gloating attention to sadistic violence."

*869 Knight, Arthur. "Russ Meyer's Supervixens." *Hollywood Reporter,* 236(27):4, 10, May 21, 1975.

Knight's fine review notes that while Meyer's camerawork and editing are excellent, the violence in *Supervixens* (exemplified by the bathtub murder scene) lacks the "sense of detachment" in Hitchcock's *Psycho* even though it "is every bit as expert in its suggestion of gory death." Although the film is Meyer's best since *Vixen,* Knight concludes that it ultimately "demeans its audiences by encouraging them to enjoy vicariously the violent and the vicious." Recommended.

870 Koch, John. "Sex, Violence Dominate 'Supervixens'." *Boston*

Herald American, p. 18, July 31, 1975.

Koch criticizes the film's heavy doses of "super-sex and super-violence" and accuses Meyer of not being a satirist of the "sado-skin genre," but rather a filmmaker who "revels and grovels in it."

871   Lenne, Gérard. "Supervixens." *Revue du Cinéma,* 377:46–48, Nov. 1982.

Prior to reviewing the film, Lenne announces that *Supervixens* will be broadcast in January 1983 on Antenne 2 (French television) preceded by a portrait of Meyer on "Cinema/Cinemas." Calling it the "most representative" of Meyer's films, Lenne compares it to an animated cartoon replete with the Meyeresque elements of "door-busting, bath-tub stomping, (and) apocalyptic electro-cution." He concludes that while Meyer is obsessed he is a perfectionist deserving of our respect. (2 illus.)

872   Lyons, Donald. "Screenscenes." *Andy Warhol's Interview,* 5(9): 40, Sept. 1975.

An accurate, and strongly positive review of *Supervixens* noting that the film combines elements of a Morality Play or Noh Theater with fast-paced self-parody. Lyons assesses Meyer as an original "working the midnight border between nightmare and orgasm." Note: the tabloid is incorrectly numbered as 6(9).

873   Martin, James. "Super Vixens." *Hustler,* 2(3):24, Sept. 1975.

A humorous, but unerotic parody of all of Meyer's previous films. Rated "one-quarter erect" on *Hustler*'s phallic rating guide. (2 illus.)

*874   McMahon, T.K. "Russ Meyer's Supervixens: Meyer Über Alles." *Take One,* 4(11):28–30, 1975.

In a totally unique interpretation of *Supervixens* and the *auteur's* other films, McMahon identifies "Meyer's creative vision" as consisting of two threads: "the comedic narrative with socio-political overtones" *(Vixen, Beyond the Valley of the Dolls, The Seven Minutes)* and the

"film-poem" in which narrative is seemingly replaced by the "free-form outflowing of images and ideas" *(Cherry, Harry & Raquel). Supervixens* represents the synthesis of these elements in a film McMahon forcefully argues is based upon the "Teutonic ideal" professed by National Socialism. Recommended. (2 illus.)

875   McQuay, David. "Supervixen—Satire, Sex, Seduction, Sadism." *The News American,* sec. D, pp. 6, 8, July 18, 1975.

McQuay criticizes the film as a "perverse macho/sexual cartoon" in which any "humor is devoured by . . . violence."

876   Munroe. "'Supervixens'." *Film Bulletin,* UNKNOWN, June 1975.

The film is typical of Meyer's fascination with sex and violence, but also atypical in that he consciously parodies his own style.

877   Niepold, Mary Martin. "Nausea, Not Laughter, Evoked by 'Super-vixens'." *Philadelphia Inquirer,* sec. C, p. 4, July 10, 1975.

According to Niepold, only an "unconfessed psychopath" could enjoy the nauseating scenes of sadistic sex and violence in *Supervixens*. Niepold mistakenly attributes the film to "Ron Avery" rather than to Meyer who is never mentioned.

878   Peary, Danny. "Supervixens." *Guide for the Film Fanatic,* p. 516. New York: Simon & Schuster, 1986.

Supervixens is included in the "Additional 'Must See' Films" section at the end of Peary's 1986 tome.

879   Philbert, Bertrand. "Supervixens." *Cinématographe,* 84:52, Dec. 1982.

Like his American counterpart John Waters, Meyer's films "jubilantly attack the codes of deepest America." In this short review, saying little, Philbert does acknowledge Meyer's technical proficiency.

880 Phillips, Lou. "Russ Meyer's 'Supervixen'." *Dallas Post Tribune,*
28(14):19, Apr. 5, 1975.
A review in the black weekly
newspaper *The Post Tribune* ("serving
24,000 Customers in the Dallas–Fort
Worth Metroplex") cites *Supervixens* "as
an exotic escape" featuring Meyer's
"Bosom Brigade." Phillips also reports
that Meyer was approached by a black en-
trepreneur who suggested he shoot a
"Black Vixen" based on his 1968 hit
Vixen.

881 Rayns, Tony. "Supervixens."
Monthly Film Bulletin, 44(520):
108, May 1977.
British critic Rayns comments on
the stylistic effects Meyer's brief association with 20th Century–Fox has had on
Supervixens. According to Rayns, Fox
". . . helped to focus his gift for caricature
in the direction of satire" as well as "gave
him the opportunity to develop his
idiosyncratic editing style." Interestingly, the British censor removed the infamous bathroom stomping and elec-
trocution scene as well as the escalation of
violence leading up to it.

882 Rimmer, Robert. "Supervixens."
The X-Rated Videotape Guide,
pp. 139–140. New York: Arlington House, 1984.
Supervixens will never appear uncut on cable or subscription television
because of its unsettling combination of
sex and violence which leaves the viewer
undecided as to "whether to scream or
chuckle."

883 Rotsler, William. "Supervixens."
Cinema X Monthly, 6(10):22,
Feb. 1976.
Rostler's scathing review berates
Meyer for his lack of artistic discipline
and seeming unwillingness to take cine-
matic chances.

884 Sachs, L. "Super Vixens." *Variety,* 279:20, Mar. 12, 1975.
A dull, overly long and violent
skin film with pretensions to be more
than a skin film.

*885 Sarris, Andrew. "Reflections on
the New Porn." *Village Voice,*
20(35):71–72, Sept. 1, 1975.
In a fine article on the uneasy
relationship between humor and sex in
contemporary porn films, self-professed
"licensed lecher before the silver screen"
Andrew Sarris criticizes *Supervixens* for
its pretentiously mindless allegorical con-
tinuities and its poor acting (except for
Charles Napier's "interestingly malig-
nant performance" which Sarris incorrectly identifies as Charles Pitts). For Sarris, Meyer who "seems to be auditioning
for the role of the Frank Tashlin of the
70's," unfortunately "represents another
talent lost to pop attitudinizing." Recommended. (1 illus.)

886 Saunders, Dudley. "Warning:
'Supervixens' Is a Grisly Turn-
Off, Instead of a Turn-On."
Louisville Times, sec. C, p. 13,
June 12, 1975.
Patrons interested in sex films are
advised to either wait awhile for a less
violent film or to visit a local porno
theatre. Meyer is severely criticized for
the film's graphic violence and is characterized as a filmmaker linking sex with
violence to appeal to a new audience
bored with conventional screen sexuality.

887 Schubert, Sunny. "Sex in My
Films Just for Laughs, Says Russ
Meyer." *Bloomington Herald
Telephone & Bedford Daily
Times-Mail,* sec. 1, p. 1, June 29,
1975.
In Bloomington, Indiana, to do
pre-promotion for *Supervixens,* Meyer
comments on the portrayal of sex in his
films, likening it to a parody of a "pornographic decathlon." (1 illus.)

888 Siclier, Jacques. "Supervixens."
Le Monde, p. 26, Nov. 26, 1982.
Thanks largely to the efforts of
French film distributor and Meyer biog-
rapher Jean-Pierre Jackson, a renewed in-
terest in Meyer is occurring in France.
Siclier sees Meyer's originality stemming
from the humor he has "inherited

from the comic strips"—a humor which takes the form in *Supervixens* of a series of "eroto-surrealist gags" which effectively parody many "Hollywood genres."

889 Simon, John. "Nashville Without Tears." *New York,* 8(32):66–67, Aug. 11, 1975.

Simon's condemnation of *Supervixens* goes well beyond film criticism to the level of a personal attack on Meyer whom he describes as an "abject no-talent" filmmaker who is "arrested technically somewhere between home movies and television commercials." Film critics like Richard Schickel and Raymond Durgnat are also blasted for writing serious analyses of this "Neanderthal hack." (1 illus.)

890 Siskel, Gene. "'Supervixens' Isn't; the Porn's Forlorn...." *Chicago Tribune,* sec. 3, p. 3, May 2, 1975.

Siskel observes that Meyer's occasionally enjoyable sense of humor is replaced in the film by an unsettling "violence and ridicule directed toward women...." Rated one star out of four.

891 Smith, Kent. "Supervixens." *Adam Film World Guide,* 2(10): 145, Mar. 1986.

A rave review citing the cartoon-like intensity of the film's manic plot and characterizations. Smith: "the classic example of Russ Meyer's rather exotic erotic style." Rated 4 stars out of 5, *Adam Film World Guide* considers *Supervixens* to be an adult classic. (1 illus.)

892 Smith, Monty. "Supervixens." *New Musical Express,* UN-KNOWN, Apr. 16, 1977.

Reviewing a heavily censored print of *Supervixens,* British critic Smith still finds the film's cartoon humor to be irresistible. The work of Meyer ("an astute film-maker") is likened to that of "a particularly deranged Mel Brooks." (2 illus.)

893 Stark, Susan. "Meyer's Porn Is Obsolete." *Detroit Free Press,* sec. C, p. 5, June 18, 1975.

Stark maintains that the more slickly produced hardcore pornographic films now in wide distribution have made "King Leer's" softcore product obsolete and Meyer himself "the epitome of obsolete royalty." *Supervixens* is dismissed as "flat-out boring." (1 illus.)

894 Stewart, Perry. "Meyer Fame of 2 Worlds." *Fort Worth Star-Telegram,* sec. C, p. 10, Apr. 3, 1975.

In Fort Worth for the local premiere of *Supervixens,* a still grateful Meyer recalls a late 1940s incident when he, an unknown industrial filmmaker, was mistaken for Russ Meyer, a popular pitcher for the Philadelphia Phillies and Chicago Cubs, by an adoring female baseball fan. The film is mildly criticized.

895 "Supervixens." *Playboy,* 22(11): 36, Nov. 1975.

Viewers not familiar with Meyer's legendary sense of overstated sex and violence may be shocked, but longtime fans will recognize the film as an "outright spoof" of the genre.

896 "Supervixens." *Boxoffice,* UN-KNOWN, May 12, 1975.

Actor Charles Napier is praised, but the film is condemned for its sex and violence.

897 Tesson, Charles. "Supervixens." *Cahiers du Cinéma,* 342:58, Dec. 1982.

Tesson notes that the construction of the film serves as a pretext for a series of boring sketches that lack rhythm and add to the film's general disequilibrium. (1 illus.)

*898 Thomas, Kevin. "Violence Bared in 'Supervixens.' *Los Angeles Times,* pt. IV, p. 14, May 14, 1975.

The "direct connection between sex and violence" made by Meyer in the "dazzlingly staged" bathtub stomping scene in *Supervixens* marks the filmmaker's most serious attempt yet to explore "the dark underside of his erotic myths." Recommended.

899 Wasserman, John L. "'Super Vixens' on the Couch." *San Francisco
Chronicle,* p. 40, July 28, 1975.
The only person qualified to
discuss the "terminal case of misogyny
(and) gynephobia" in *Supervixens* is a
"psychiatrist."

900 Wolf, William. "Supervixens."
Cue, 44(29):21, Aug. 11–17, 1975.
Wolf's totally negative review
identifies Meyer's audience as "super-
morons" who seemingly enjoy low humor
and sadistic violence.

Up! (1976)

PROMOTION

901 Baum, Robert. "When Russ
Meyer Brought His Raven to
Lunch." *Patriot Ledger,* sec. Limelight, p. 14, Oct. 30, 1976.
Raven De La Croix talks about her
literary aspirations and Meyer surveys
censorship standards in various countries
at a promotional luncheon in Boston to
publicize *Up!* (1 illus.)

902 Berger, Rick H. "Laugh at the
Establishment: Meyer's Sexploitation Films Soft-Core." *Daily
Trojan,* pp. 5, 7, Jan. 8, 1976.
Meyer promises the readership of
the University of Southern California's
student newspaper that his film currently
in the editing process, *Up!,* will contain
extensive male nudity designed to cater
to females in the audience. Other topics
discussed include Canadian film censorship, feminist attacks on his work, and
the myriad difficulties encountered in
casting the female roles in his films. (2
illus.)

903 Boyd, Richard. "First Fling: She
Knew the Score Before Shooting
Started." *The States-Item,* sec. B,
p. 3, Oct. 20, 1976.
Raven De La Croix is featured in
a biographical piece written while she
and Meyer were in New Orleans to promote the October 29 opening of *Up!* (1
illus.)

904 Brown, Barbara. "Slick Flicks Play
Sex for Grins." *Here's Boston,*
UNKNOWN, Oct. 29, 1976.
At a promotional luncheon in
Boston for *Up!,* Meyer categorically states
that a viewer with "any real hangups" can
not watch his films. Reviewer Brown,
who walked out on the picture, tends to
agree. (2 illus.)

905 Bryan, Howard. "Off the Beaten
Path." *Albuquerque Tribune,*
sec. A, pp. 1, 10, Feb. 3, 1977.
The filmmaker is interviewed in
Albuquerque during a promotional stop
for *Up!* by columnist Bryan who admits
to knowing nothing more about Meyer
than details provided by a three-page
mimeographed biography.

906 "Cleveland." *Boxoffice,* 108(17):
ME-2, Feb. 2, 1976.
Meyer promotes *Up!* in Cleveland
where he tells reporters that three months
of editing should ready the film for
exhibition.

907 Furcolow, John. "Blue Movies
Defended: X-Rated Actress, Producer 'Believes' in Her Business."
Lexington Herald-Leader, sec. D,
p. 14, Nov. 21, 1976.
In Lexington with Meyer to promote *Up!,* Uschi Digard, frequent Meyer
star and the film's producer, explains
what it is like to work with the "perfectionist" filmmaker. (1 illus.)

908 Gerber, Eric. "King Leer, Bad
Taste Don't Want Respectabil-
ity." *Houston Post,* sec. C, p. 12,
Oct. 8, 1976.
Accompanied by actress Raven
De La Croix during a promotional stop in
Houston to plug *Up!,* Meyer describes
her discovery and refutes charges con-
cerning his exploitation of women. De La
Croix comments on the physical chal-
lenges posed by performing outdoor
nude scenes. (2 illus.)

909 Hale, David. "'A Dirty Old Man':
Russ Meyer Goes Beyond Valley
of Skin-Flicks." *Fresno Bee,* sec.
C, pp. 1, 3, Mar. 18, 1977.

During a promotional tour of Fresno, California, to publicize *Up!*, Meyer (accompanied by the film's star Francesca "Kitten" Natividad), discusses the evolution of the "Russ Meyer genre." (1 illus.)

910　Hartl, John. "'King Leer' Back with a Downer Called 'Up!'" *Seattle Times,* sec. C, p. 1, Jan. 23, 1977.

Hartl interviews Meyer during the director's swing through Seattle to tout *Up!* and inquires about a project, *Up the Valley of the Beyond,* Meyer had mentioned in a years-earlier discussion with him. The film, coscripted by Roger Ebert, was never made because a nervous American-International Pictures refused to finance the effort for fear that Meyer's name would guarantee the production an X-rating. (1 illus.)

911　Henderson, Mike. "A Conversation with the King of Soft-Core." *Seattle Post-Intelligencer,* sec. "206," p. 23, Jan. 21, 1977.

The filmmaker answers questions concerning the audience for his films, his refusal to do hardcore, and aspects of his personal life while in Seattle to promote *Up!* (1 illus.)

912　Kaminsky, Ralph. "Russ Meyer's 'Up!' Has Appeal as Erotic Film for Women, Too." *Boxoffice,* 110(1):15, Oct. 11, 1976.

Prior to hitting the road with Raven De La Croix for a three-month, thirty-five-city publicity tour to support *Up!*, Meyer notes that the film's inclusion of tastefully photographed, "fleeting glimpses of . . . well-endowed men" marks his first attempt to play more directly to the women in the audience.

913　Marks, Arnold. "Producer Sees Movie Change." *Oregon Journal,* p. 14, Dec. 18, 1976.

Meyer states audiences are bored with morbid sex, crime, and violence in films and are now more interested in "comedy and hokum." Describing *Up!* as "my first intentional farce," Meyer notes

the film is currently playing in "main stream" theatres in 25 U.S. cities. Meyer also relates a wartime story that served as the basis for "Mick" Nathanson's bestselling novel, *The Dirty Dozen.* (1 illus.)

914　McCabe, Bruce. "Russ Meyer's Comedy Quest." *Boston Globe,* p. 13, Oct. 30, 1976.

In Boston with actress Raven De La Croix to promote *Up!*, Meyer describes the film as his "first intentional comedy."

915　"Meyer Fakes Quote." *Variety,* 285:56, Jan. 12, 1977.

Controversy is caused by Meyer's inclusion of a faked quote attributed to Nazi war criminal Martin Bormann in the newspaper advertising for his current release *Up!* Though pulled from the *New York Times* after a one-day run, the ad continued to run in the *New York Daily News* and *New York Post.*

916　Millar, Jeff. "Meyer Pokes Outrageous Fun at Sex." *Houston Chronicle,* sec. 2, p. 7, Oct. 6, 1976.

Meyer attributes his longstanding commercial success in softcore sex films to his cinematic style of "playing sex for laughs." (1 illus.)

917　Mittlestadt, Chuck. "Russ Meyer: Still King Leer." *Albuquerque Journal,* sec. D, p. 4, Feb. 6, 1977.

Promoting *Up!* in Albuquerque, Meyer presents his thoughts on film censorship and the competition his simulated sex farces face from the increased nudity in major studio-produced films. The filmmaker also mentions his plan to anonymously make a PG-rated movie shot in Georgia that will only be exhibited in mid–America for rural audiences. Meyer promises, "The sex will be all Disney-like." (1 illus.)

918　"Russ Meyer Likes 'Warm Weather' for Winter Exhib'n." *Daily Variety,* 174(40):14, Jan. 28, 1977.

The freedom of being an inde-

pendent producer/distributor, according to Meyer in a statement made by him while in Seattle for the opening of *Up!*, is the power to pull a film if business is poor and to reinstate it when times improve. Meyer's release strategy of playing *Up!* only in "warm weather" sites has paid off with the film already recouping its production and distribution costs.

919   "Russ Meyer Visits Kaycee to Beat Drums for 'Up!'" *Boxoffice*, UN-KNOWN, Jan. 3, 1977.

While in Kansas City, Missouri, to promote *Up!*, Meyer appears on a local radio call-in talk show, and responds to questions ranging from why he will not give up "manufacturing filth" to if his films have any therapeutic value in regenerating the libido of elderly men. *Up!* opened in the Kansas City area on December 22, 1976.

*920   Safran, Don. "Meyer, Following Sexy Film Trail, Sacrifices Marriage for His Fans." *Dallas Times Herald*, sec. I, p. 1, Oct. 10, 1976.

With Raven De La Croix in Dallas to publicize *Up!*, Meyer discusses his failed marriage to actress Edy Williams. In an equation comparing the influence of Meyer on filmmaking with that of Elvis Presley on pop music, Safran concludes that both men served as "a kind of catalytic liberating force" for their respective mediums. Meyer also traces the secret of his cinematic success to his ability to "strike deeply at the core of sensuality in the common man." Recommended. (1 illus.)

921   Seeley, Richard. "Russ Meyer Enjoys His Work." *Detroit Register*, sec. D, p. 16, Nov. 28, 1979.

A typical biographical piece written during the time Meyer was in Detroit promoting *Up!*

922   Stanley, John. "'Blazing Bosoms' and the King of Sexploitation." *San Francisco Chronicle*, p. 45, Mar. 17, 1977.

Meyer and Uschi Digard, the film's producer, discuss *Up!* while in San Francisco to promote the film. Asked if the work represents his ultimate classic, Meyer quickly responds that the "ultimate Meyer film has already been made," *Beyond the Valley of the Dolls,* and that he would never again be able to approach that cult masterpiece. (1 illus.)

923   Thomas, J.N. "Sex Film Maker: 'I'll Admit to Anything'." *Berkeley Barb*, 605:7, Mar. 18–24, 1977.

In San Francisco promoting *Up!* with the film's star "Kitten" Natividad, Meyer describes the basis of his brief friendship with the late actor James Dean and tells Thomas that he will "admit to anything" in order to convert controversy into publicity for his films. (1 illus.)

924   Tubert, Jack. "Producer Russ Meyer Comes to Town Promoting His New Film 'Up'." *Worcester Sunday Telegram*, sec. A, p. 20, Oct. 31, 1976.

Meyer and Raven De La Croix promote *Up!* in Worcester, Massachusetts. (2 illus.)

925   Turan, Kenneth. "Russ Meyer, Almost an American Institution." *Washington Post*, sec. B, p. 1, Nov. 9, 1976.

Turan characterizes Meyer, the "58-million dollar man," as a survivor who after the personal trials involved in a lengthy film career has finally gained the financial rewards, peace of mind, recognition, and status accorded to "an American institution." Accompanied by Uschi Digard on a promotional tour of

---

Opposite, left: Up! (1976): Testing the limits of softcore . . . sex, violence, Nazis, and "Kitten" Natividad as a Greek Chorus of one intoning Roger Ebert's purple prose! *Right:* The campaign manual for *Up!* came complete with various "pasties," a smokey's hat to cover the film's phallic logo and a fishnet bra to obscure Raven De La Croix's "busty signature," in the event local media might balk at running uncensored ads.

Washington, D.C., to tout *Up!*, Meyer reflects on his remarkable staying power in a filmmaking genre rapidly shifting towards hardcore sexual explicitness. (2 illus.)

926   "'Up!' Premieres Friday." *Chicago Daily Defender*, p. 21, Nov. 4, 1986.

While ostensibly an announcement of the Chicago premiere of *Up!* at the Loop Theatre on November 5, 1976, the article features a biographical sketch of Raven De La Croix, the film's star. (1 illus.)

927   Verrill, Addison. "Preposterous Sex Dimensions, and Russ Meyer's Hang-Ups." *Variety*, 285:27, Nov. 10, 1976.

With *Up!*, Meyer experiments for the first time with showing male frontal nudity which he feels will expand his audience to include women. In New York City for the opening of *Up!*, Meyer also discusses the distribution network and advertising procedures he employs for his independent features. Other topics include Meyer's reported efforts to convince 20th Century–Fox to permit him to recut *Beyond the Valley of the Dolls* from an "X" to an "R" rating for re-release and the studio's purported lack of interest in a sequel to the film entitled *Beyond the Valley of the Beyond*, coscripted by Roger Ebert.

928   Weimers, Leigh. "Meyer's Living His Fantasy as King of Porn Producers." *San Jose Mercury-News*, sec. L, p. 1, Mar. 10, 1977.

Meyer identifies pro football as the only real competition against his films during a promotional stop in San Jose for *Up!* (1 illus.)

929   White, Maggi. "The 'Dirty Old Man' Swings Through." *Downtowner*, p. 22, Dec. 27, 1976.

Meyer tells White that critics now have less influence on his audience than in the past due to the shortage of slickly made, interesting films available to theatres. In Portland promoting *Up!*, he

also maintains that the ultimate critical yardstick is the number of people in the audience. (1 illus.)

930   White, Mel. "Russ Meyer's New Film Staid Fare: **, ***." *Arkansas Democrat*, sec. A, p. 9, Oct. 14, 1976.

An embarrassed White humorously comments on his meeting with Meyer and Raven De La Croix while the duo were in Little Rock promoting *Up!* (1 illus.)

*931   White, Tricia. "Russ Meyer Is Porno's DeMille." *Las Vegas Sun*, p. 13, Mar. 23, 1977.

Reflecting on today's "permissive society," Meyer predicts serious censorship problems ahead for hardcore, but not softcore pornography. In Las Vegas for the local premiere of *Up!*, he also defines the two types of pornography and credits *Playboy* publisher Hugh Hefner with being the catalyst behind the increasing permissiveness in U.S. society. Recommended. (1 illus.)

MISCELLANEOUS

932   Anders, John. "Of Respectability." *Dallas Morning News*, sec. A, p. 12, Oct. 10, 1976.

Anders maintains that regardless of what one thinks of Meyer's films, the filmmaker has become part of the Establishment, "a permanent fixture in our collective movie consciousness...." *Up!* and the film's star, Raven De La Croix, are also discussed.

933   Grant, Hank. "Rambling Reporter." *Hollywood Reporter*, 237(29):2, Aug. 5, 1975.

Meyer's exhaustive search for an "outrageously abundant" actress to star in *Up!* has to date been unsuccessful.

934   Worsham, Doris G. "X-Rated Russ Meyer's Latest Up for Discussion." *Oakland Tribune*, p. 11, Mar. 12, 1977.

Reacting to criticism over the violence in his films, Meyer states that he finds it "entertaining, providing it is cardboard." *Up!* is briefly mentioned. (1 illus.)

REVIEWS

935 Bartholomew, D. "Up!" *Film Bulletin*, 45(11/12):44, Nov./ Dec. 1976.
A dull "quagmire" of sex and violence that should do well among action fans and male voyeurs in urban theatre and drive-in settings.

936 Brenner, Wolfgang. "Herbst für Hitler." *Tip: Berlin Magazin*, 15(16):40–41, Juli 24-Aug. 6, 1986.
Drunter, drüber und drauf (Up!) is discussed as Meyer's attempt to confront the competition of hardcore while still remaining true to his roots of softcore sexploitation. Brenner writes that Meyer, "the Great Primitive," is still a joy to watch even if he is a bit old-fashioned and with *Up!* he has created a "furious ballet of sex and magnitude." (3 illus.)

937 Churchod, Olivier. "Megavixens et l'art d'aimer: rut et bromure." *Positif*, 276:58–59, Feb. 1984.
Megavixens (Up!) and Walerian Borowczyk's *L'Art d'aimer* are compared, contrasted, then mercilessly ridiculed by Churchod for being respectively, "too full" and "too empty." Noting that it is now "toney" to wax poetic over each new film by the American *"auteur,"* he terms Meyer's directorial style to be that of a "truckdriver" and his cinematic eroticism to be "to love what hardtack is to the new cuisine." Churchod does, grudgingly, appreciate the force of Meyer's direction and his use of parody, but can not bring himself to like his films. (2 illus.)

938 Cosford, Bill. "Meyer's 'Up' — Excess, Comedy." *Miami Herald*, sec. D, p. 6, Nov. 23, 1976.
Up! is panned as the latest in Meyer's catalog of "cinematic excess." (1 illus.)

939 Cowan, Ari. "On Cantilevered Ladies and Square-Jawed Men."
Daily Journal-American, p. 8, Jan. 28, 1977.
Up! is characterized as "a fantasy of adolescent scope" which is "not too bad technically."

940 El Guedj, Frédéric. "Megavixens." *Cinématographe*, 96:54–55, Jan. 1984.
El Guedj divides American films into two camps represented by the "pre-adolescence" of George *(Star Wars)* Lucas and the "maturity" of Meyer. While ostensibly a review of *Megavixens (Up!)*, El Guedj is seemingly more interested in comparing Meyer to other American filmmakers like Martin Scorsese. (1 illus.)

941 Furcolow, John. "'Up' Just Another Runaround Film." *Lexington Herald-Leader*, sec. B, p. 11, Nov. 19, 1976.
Furcolow depicts Meyer as an undeniably talented filmmaker with a unique style, but criticizes *Up!* as well as his other films as displaying "a one-track mind." (1 illus.)

942 Garrett, Robert. "'Up' Is Straight Up in Violence, Sex." *Boston Herald-American*, p. 25, Oct. 28, 1976.
An essentially non-critical review that deems *Up!* as purposely inane, or as Meyer describes the film, as "arrested adolescence."

943 Henderson, Mike. "Meyer's Soft-Core 'Up' Is a Downer." *Seattle Post-Intelligencer*, sec. A, p. 8, Jan. 22, 1977.
Up! is described by Henderson as a "professional-looking home movie" that just happens to contain nudity. The reviewer also warns Meyer that since he is no longer the sole producer of softcore pornography he needs to improve his product in order to avoid being caught by the competition.

944 Koshner, Karen. "Something for the Ladies." *Chicago Sun-Times*, p. 103, Nov. 18, 1976.
Up! is reviewed as a "sort of funny film" that marks Meyer's first time use of

male actors as artificially over-endowed as his actresses. Koshner rates the film two stars out of a possible four.

945 Lewis, Bill. "King of Soft-Core Pornography Is Back with Latest Work of Art." *Arkansas Gazette,* sec. E, p. 9, Oct. 17, 1976.
    A non-critical review of *Up!* The "work of art" alluded to in the article's title refers to the film's star, Raven De La Croix, who accompanied Meyer to Little Rock to help promote the film. (1 illus.)

946 Lusting, John. "You Guessed It—It's a Russ Meyer Film." *University of Washington Daily,* 51:15, Jan. 20, 1977.
    Up!, while not as violent as *Supervixens,* is enjoyable providing the viewer has "a strong stomach and a very strange sense of humor." (1 illus.)

947 Mahar, Ted. "Up the Valley with Russ Meyer." *The Oregonian,* sec. C, p. 9, Feb. 2, 1977.
    Up! is described as faithfully following Meyer's successful formula of big bosoms and square jaws. Though "overplotted," Meyer's rapid fire editing moves the film briskly along, leading Mahar to comment: "If anyone else had made it, it would have been five hours long with two intermissions." (1 illus.)

948 McGillivray, David. "Up!" *Monthly Film Bulletin,* 48(568): 98, May 1981.
    While *Up!* follows the standard Meyer formula of big breasts and square jaws combined with "Tom and Jerry–style violence," McGillivray maintains Meyer's exceptional technical expertise prevents this formula from failing. The British critic concludes that *Up!* is an "indisputably superior . . . contribution to the genre" Meyer invented.

949 Mittlestadt, Chuck. "'Up!': Meyer's Best Movie Yet." *Albuquerque Journal,* sec. D, p. 4, Feb. 6, 1977.
    Pronouncing *Up!* to be a classic in the softcore field, Mittlestadt calls it Meyer's "happiest, campiest, brightest film." Raven De La Croix receives high marks for her beauty and comedic flair.

950 Ostria, V. "Megavixens." *Cahiers du Cinéma,* 356:64–65, Feb. 1984.
    While Meyer is not to be disregarded as a director, *Up!,* a "droll sketch based on sex and violence," fails to satisfy because it does not sustain its lunacy.

951 Peary, Danny. "Up!" *Guide for the Film Fanatic,* p. 453. New York: Simon & Schuster, 1986.
    The film is totally devoid of Meyer's usual humor and contains sex scenes "more graphic and repulsive" than usually found in his work.

952 Pennington, Ron. "Russ Meyer's Up!" *Hollywood Reporter,* UNKNOWN, Feb. 1, 1977.
    Overly violent and too thinly plotted to avoid tedium, Meyer's photography and editing are, however, termed "excellent."

953 Perchaluk, E. "Up!" *Independent Film Journal,* 78:9, Nov. 26, 1976.
    A highly graphic softcore movie which once again proves that Meyer is tops at spoofing "skin films."

954 Rimmer, Robert. "Up." *The X-Rated Videotape Guide,* p. 148. New York: Arlington House, 1984.
    This "sadistic sexual satire" is nervously funny if the viewer is "sophisticated" enough to realize Meyer is putting them on. Though dated 1979, *Up!* was released in 1976.

955 "Russ Meyer's Fans." *Gent,* 22(3): 3, Mar. 1981.
    In a letter to *Gent* thanking the magazine for Jody Charles' interview of Meyer, "J.B." from California praises the filmmaker for his depiction of sex in natural outdoor surroundings and notes that the sharp, pure color in *Up!* is reminiscent of "David Lean without the pretentiousness." (1 illus.) See entry **11.**

956 Sarris, Andrew. "Pundits Ponder the Peril of Porn." *Village Voice,* 21(49):67, Dec. 6, 1976.

Calling Meyer "the Magician of Raunch," Sarris is disappointed with the "pretentious and confusing" *Up!* In light of the emergence of European art films and domestic hardcore pornography, Sarris conjectures that Meyer now lacks a "dependable constituency" and consequently his work interests only "hard-core historians of soft-core." Linked to the review is Sarris' description of and thoughts on a panel discussion of pornography sponsored by *More* magazine. (1 illus.)

957 Siskel, Gene. "Audiences Become Shock Absorbers as Horror Fills Screens." *Chicago Tribune,* sec. 6, p. 4, Nov. 14, 1976.

Siskel offers critical comments on several films based upon his assessment that the sole purpose of much contemporary cinema is to shock the audience. Indicative of this disturbing trend is Meyer's *Up!* which he describes as "softcore sadomasochism." (1 illus.)

958 Smith, Kent. "*Up!*" *Adam Film World Guide,* 2(10):161, Mar. 1986.

Considering *Up!* to be an adult classic, Smith lauds Meyer's satirization of "sexual stereotypes and society's fascination with sex in general." Rated 4 stars out of 5. (1 illus.)

959 Stinson, Roddy. "A PG Visit with an X-Rated Movie Actress." *San Antonio Express-News,* sec. A, p. 3, Oct. 13, 1976.

In an interview with Raven De La Croix conducted while she and Meyer were in San Antonio to promote *Up!*, the actress discusses the physical rigors inherent in working on location with the filmmaker.

960 Thomas, Kevin. "'Up' a Down Due to Violence." *Los Angeles Times,* pt. IV, p. 14, Jan. 28, 1977.

Thomas is disconcerted by the film's explicit violence.

961 "*Up!*" *Film Review Digest,* 2(4): 439, Summer 1977.

Excerpts of entries **960** and **967**.

962 "*Up.*" *Filmfacts,* 20(1):9–11, 1977.

Excerpts of **960** and **964** are offered as are a detailed plot synopsis and credits. Of seven critical reviews, two were mixed and five were negative.

963 "*Up!*" *Boxoffice,* UNKNOWN, Dec. 13, 1976.

A "class sexer" with inoffensive violence presented in Meyer's "inimitable comedic style." The film's excellent production values and crisp Eastmancolor should allow playdates in houses not usually exhibiting sex features. A suggested catchline for exhibitors: "If You Don't See 'Up!' You'll Feel Down!"

964 Verrill, Addison. "*Up!*" *Variety,* 284:28, Oct. 27, 1976.

Though obviously too outrageous to be taken seriously, the scenes of sex and violence in the film distinguish it as Meyer's most graphic to date. Verrill notes that the film takes to the limit what can be considered as softcore.

965 White, Ron. "'Up'; Sexy Burlesque, Is a Downer." *San Antonio Express,* sec. C, p. 8, Oct. 15, 1976.

Though *Up!* embodies the risqué slapstick that made burlesque popular, White contends both the film and Meyer's depiction of cinematic sex are as outdated today as burlesque.

966 Williamson, Bruce. "*Up!*" *Playboy,* 24(2):26, Feb. 1977.

Williamson observes that Meyer's increased emphasis on violence begun with *Supervixens* and continued with *Up!* may spoil much of the lurid comic book fun for the more fainthearted viewer.

967 Winsten, Archer. "Porno Puff." *New York Post,* p. 37, Oct. 30, 1976.

Up!, though totally lacking in good taste, does have vitality and "a well-earned X-rating."

968 Zimmer, Jacques. "Megavixens." *Revue du Cinéma*, 389:30, Dec. 1983.

Up! offers nothing new and is only an "exaggeration" of *Supervixens* sporting larger breasts and more pronounced male members. Meyer's work is categorized as a series of "sequels." (1 illus.)

Beneath the Valley of the Ultravixens (1979)

PROMOTION

969 Andelman, Bob. "The Happy Pornographer: Revealing Conversation with Russ Meyer." *Gainesville Magazine*, 7(1):UNKNOWN, Nov. 1, 1979.

Publicizing *Beneath* in Gainesville, Florida, Meyer credits his wartime meeting with Ernest Hemingway, who arranged the services of a prostitute for him, with sparking his obsessive interest in sex. Also discussed is Meyer's practice of outlining in minute detail every sexual expression and activity in the script so that his actors know in advance what is expected of them. (1 illus.)

970 Apikian, Nevart. "'Class Porn King' Seeks to Titillate." *Syracuse Post-Standard*, p. 10, July 23, 1979.

In Syracuse to promote *Beneath,* Meyer advocates a new ratings system supported by the National Association of Theater Owners, relates his role in suggesting the idea for the book *The Dirty Dozen* to its author, Eric "Mick" Nathanson, and cites *The Story of G.I. Joe* as being the "only real war film." (1 illus.)

971 Brooks, Jackie. "Assessment of X-Rated Movies." *The State*, sec. E, p. 2, Aug. 5, 1979.

Promoting *Beneath* in "sub-key markets" like Columbia, South Carolina, Meyer describes his work as "a cinematic version" of what Al Capp did in his comic strip *L'il Abner.* (2 illus.)

972 Bustin, John. "Ample Sex 'Kitten' Is Russ Meyer's Latest Asset." *Austin Citizen,* p. 9(?), Mar. 22, 1979.

Meyer and "Kitten" Natividad answer personal and professional questions while in Austin, Texas, promoting *Beneath.* Asked why he works so hard in a genre not known for its technical accomplishments or style, Meyer answers that he takes great pride in what he does. (1 illus.)

973 Calhoun, John. "Self-Proclaimed Soft-Porn King Enjoys His Work." *Arizona Daily Wildcat,* 73(57): sec. Encore, pp. 1, 9, Nov. 15, 1979.

The filmmaker is interviewed by the University of Arizona's student newspaper, the *Arizona Daily Wildcat,* while in Tucson to tout *Beneath.* In addition to discussing his career and former wives, Meyer admits that the portrayal of sex in his films is raucous because he personally is not "a sensitive, tender guy." (2 illus.)

974 Chapin, Catherine. "Meyer's Core Is Soft, But He Thinks Big." *Charlotte Observer,* sec. F, pp. 1, 3, Aug. 5, 1979.

While promoting *Beneath* in the South, Meyer speaks of the feminist outrage directed against his films and his strategy of utilizing it as a publicity/promotional tool. (1 illus.) See entry **975**.

975 Chapin, Catherine. "Trying to Bait the Feminists." *San Francisco Examiner,* p. 23, Aug. 14, 1979.

A wire service pickup of Chapin's *Charlotte Observer* article. (1 illus.) See entry **974**.

976 Chatenever, Rick. "X-Ratings and Beyond: Russ Meyer." *Santa Cruz Sentinel,* pp. 15, 26, Sept. 21, 1979.

Meyer talks about his career and relationship with Kitten Natividad during a brief stop in Santa Cruz to promote the September 21st opening of *Beneath.* (2 illus.)

Beneath the Valley of the Ultravixens (1979): Meyer and Ebert not only send-up Thornton Wilder's *Our Town* but also pay homage to the director's early years as an industrial filmmaker by casting Stuart Lancaster as "The Man from Small Town U.S.A.," a folksy narrator who intermittently comments on the action.

977 Citron, Peter. "New Ratings Possible for Movies." *Omaha World-Herald,* p. 27, July 30, 1979.

On a pre-publicity tour of Omaha to tout *Beneath,* Meyer agrees with Citron's criticism of the Motion Picture Association of America's vague "PG" rating and tells the columnist that the National Association of Theater Operators has received MPAA permission to trial test its own more detailed ratings system in the Midwest.

978 Conway, Mike. "Rating System Criticized [By Adult Film Maker]." *Chico Enterprise-Record,* sec. C, p. 2, Sept. 12, 1979.

In Chico, California, to promote *Beneath,* Meyer criticizes the current rating system and suggests that it be separated into general and adult divisions in which those only 18 and older could gain admittance to adult movie theatres. (1 illus.)

979 Cowan, Janet. "A Controversial Filmmaker Proposes a New Film Rating: A Conversation with Russ Meyer." *On the Set,* 1(10):16, 27, Dec. 1979.

Promoting *Beneath* in Miami, Meyer proposes that the "A" (Adult) rating be created to serve as a buffer between R and X-rated films. The X-rating would be reserved for hardcore or "outrageously" violent films. (1 illus.)

980   De Blasio, Don. "Russ Meyer Enjoys Job's Fringe Benefits." *Champaign-Urbana News-Gazette*, sec. Weekend, p. 5, June 8, 1979.

In Champaign-Urbana to promote the June 15 opening of *Beneath*, Meyer admits that he steered clear of violence in the film because of his suspicion that its inclusion in *Up!* adversely affected ticket sales. The filmmaker also discusses the importance of good reviews, the disappointing *The Seven Minutes*, and his association with "R. Hyde," the screen alias Roger Ebert uses when writing with Meyer. (1 illus.)

981   Dodds, Richard. "Russ Meyer: Disney of the Skinflicks." *New Orleans Times-Picayune*, sec. 3, p. 7, Aug. 20, 1979.

During a stop in New Orleans to promote *Beneath*, Meyer insists that his films are not hardcore, but are rather "like a ripoff of Al Capp with the cantilevered women and the muscular, dumb men." (1 illus.)

982   Dresser, Norman. "Things Mostly Big and Busty in Russ Meyer's Standards." *The Blade*, sec. Peach, p. 2, July 19, 1979.

In Toledo for the July 20 opening of *Beneath*, Meyer states that his three marriages failed in part because he refused to change his lifestyle and commitment to filmmaking. (1 illus.)

983   Frago, Lee. "Movie Director's Fantasies Wind Up as Huge Profits." *Southeast Sentinel*, p. 14, Aug. 15, 1979.

In town for the August 15 Denver premiere of *Beneath*, Meyer states that the film can only play limited engagements because just 50 prints were made

of the self-imposed X-rated film. (1 illus.)

984   Frymer, Murry. "His Flicks Aren't Made in Motels." *San Jose Mercury-News*, sec. L, p. 9, Sept. 23, 1979.

In San Jose, California, to promote *Beneath*, Meyer expresses the pride he feels in being a "class pornographer" who can make quality low-budget films that successfully compete with the product of the major studios. Meyer also notes that the refusal of the *San Jose Mercury-News* to run display advertising for the film represents the only kind of censorship still operative in America. (1 illus.)

985   Garner, Jack. "Proud of His Escapism." *Democrat and Chronicle*, sec. C, p. 1, July 17, 1979.

Describing *Beneath* as "Al Capp brought to life," Meyer states that he is extremely proud that his escapist films have entertained a wide audience. Interviewed while in Rochester, New York, to promote the film, Meyer also candidly discusses the role women occupy in his private life and what he considers to be the mutual responsibilities each party must fulfill in a satisfying relationship. (1 illus.)

*986   Gire, Dann. "'King Leer' Sticks Chest Out in Pride." *Arlington Daily Herald*, sec. 4, pp. 1, 3, Aug. 31, 1979.

A literate interview with Meyer conducted by Gire during a publicity tour through the Chicago area for *Beneath* explores the filmmaker's attitudes toward Women's Liberation, women in general, and "commercial" religion. Recommended. (2 illus.)

987   Gosney, Jim. "Lust and Profit: Russ Meyer's Film Formula: 'Big Bosoms and a Lot of Sex'." *Yakima Herald-Republic*, p. 3, June 16, 1979.

Meyer discusses the elements that distinguish his softcore films (humor,

Meyer, the complete filmmaker, is not content to only produce, direct, write, photograph, and edit his films. He also travels widely to promote them. Here, he appears under his writing persona, "Buster Callum," in an ad for *Beneath the Valley of the Ultravixens.*

technical quality, big bosoms, lots of sex) while in Yakima, Washington, to promote *Beneath*. The self-crowned "leading male chauvinist pig in the world" also unashamedly admits to gleefully exploiting women for "lust and profit." (1 illus.)

988 Herman, Fred. "Movies, Morality and the Big Hype: Skin Flick Chief Bares 23rd Film." *Modesto Bee,* sec. F, pp. 1, 6, Sept. 23, 1979.

Former Modesto, California, inhabitant Meyer promotes *Beneath* in the city he lived in between the ages of seven and twelve. Meyer describes the film as "a cinematic smorgasbord of erotic fantasy." (2 illus.)

989 Hicks, Bob. "For King of the Soft Cores, It's Lust and Profit." *Oregon Journal,* p. 21, Apr. 26, 1979.

While in Portland with Meyer to promote *Beneath*, "Kitten" Natividad comments on her professional and personal relationship with the filmmaker and shares her thoughts regarding the inherent sexism in Meyer's films. Meyer, who discusses his view of cinematic sex, is characterized by Hicks as a "cultur chic" having "attained a position teetering on the edge of respectability." (1 illus.)

990 Holmes, Kendall. "'Lust and

Profit' King Pans X-Rating." *Portland Press Herald,* p. 22, June 26, 1979.

The "lust and profit" king visits Portland to promote *Beneath* and voices his opposition to the MPAA's ratings system that labels all his softcore films "X." (2 illus.)

991 Huff, Dan. "'High Class Pornographer' Enjoys Flak, All the Way to the Bank." *Tucson Citizen,* sec. B, p. 1, Nov. 13, 1979.

While in Tucson to promote *Beneath*, his outrageous satire on radio evangelism, Meyer admits that had he not become a "high class pornographer" he would have made "one hell of a fundamentalist preacher." (1 illus.)

*992 Hunter, Stephen. "King of the D-Cups Is Back with Another 'Vixen'." *Baltimore Sun,* sec. B, pp. 1, 5, May 21, 1982.

Hunter's thought-provoking interview conducted during Meyer's promotional tour of Baltimore to tout *Beneath*, characterizes Meyer as a sort of "Beast from 20,000 D-Cups"; a colossal anachronism with a 1959 *Playboy* mindset who still insists on viewing women solely on the basis of their anatomical measurements. Hunter does concede that Meyer's calculatedly outrageous

180 RUSS MEYER

statements concerning women have been used effectively to promote his films. Recommended. (1 illus.)

993 Iggulden, Sue. "Porno Star 'Kitten' X-Pelled from Campus." *Portland State University Vanguard*, 34(56):1, Apr. 27, 1979.

"Kitten" Natividad is escorted off the campus of Portland State University by guards acting under orders from a school officer who stated that her promotion of *Beneath* violated a university policy prohibiting the unauthorized "distribution of material for commercial, promotional, or private gains" on PSU's grounds. (1 illus.)

994 Jones, Bill. "King Leer of Movies Retains Softcore Throne." *Phoenix Gazette*, pp. 16–17, Dec. 8, 1979.

After citing three reasons why he has remained adamant about not making hardcore films, Meyer explains the basis for his unique relationship with Roger Ebert. "Kitten" Natividad, who accompanied Meyer to Phoenix to help promote *Beneath*, discusses their stormy working relationship. (2 illus.)

995 King, Ben. "To Russ Meyer: It's What's Up Front That Counts." *San Antonio Express-News*, sec. Weekender, p. 10, Apr. 13, 1979.

In San Antonio to promote *Beneath*, Meyer and Francesca "Kitten" Natividad discuss their offscreen relationship to the embarrassment of writer Ben King. The columnist does, however, suspect that the tactic serves a useful promotional purpose. (3 illus.)

996 Kogut, William. "Hitting Them Over the Head with a Sledgehammer: Russ Meyer Exposes Himself." *Oregon Daily Emerald*, sec. B, p. 7, Oct. 4, 1979.

Promoting *Beneath* in Eugene, Meyer tells a reporter for the University of Oregon student newspaper that many moviegoers are not interested in thought-provoking films, but instead go to the

movies to "receive sledge-hammer blows of sex, action or violence." Meyer also comments on his offscreen relationship with "Kitten" Natividad and the tendency for some critics to misinterpret or invent complicated social and sexual symbolism for his films. (2 illus.)

997 Lamb, Jamie. "Meet the Man Who Brought You Sex in a Coffin." *Vancouver Sun*, sec. C, p. 6, June 9, 1980.

In Vancouver to promote *Beneath*, Meyer says his films are not meant to be great art, just fun. (1 illus.)

998 Mahar, Ted. "Meyer 'King Leer' of Soft-Core Cinema." *Sunday Oregonian*, sec. SUNDAY, p. 19, Apr. 29, 1979.

In Portland to publicize *Beneath*, Meyer outlines his philosophy of film promotion which includes personally accompanying his films to the major markets to ensure they play only in first class theatres. (2 illus.)

999 Mastroianni, Tony. "Beneath the Valley of the Skin Flicker." *Cleveland Press*, sec. D, p. 3, Aug. 23, 1979.

Meyer is interviewed in Cleveland while on a promotional tour for *Beneath* that started in upstate New York and will end in Anchorage, Alaska. While enthusiastically describing his films as translations of Al Capp's comics, Meyer speaks more fondly of the ex-army buddies he has visited in the region and admits that for him it is more exciting to rediscover them than to find buxom women for his films. (2 illus.)

1000 Masullo, Robert A. "Russ Meyer—He Relishes Lecher Role." *Sacramento Bee*, sec. H, p. 3, Sept. 16, 1979.

Meyer states that far from exploiting women, his "outrageous" films cast them as dominators of "square-jawed, stupid" men. Pointing to his personal relationship with Francesca "Kitten" Natividad, star of *Beneath*, he insists that she manage her own business interests and funds. (2 illus.)

1001 McElwain, Bill. "Porno King Visits Q-C." *Daily Dispatch*, p. 17, June 1, 1979.

Meyer, promoting *Beneath* in the Quad-City area, mentions that Roger Ebert who collaborated with him under the name "R. Hyde" recently took the film to the Cannes Film Festival where "it was a smash hit with festival-goers." He also discusses his Hollywood Hills home which doubles as a studio and the initial neighborhood fears transmitted via anonymous letters that he "would be taking pictures of naked ladies running through the back yard." (1 illus.)

1002 "Meyer Shuns H'wood to Make Pix When 'Inspiration Hits Me'." *Daily Variety*, 185(3):6, Sept. 10, 1979.

Confessing that he lacks the patience to wait for studio executives to bankroll his films, Meyer states that he enjoys his status as an independent *"auteur"* and the complete freedom it gives him to film his own fantasies. Promoting *Beneath* in Chicago, Meyer admits he is apprehensive over the film's reception in the neighborhood theatres where he has chosen to exhibit it in order to escape the prohibitive expense of a downtown opening.

1003 "Meyer's 'Ultravixens' Will Unspool Tonight." *Daily Variety*, 183(29):14, Apr. 13, 1979.

A blurb announcing the west coast opening of *Beneath* at the Nuart Theatre in West Los Angeles as a benefit for the Sepulveda Convalescent Center in Encino.

1004 Miller, Howard L. "Exclusive Entertainer Interview: Russ Meyer." *The Louisville Entertainer*, p. 25, June 12–25, 1979.

In an interview conducted in New York to promote *Beneath*, Meyer maintained that production to be superior in every detail (lighting, sound, music, color) to any film he has yet made.

1005 Neff, Andrew J. "Meyer Mounts Clip Montage for Sexpo Film." *Daily Variety*, 185(46):10, Nov. 7, 1979.

While in Los Angeles promoting *Beneath*, Meyer outlines his next project, *Jaws of Vixen*, as a semi-biographical picture consisting of clips from his earlier films. The filmmaker also discusses his limited use of paid advertising to promote his films.

1006 O'Brien, Mike. "'King of Nudies' Bares His Career." *Eugene Register-Guard*, sec. B, p. 1, May 14, 1975.

Meyer discusses the evolution of his career during a promotional stop in Eugene, Oregon, for *Beneath*. Of special interest is Meyer's reported assertion that famed stripper Tempest Storm was first responsible for putting him in contact with burlesque theatre owner Peter DeCenzie, future producer of *The Immoral Mr. Teas*. (1 illus.)

1007 O'Connor, Matt. "'King Leer' Here to Promote Movie." *Peoria Journal Star*, sec. D, p. 14, July 25, 1979.

Although *Vixen* played six months in Peoria, Illinois, in 1968, Meyer's first trip to the city is to promote his current release *Beneath*. Accompanying Meyer was the manager of the Kerasotes Theaters, who mentioned that the film would be followed in the Varsity Theater by Walt Disney's latest release. (2 illus.)

1008 Panek, Richard. "Behind 'Beneath the Valley...'." *Skokie News*, p. 13, Sept. 6, 1979.

Meyer discusses the media problems he faces in trying to promote *Beneath*.

1009 Picard, Peter, "Interview: Hey! It's Uncle Russ Cartoon Time Again!" *Minnesota Daily*, 81(9): sec. 2, p. 10, June 29, 1979.

Interviewed for the University of Minnesota student newspaper while in Minneapolis to promote *Beneath*, Meyer touches on the type of audiences his films attract, the reasons why most of the actresses are strippers, and critics who interpret more to his work than he does. (1 illus.)

1010 Platt, Alan. "Uncle Dirty." *Soho Weekly News,* p. 61, May 24, 1979.

In a forthright interview conducted during the opening week of *Beneath,* Meyer discusses the film's unusual sound effects, his contribution ("sexual honesty") to film, his diverse audience, and the reasons for the cancellation of his proposed film, *Who Killed Bambi?,* featuring the English punk rock band the Sex Pistols. (2 illus.)

1011 Raidt, Rose. "'I Couldn't Survive on the Raincoat Brigade'." *Up the Creek,* 5(32):6–7, Aug. 17, 1979.

Promoting *Beneath* in Denver, Meyer discusses his audience, his longtime friendship with collaborator and film critic Roger Ebert, and his association with Sex Pistols guitarist Sid Vicious whom he met during a planned film project on the English punk rock band. (2 illus.)

1012 Rainer, Peter. "The Immortal Mr. Meyer." *Los Angeles Herald Examiner,* sec. B, pp. 1, 6, Nov. 9, 1979.

Identical to author's *Chicago Tribune* article entry **1013.**

1013 Rainer, Peter. "Russ Meyer: 'King Leer' Reigns in Male-Fantasy Land." *Chicago Tribune,* sec. 6, p. 23, Nov. 25, 1979.

A brief interview with Meyer conducted during a promotional luncheon for his current film *Beneath.* Despite Meyer's claim that his films depict his own sexual fantasies, Rainer contends Meyer's "fantasies have a way of shifting with the commercial winds." Meyer's inclusion of explicit, but simulated, sex scenes is viewed as a commercially motivated reaction to hardcore sex films. Likewise, the scenes of shocking violence

which many viewers found offensive in *Up!,* are noticeably absent in Meyer's follow-up film *Beneath.* See entry **1012.**

1014 Rayns, Tony. "Portrait of the Pornographer with His Ass to the Wall." *Time Out,* UNKNOWN, Dec. 14, 1979.

Meyer discusses the difficulties he encountered during the preproduction planning and abortive filming for the proposed Sex Pistols movie *Who Killed Bambi?* He credits the failed project with creating a sense of personal crisis ("my ass is to the wall") that spurred him on to create one of his best works, *Beneath.* Meyer is in London to promote the film. (4 illus.)

1015 Ringel, Eleanor. "Meyer Likes Put-Downs of Skin Flicks." *Atlanta Constitution,* sec. B, p. 15, Sept. 7, 1979.

Meyer explains the significance of the title *Beneath the Valley of the Ultravixens* as an attempt to capitalize on the public's name recognition of two past Meyer hits—*Vixen* and *Beyond the Valley of the Dolls.* Meyer's next film, *Jaws of Vixen* is also discussed. (1 illus.)

1016 Royalty, Doug. "Oral Treats Lighten Meyer's Load." *The Daily Illini,* 108(159):14–15, June 19, 1979.

Interviewed by the University of Illinois student newspaper while in Champaign promoting *Beneath,* Meyer discusses the interrelationship between his lifestyle and the content of his films. (1 illus.) For a reaction to this article see entry **1032.**

1017 Scott, Bruce. "In His New Film, Russ Meyer Aims for 'Lust and Profit'." *Anchorage Daily News,* sec. D, p. 1, Aug. 3, 1979.

In Anchorage with Francesca "Kitten" Natividad for the opening of *Beneath,* Meyer discusses several aspects of his career to date, most notably his interactions with feminist groups who charge him with exploiting women. (2 illus.)

1018 Shea, Al. "Russ Meyer Presents Russ Meyer." *West Bank Guide*, sec. 3, p. 6, Aug. 29, 1979.

Meyer, a self-described "high class pornographer," explains the numerous differences between his outrageously humorous softcore erotica and hardcore pornography during a promotional interview for *Beneath*. (1 illus.)

1019 Smith, Steven. "Soft-Porn King Makes No Apologies." *Eugene Register-Guard*, sec. D, p. 16, Sept. 27, 1979.

Interviewed while in Eugene to promote *Beneath*, Meyer accuses the major studio bosses with not knowing their audience and neglecting the rural, largely unsophisticated drive-in moviegoing public who have traditionally flocked to his films in pickups filled with six-packs of beer. Smith describes *Beneath* as "definitive Meyer ... incredibly fast-paced, totally irreverent and lewd as hell." (1 illus.)

1020 Talbot, Maggie. "His Films and Reputation Are Naughty." *Tallahassee Democrat*, sec. D, pp. 1, 4, Oct. 4, 1979.

Publicizing *Beneath* in Tallahassee, Meyer addresses an "Elements in Film" class at Florida State University on the problems facing his productions and the reasons for the universal appeal of his films. (1 illus.)

*1021 Turnquist, Kristi. "Russ Meyer: Porno Potentate and Proud of It." *Willamette Valley Observer*, 5(39):6–7, Sept. 28, 1979.

In a publicity interview for *Beneath* currently playing in Eugene, Oregon, Meyer admits that his heavy personal promotion of the film is to compensate for the fact that it contains no name talent yet must compete directly with star-studded major studio releases. Also, Meyer insists that since he makes films essentially for himself, he is not concerned with feminist reaction, although he needs audience acceptance of his work to feel gratified. Recommended.

(1 illus.) For a reaction to this article see entry **1030**.

1022 Vadeboncoeur, Joan E. "Russ Meyer: Kingpin at the Box Office." *Syracuse Herald-Journal*, p. 34, July 19, 1979.

On a publicity tour of Syracuse, New York, for *Beneath*, a proud Meyer discusses three talented and prospering actors to whom he gave significant career breaks: Harrison Page *(Vixen, Beyond the Valley of the Dolls)*, Alex Rocco *(Motorpsycho!)*, and Charles Napier *(Cherry, Harry & Raquel, Beyond the Valley of the Dolls, The Seven Minutes, Supervixens)*. (1 illus.)

1023 Ward, Michael. "Following Fellini: Soft-Porn King Is Turning Cincinnati Defeat into Triumph." *Cleveland Plain Dealer*, sec. D, pp. 1, 5, Oct. 26, 1980.

Though Meyer is in Cleveland to promote *Beneath*, he tells Ward that much of his upcoming autobiographical "Fellini film," *The Breast of Russ Meyer*, will feature Cincinnati where he unsuccessfully defended *Vixen* against obscenity prosecution. (2 illus.)

1024 Ward, Michael. "Search No More, Diogenes: Filmmaker Russ Meyer Is Honest Man." *Cleveland Plain Dealer*, sec. B, p. 8, July 11, 1979.

During a promotional stop in Cleveland to publicize *Beneath*, Meyer is profiled as an honest man who knows exactly what he wants to accomplish with his films — "lust and profit." (1 illus.)

1025 Webb, Steve. "Film Maker Says He Doesn't Take Sex Too Seriously." *Rochester Post-Bulletin*, p. 3, June 23, 1979.

In Rochester, Minnesota, as part of a 40-city tour to promote *Beneath*, Meyer explains that he does not treat sex too seriously in his films because society as a whole already has too many "sexual hangups." (1 illus.)

1026 White, Maggi. "The King of the Nudies." *Downtowner*, 5(31):

UNKNOWN, Apr. 30, 1979.
Meyer and "Kitten" Natividad frankly discuss their personal relationship during a promotional stop in Portland for *Beneath*. According to Natividad, the filmmaker likes to be constantly mothered, while Meyer admits that he is "closer to this woman than anyone." (2 illus.)

1027 Winsten, Archer. "Russ & Friends Come to Town." *New York Post*, p. 20, May 12, 1979.
Promoting *Beneath* in New York City, Meyer briefly discusses the financial aspects of independent film production. (1 illus.)

1028 Wohlwend, Chris. "Russ Meyer Is America's 'Dirty Old Man'." *Louisville Times*, sec. Scene, p. 29, May 26, 1979.
An unabashed interview with Meyer conducted while the filmmaker was in Louisville promoting *Beneath*.

1029 "Yank Girls Way in Front!" *Sydney Truth*, 4912:3, May 2, 1981.
Promoting *Beneath* in Sydney, Australia, Meyer "slur(s) . . . Australian womanhood" by observing that while in the country he has not seen one female with the "mammarian munificence" necessary to be in his movies. (1 illus.)

MISCELLANEOUS

1030 Detroy, S. "Part of the Porn Problem." *Willamette Valley Observer*, 5(41):2, Oct. 12, 1979.
Detroy's bitter letter to the editor berates the paper for its coverage of Meyer and argues that "such irresponsible journalism only serves to perpetuate the idea that it's okay to objectify and use women." Kristi Turnquist, the article's author, is charged with the responsibility for the "continuation of violence against women." See entry **1021**.

1031 Nelson, Bonnie Weinstein. "Turn to the Tribune." *Reader: Chicago's Free Weekly*, 8(50): sec. 1, p. 2, Sept. 14, 1970.

Nelson protests in a letter to the editor against the "degrading" ad for *Beneath* which reads "Six Chicks in Search of a Cluck." Where can readers turn, she asks, if an allegedly liberal publication like the *Reader* "condones the degradation of women"?

1032 White, Nancy. "Sexist Meyer's Views Don't Deserve Story." *The Daily Illini*, 108(164):9, June 27, 1979.
Reacting to Doug Royalty's article entitled "Oral Treats Lighten Meyer's Load" which appeared in the June 19 issue of *The Daily Illini*, Nancy White, in a letter to the editor, criticizes the paper's publishing of "sexist articles." Meyer is characterized as a "fool" who judges half the population "by their cup size." See entry **1016**.

CENSORSHIP — AUSTRALIA

1033 Coster, Peter. "Meyer on the Prowl." *Melbourne Herald*, p. 7, Oct. 7, 1980.
In Sydney to edit *Beneath* for the Australian censor, Meyer states that he will return with two of his stars in March 1981 to scout locations around Alice Springs and the Great Barrier Reef. (2 illus.)

1034 Tame, Adrian. "Joh Says No to 'Vixens'." *Sydney Truth*, 4912:9, May 2, 1981.
After exhibiting three days in a suburb of Brisbane, Queensland, censors ban the exhibition of *Beneath* in their state. (1 illus.)

1035 White, Matt. "Australian Film Industry in Danger as 'Offshore Factory'." *Hollywood Reporter*, 266(34):4, May 5, 1981.
After playing for only two days in Brisbane, the Queensland State Censorship Board orders *Beneath* taken off. Meyer, in Brisbane to promote the film, notes that the incident represents the first time one of his movies has ever been banned.

An attentive Francesca "Kitten" Natividad listens to Meyer's direction for an upcoming take in *Beneath the Valley of the Ultravixens.*

CENSORSHIP — CALIFORNIA

1036 Empey, R. Wayne. "Police Don't Make Good Movie Critics." *San Jose Mercury-News,* sec. B, p. 10, Oct. 10, 1979.

The pulling by vice squad officers of *Beneath* from San Jose, California, theatres prompts an outraged citizen to question why a "silly sex-comedy" should be deemed evil when the violence-filled, PG-rated *Escape from Alcatraz* plays uncensored at the same theatre.

1037 Frymer, Murry. "'Ultravixens' Experiences Abbreviated Run." *San Jose Mercury-News,* sec. C, p. 13, Sept. 28, 1979.

Beneath is closed after a one-week run by San Jose, California, vice squad officers who cite a city ordinance which prohibits the exhibition of a pornographic film within 1000 feet of residential areas or hotels. The theatre owner, citing the film's poor box office and the prohibitive costs of legal fees, refused to risk possible negative community reaction by attempting to secure a conditional use permit from the city which would allow him to exhibit a film deemed pornographic.

1038 Hoyt, Bernard W. "Police Don't Make Good Movie Critics." *San Jose Mercury-News,* sec. B, p. 10, Oct. 10, 1979.

A San Jose citizen resents the "police-state atmosphere" perpetuated by the vice squad's closing of *Beneath.*

CENSORSHIP — TEXAS

1039 "Yank Russ Meyer's 'Vixens' Film Spoofing Fundamentalist Faith." *Variety,* 294:50, Mar. 21, 1979.

Local opposition to what Meyer terms the "comic put-on of faith healing (and) born again immersion" depicted in *Beneath* compels the management of the United Artists Theatre Circuit to pull the film from its Hurst Four Theatre in Arlington, Texas.

REVIEWS

1040 Bliss, Michael. "Beneath the Valley of the Ultravixens." *Minnesota Daily*, 81(9):sec. 2, p. 14, June 29, 1979.
A slickly edited hit-and-miss sex satire that stretches too little material too far. Rated 1 star—"Proceed with caution."

1041 Blowen, Michael. "Sex and Violence." *Boston Globe*, p. 51, May 30, 1979.
The humor in Meyer's *Beneath* is compared unfavorably to that in George Romero's *Dawn of the Dead*. For Blowen, Meyer's "sledgehammer directorial style" fails to raise Roger Ebert's "sophomoric" screenplay from the level of "bathroom humor" to that of "genuine satire."

1042 Brien, Alan. "The Vampire in the Dark." *London Sunday Times*, p. 39, Nov. 25, 1979.
Brien reviews among other films *Beneath* and horror specialist George A. Romero's *Martin*. Dubbing Meyer "the Romero of porn," Brien is disappointed by Meyer's inability to "transmute a sexy soap-opera into an erotic essay on the human condition."

1043 "Can Russ Meyer Keep on Doing It?" *Gent*, 21(3):82, Mar. 1980.
Gent, "Home of the D-Cups," features four stills from *Beneath* incorrectly referred to as *Beneath the Planet of the Ultravixens*. Though predicting probable commercial failure for the film, *Gent* concedes that it does contain excellent cinematography and like Meyer's past work is "a tit man's dream." (4 illus.)

1044 Canby, Vincent. "Movie: 'Beneath the Valley of the Ultravixens'." *New York Times*, p. 13, May 12, 1979.
A non-critical review attributing the enduring quality of Meyer's "particular brand of super-soft-core pornography" to the fantasy element of sex and violence in it. A brief discussion of Meyer's technical prowess cites the crystal clarity of the photography "that makes everything look as if it had just been washed squeaky clean."

1045 Cargin, Peter. "The 'Other Cannes'." *Film*, 76:6–7, Aug. 1979.
Shown at Cannes to potential film distributors, *Beneath* is described as "a lovely sendup" of much television fare distinguished by its "fast paced, zippy editing." (6 illus.)

*1046 Chute, David. "Beyond the Valley of Russ Meyer." *Boston Phoenix*, sec. 3, pp. 7(?), 12, May 22, 1979.
Chute's review of the film accompanied by an interview with Meyer provides the basis for an interesting perspective on the filmmaker's place in cinema history. Describing *Beneath* as "a romantic farce-cum-morality play—with skin," Chute notes that Meyer's 16 months of painstaking post-production work have resulted in a technically excellent film. However, the film's emphasis on unrelenting sex at the cost of the intermittent action scenes found in Meyer's earlier work, leads Chute to call the film "a bit dull." Recommended. (2 illus.)

1047 Coleman, John. "If Only...." *New Statesman*, 98:825, Nov. 23, 1979.
British critic Coleman's one-line review describes the film as Meyer's "hymn to gargantuan mammaries."

1048 Crawford, Mark. "Ribald Film Makes Russ Meyer a 'Class Pornographer'." *Reno Evening Gazette*, p. 16, Sept. 14, 1979.

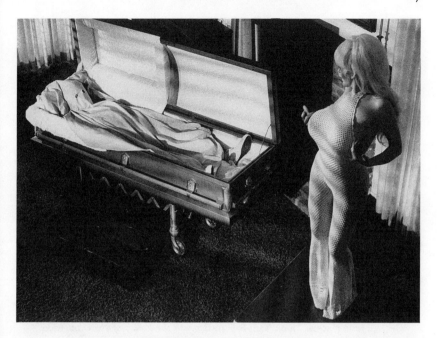

Radio evangelist "Eufaula Roop" (Ann Marie) "ministers" to "Martin Bormann" (Henry Rowland) in *Beneath the Valley of the Ultravixens,* cowritten with Meyer by Pulitzer Prize winning film critic Roger Ebert under his pseudonym "R. Hyde."

Meyer explains that it is to his financial advantage to promote *Beneath* in cities like Reno where it opens on September 21. A self-described "class pornographer," Meyer also admits that while he admires Woody Allen's comedy he does not find it amusing. (1 illus.)

1049 Dresser, Norman. "Only the Plot Isn't Heavy." *The Blade,* sec. Peach, p. 2, July 19, 1979.

The plot never interferes with a 93-minute "parade of nude women and simulated sex acts."

1050 Frymer, Murry. "'Ultra Vixens' Is an Assault to the Senses." *San Jose Mercury-News,* sec. L, p. 9, Sept. 23, 1979.

The progressively larger bosoms which adorn every subsequent Meyer film lead Frymer to conclude that he is no longer making sexual satires, but rather "horror films."

1051 Gire, Dann. "Prurient Interest Stars in 'Beneath'." *Arlington Daily Herald,* sec. 4, p. 3, Aug. 31, 1979.

Although Gire identifies the major appeal of *Beneath* to be "prurient interest," the film's abundant humor and satire should find a receptive, if undiscriminating, audience.

1052 Hogue, Peter. "Beneath the Valley of the Ultravixens." *Movie-tone News,* 64/65:51–52, Mar. 1980.

An unreservedly rave review in which Hogue describes Meyer's film as "one of the livelier entertainments of 1979" and possibly "this middle–American Rabelais's . . . masterpiece." Hogue is most impressed by the film's employment of a "mock-serious *Our Town*–style narration" and Meyer's "Russian-style editing" which enlists "Eisensteinian montage" for comedic purposes.

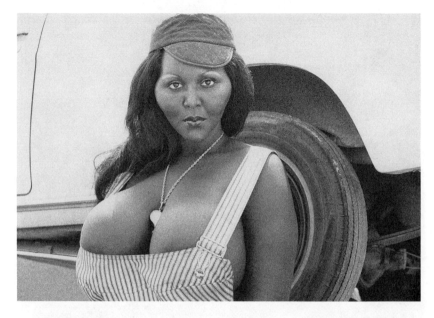

The late June Mack as "Junk Yard Sal" in *Beneath the Valley of the Ultravixens.*

1053 Hunter, Stephen. "'Voyage' Versus 'Ultra Vixens': Less Is More." *Baltimore Sun,* sec. B, p. 11, May 21, 1982.

In perhaps one of the most scathing reviews ever written on a Meyer film, Hunter blasts *Beneath* as "overendowed, overloud (and) overlong." Meyer is characterized as a filmmaker whose only two talents lie in his ability to convince big-busted women to strip and "subsequently keep them in focus long enough to get enough film together to stitch into a movie." (1 illus.)

*1054 Kehr, Dave. "Only the Style Survives." *Reader: Chicago's Free Weekly,* 8(48):sec. 1, pp. 14, 21, Aug. 31, 1979.

Kehr's perceptive review of *Beneath* argues that the isolated position Meyer's recent softcore movies occupy midway between hardcore (which he refuses to make) and the Hollywood mainstream (which he still goes well beyond) has resulted for him in an emphasis on directorial "style" in order to compensate for the devalued commercial appeal of film sex. In *Beneath,* which Kehr terms a "technical exercise," Meyer's style completely squeezes out the film's content until it becomes an overlong Disney-type sex cartoon which psychologically numbs the viewer. Still, Kehr maintains, that at a time when mainstream films lack individuality, Meyer's creation of a "comic universe" with an internal consistency represents a cinematic "world of his own, as unique and recognizable as John Ford's." Rated two stars ("worth seeing") out of four. Highly recommended. (1 illus.)

1055 Kimsey, Gary. "Russ Meyer and His Vixens." *Denver Monthly,* pp. 69–70, Sept. 1979.

Kimsey portrays Meyer as a con artist perpetrating a long-running scam on any one foolish enough to attend his films. As for *Beneath,* Kimsey can suggest only two reasons to see it: if the viewer needs a nap or is interested in a shallow "satirical cinematic work." Kimsey does, however, grudgingly admit

Meyer knows how to publicize his films. (3 illus.)

1056 Knight, Arthur. "Russ Meyer's Beneath the Valley of the Ultravixens." *Hollywood Reporter,* 256(14):2, Apr. 17, 1979.

Knight considers Meyer to be "as close to a full-fledged 'auteur' as any filmmaker in this country today." No critical comment on the film is offered.

1057 Kogan, Rick. "Really Big Show: Meyer's Latest Tape-Measure Epic." *Chicago Sun-Times,* p. 69, Sept. 5, 1979.

A whimsical review of *Beneath* by Roger Ebert's movie reviewer colleague on the *Chicago Sun-Times* who diplomatically concludes that while the film is not too good, it is also not that bad. Though admitting that Meyer is "a film maker of undeniable talent," Kogan wonders if a market still exists for the type of films Meyer makes.

1058 Lee. "Beneath the Valley of the Ultravixens: A Hot Russ Meyer Time in the Old Town Tonight." *Variety,* 294:22, Apr. 18, 1979.

For Lee., regardless of what Meyer is trying to achieve in this film—satire, fantasy, or both—it is amusing "in a dirty joke way" that "gives his customers their money's worth."

1059 Millar, Jeff. "Film Will Satisfy Most Fans." *Houston Chronicle,* sec. 6, p. 1, Mar. 23, 1979.

According to Millar, *Beneath* will satisfy the 98 percent of Meyer's audience who go to his films to "have their prurience interested," while the 2 percent (himself included) who go for the height in low humor will be disappointed.

1060 Nelson, Brian, and Haugen, Peter. "Cinema Capsules: Beneath the Valley of the Ultravixens." *Daily Dispatch,* sec. A, p. 5, June 3, 1979.

The reviewers can not believe that Pulitzer Prize–winning film critic Roger Ebert collaborated on the screenplay under the alias "R. Hyde."

1061 Patoski, Joe Nick. "'Beneath Valley of Ultravixens': Russ Meyer Overdoes It Again." *Austin American-Statesman,* p. 20, Mar. 24, 1979.

Meyer is taken to task for failing to please the "overcoat crowd" who go to his films for titillation or the "high brows" who view his work as "Serious Art."

1062 Peary, Danny. "Beneath the Valley of the Ultravixens." *Guide for the Film Fanatic,* p. 492. New York: Simon & Schuster, 1986.

Peary lists the film as a "cult movie" in the "Additional 'Must See' Films" section at the end of his book, *Guide for the Film Fanatic.*

1063 Rayns, Tony. "Beneath the Valley of the Ultravixens." *Monthly Film Bulletin,* 47(552):4, Jan. 1980.

British critic Rayns laments Meyer's decision in *Beneath* to "...condemn himself to endless variations on the formula he pioneered in *Vixen* in 1968." Despite these shortcomings, however, Rayns concludes that Meyer repeating himself "is still many times livelier than much of the rest of contemporary American cinema."

1064 Richmond, Rocsan. "Beneath the Valley of the Ultravixens: Another Meyer Hit." *Chicago Metro News,* p. 10, Sept. 8, 1979.

Reviewing for Chicago's weekly black newspaper, Richmond enthusiastically declares the film to be "a sexual satire of the very best caliber." (2 illus.)

1065 Rimmer, Robert. "Beneath the Valley of the Ultravixens." *The X-Rated Videotape Guide,* p. 63. New York: Arlington House, 1984.

Comparing the narrative structure of the film to Thornton Wilder's *Our Town,* Rimmer announces the *Vixen* saga will continue with the soon-to-be-released *Jaws of Vixen. Beneath* is incorrectly dated as 1980 rather than 1979.

*1066 Roberts, Bradford. "Uncle Russ." *Twin Cities Reader,* 4(23): 11, 14, June 29–July 6, 1979.

Roberts impressively notes that Meyer's early background as a maker of industrial films reaches its full expression in *Beneath,* a "lusty industrial" that parodies the photographic clarity ("the better to see the product"), fluid editing, and obvious narration of the genre. Highly recommended. (2 illus.)

1067 Rotsler, William. "Russ Meyer's Beneath the Valley of the Ultra-Vixens." *Adam Film World,* 7 (10):58, May 1980.

Rotsler likes the film's "exuberant over-indulgence," but laments its "sameness" to past Meyer efforts. Rated 2 stars out of 4. (1 illus.)

1068 Roy, Jean. "Beyond the Valley of the Ultravixens." *Cinéma,* 247/248:38–39, July/Aug. 1979.

Beneath promised to be better than *Beyond the Valley of the Dolls, Vixen,* and *Supervixens* combined and was. Roy, obviously a big fan, feels that Meyer's work merits a choice place among the premieres at the Cannes Film Festival.

1069 Royalty, Doug. "Bigger and Better? Only at the Chest Level: Flat Ebert Script Dooms Titilating [sic] Movie." *The Daily Illini,* 108(159):15, June 19, 1979.

Reviewing for the student newspaper of the University of Illinois, Royalty praises Meyer's technical expertise which makes *Beneath* look like "a 90-minute cartoon," but blames the failure of this "inane . . . (and) least erotic skinflick ever produced" on UI graduate Roger Ebert's unfunny script. (1 illus.)

1070 Sanders, Charles H. "Skinflick King Seeking Lust & Profit." *The Argus,* sec. Sunday Argus Quad-Citian, p. 14, June 3, 1979.

Interviewed while in the Quad Cities area to promote *Beneath,* Meyer characterizes his close personal friend and the film's scriptwriter, Roger Ebert, as an honest man who refuses to review his work in order to avoid being accused of trying to influence critical opinion and public acceptance in the filmmaker's favor. (1 illus.)

1071 Siskel, Gene. "Meyer's 'Ultra Vixens' Goes Beyond the Valley of the Shadow of Boredom." *Chicago Tribune,* sec. 2, p. 7, Sept. 6, 1979.

A scathing review highlighted by comments like "tedious," "not erotic," and "childish trash." Both Meyer and Ebert are criticized for writing a script filled with a cruel humor that betrays a dislike for the characters. Rated one star out of a possible four.

1072 Smith, Kent. "Beneath the Valley of the Ultravixens." *Adam Film World Guide,* 2(10):32, Mar. 1986.

Smith says "too much" to Meyer's quick cut editing and directorial style. Rated 3 ½ out of 5 stars (between "good" and "excellent"). (1 illus.)

1073 Stark, John. "A Review Shorter Than the Title." *San Francisco Examiner,* p. 7, Sept. 22, 1979.

Confining his critical comments on *Beneath* to "yuk," reviewer Stark caustically notes Meyer's refusal to submit the film to the Motion Picture Association of America's ratings board.

1074 Sterritt, David. "Movie Guide: 'Beneath the Valley of the Ultravixens'." *Christian Science Monitor,* p. 18, May 31, 1979.

Labelling *Beneath* ". . . a mean-spirited, rampantly sexist, stupidly cartoonish muddle," Sterritt accuses Meyer of disappointing many critics who espoused the belief that he would one day develop into a "film artist."

1075 Taggart, Patrick. "Russ Meyer's Films X-Rated, But Don't Call Him a Pornographer." *Austin American-Statesman,* sec. C, p. 14, Mar. 22, 1979.

Meyer speaks out about the inequity in the current ratings system that fails to recognize a distinction between hardcore and his softcore films. Meyer also explains his refusal to submit his films to the MPAA's ratings board. A few critical comments are offered.

1076 Tessier, Max. "Beneath the Valley of the Ultravixens." *Ecran*, 82:20, July 15, 1979.

After a brilliant beginning the film loses its "virulence" through overly repetitive "comic strip" ruttings and is saved from boredom only in its final moments by the appearance of Meyer himself. While it will please "unconditional Meyerites," it will not make viewers forget his masterpiece, *Beyond the Valley of the Dolls*.

1077 Thomas, Kevin. "'Valley' Satirizes Sexual Mores." *Los Angeles Times*, pt. IV, p. 31, Nov. 8, 1979.

The two years Meyer spent in post-production, Thomas asserts, have resulted in a film "as dazzlingly structured as any of its stars." High marks are awarded for every aspect of the film which Thomas deems Meyer's most amusing and ambitious effort.

1078 Turnquist, Kristi. "Beneath the Valley of the Ultravixens." *Willamette Valley Observer*, 5(39): sec. B, p. 10, Sept. 28, 1979.

After a good start which successfully parodies *Our Town*, *Beneath* turns into an offensive "bummer."

1079 Uhl, Jake. "Ultra Vixens." *Cinemonkey*, 5(2):57, Spring 1979.

A glowing review of *Beneath* filled with superlatives for Meyer's cinematic style and technical virtuosity.

1080 Walsh, Michael. "Russ Meyer Finds His Fun in 40-D Cup." *The Province*, sec. D, p. 2, June 12, 1980.

A review in which Walsh characterizes Meyer as an *auteur* to be considered "with Chaplin and Keaton and rather higher than either Woody Allen or Mel Brooks." Like these filmmakers, the body of Meyer's work offers a unique and consistent vision of the world and as such

can be viewed as more than just slick exploitation.

1081 Walton, Kelly. "I've Got You Under My Skin (Flick) ... a Conversation with Russ Meyer." *Scottsdale Daily Progress*, sec. Weekend, pp. 14–15, Nov. 30, 1979.

Based on the strength of her comedic performance in *Beneath*, Walton agrees with Meyer's assessment of Francesca "Kitten" Natividad's potential as a comedienne in the same vein as Jean Harlow and/or Marilyn Monroe. Elsewhere in the piece, Meyer explains and defends the differences between his casting procedures and those employed by some Hollywood "casting couch" producers. (2 illus.)

1082 Ward, Michael. "Flimsy Plot Doesn't Cover Bare Essentials." *Cleveland Plain Dealer*, sec. B, p. 4, Oct. 21, 1980.

There is nothing in *Beneath* to be taken seriously.

1083 Williamson, Bruce. "Beneath the Valley of the Ultravixens." *Playboy*, 26(9):52, 54, Sept. 1979.

Quoting extensively from Meyer's own tongue-in-cheek plot synopsis, Williamson notes *Beneath* "remains fairly constant" to the filmmaker's "patented brand of soft-core cornography."

1084 Winsten, Archer. "Ultravulgar Ultravixens." *New York Post*, p. 33, May 11, 1979.

While Winsten considers the film to be "vulgarity triumphant," he admits "it does have a velocity and explosive spirit that's in a class by itself." (1 illus.)

1085 Wohlwend, Chris. "'Beneath' Is Soft-Core Silliness." *Louisville Times*, sec. Scene, p. 29, May 26, 1979.

A lukewarm review citing the film's "pie-in-the-face" humor and its total lack of sensuous sex. Ann Marie's performance as radio evangelist "Eufaula Roop" is praised. Rated 2 stars out of 4.

XI. FILMS IN PROGRESS

The Breast of Russ Meyer (1979–)

1086 "Russ Meyer Puts Together Excerpts from 21 Features." *Hollywood Reporter,* 219(34):11, Jan. 18, 1972.

At the suggestion of distributors around the country, Meyer plans to compile clips from his 21 previous features and add new scenes for a 90-minute retrospective film entitled *Hotsa! Hotsa!* to be ready in late 1972. Obviously, the prototypical conception for Meyer's magnum opus, *The Breast of Russ Meyer.*

1087 "Russ Meyer's 12-Hour Autobiopic Approaching $2-Mil Prod. Costs." *Variety,* 321(4):24, Nov. 20, 1985.

Meyer's filmic magnum opus, *The Breast of Russ Meyer,* is rapidly approaching $2 million in production costs and nearly 12 hours in length. Meyer plans to show the film, five years in the making, at festivals and to release it on four videocassettes.

1088 Stark, Susan. "And Now for Something Completely Different." *Detroit News,* sec. F, p. 3, June 26, 1981.

Two weeks after an article by Stark in which Meyer laments the difficulty of finding spectacularly endowed stars for *The Breast of Russ Meyer,* the filmmaker sends the columnist a letter which includes photos of the protu-berant Darlene Grey and Frances De Mass. Meyer closes the letter by offering to shoot a better logo photo of the "wan" Stark, but only "from the neck up, of course." See entry **1092.**

1089 Stevens, Dale. "Proud of Image: Self-Proclaimed Pornographer Visits City." *Cincinnati Post,* sec. B, p. 12, Nov. 1, 1980.

In Cincinnati to shoot footage for *The Breast of Russ Meyer,* the filmmaker discusses his image, his attitude towards the Hollywood Establishment, and "Legacy RMF" (Russ Meyer Films), a co-operative foundation formed by Meyer to preserve his films and to direct all profits to the American Cancer Society after his death. (1 illus.)

1090 Thissen, Rolf. "Meyer's Busen-show." *Quick,* 18:66–67, Apr. 1985.

The filmmaker discusses his "monument in celluloid," the multi-hour filmic autobiography *The Breast of Russ Meyer,* and notes that there are perhaps only 20 women in the world that fulfill his anatomical criteria of large breasts, wasp-waist, and slender legs. (2 illus.)

Jaws of Vixen (1979–)

1091 "The 'Jaws' of Russ Meyer." *Variety,* 297(2):34, Nov. 14, 1979.

Jaws of Vixen, a compilation of his earlier work with an added 45 minutes of new footage, will star Morganna, baseball's kissing bandit, and buxom West German discovery Dolly Dollar. Meyer promises *Jaws* will be a "personal film" that "will lampoon some of the famous sex scenes of all time."

Jaws of Lorna (1981–)

1092 Stark, Susan. "Return of King Leer: New Film from Meyer." *Detroit News*, sec. F, p. 3, June 12, 1981.

Meyer discusses the postponement of his semi-documentary film *The Breast of Russ Meyer* in order to develop *The Jaws of Lorna*, an "arch-parody" of his 1964 film *Lorna*. (1 illus.)

Blitzen, Vixen and Harry (1982–)

1093 Segers, Frank. "Meyer Bares New Int'l Distrib'n Pact." *Daily Variety*, 195(12):16, Mar. 23, 1982.

Blitzen, Vixen and Harry, a parody of *Dirty Harry*, will be an international coproduction between Meyer's R.M. Films, Inc. and Laurens Straub's Munich-based distributorship Filmwelt Verleih-Und Vertribs. Shooting is set to begin in Fall 1982 on the $1.5 million softcore epic to star Charles Napier, Henry Rowland, and seven *Playboy* playmates.

XII. FILMS PLANNED
BUT NEVER MADE

The Eleven (1971)

1094 Archerd, Army. "Just for Variety." *Daily Variety*, 152(59):2, Aug. 27, 1971.

Recuperating from surgery, Meyer awaits word from Richard D. Zanuck at Warner Bros. to begin *Choice Cuts*, rescripted by Meyer and Jerome Kilty. The filmmaker, who became a member of the Writers Guild on August 25, 1971, also plans in April 1972 to shoot a horror film, *Eleven*, for Tempo Productions on location in Savannah, Georgia.

1095 "Concessions for '11'." *Daily Variety*, 153(37):8, Oct. 28, 1971.

The Eleven is approved for labor concessions given to films with a budget under $1 million.

1096 "Even Russ Meyer Bypasses Sexpo." *Variety*, 264(11):6, Oct. 27, 1971.

The Macon, Georgia, Chamber of Commerce happily aids Meyer in his search for an antebellum mansion to "star" in the "horror mystery" film *The Eleven* to be shot in the area.

1097 Grant, Hank. "Rambling Reporter." *Hollywood Reporter*, 222(5):2, July 10, 1972.

Meyer announces that his next movie, *Beyond ... Beyond*, will be shot in Europe and that while he initially envisioned making the horror film *The*

Eleven in Mississippi, he now plans to shoot it in either Holland or Austria.

1098 "Russ Meyer Sets Next 'Eleven' for Tempo." *Hollywood Reporter*, 218(12):2, Oct. 5, 1971.

Accompanied by art director Roger Maus, Meyer leaves October 12, 1971, to search locations in Waynesboro, Georgia, for *The Eleven*, a film financed by Tempo set to roll on an eight-to-ten-week schedule beginning in March 1972. En route, the director will attend the "Russ Meyer Night" at the Museum of Modern Art.

1099 "Russ Meyer to Direct 'Eleven' for Tempo Firm." *Hollywood Reporter*, 217(46):8, Sept. 13, 1971.

Atlanta-based Tempo Productions completes a deal with Meyer calling on him to produce and direct the $750,000-budgeted horror mystery *The Eleven* to begin preproduction January 1, 1972. Meyer teamed with Manny Diez to write the script.

Foxy (1972–73)

1100 Bacon, James. "Edy Dressed Like a Barbed Wire Fence." *Los Angeles Herald-Examiner*, sec. B, p. 9, Oct. 6, 1972.

Edy Williams relishes the opportunity her starring role in *Foxy* affords her for treating men as sex objects.

*1101 Beaupre, Lee. "Can't Risk Investors Coin Anymore Russ Meyer Cancels $400,000 'Foxy'; Raps 'Schlock' Films as Spoilsports." *Variety*, 271(8):5, July 4, 1973.

Reacting to the Supreme Court's ruling on obscenity which permits each community to set its own standard as to what is obscene, Meyer cancels *Foxy* over fears that his investors' money will be lost on a film that can be effectively harassed by various communities. Meyer blames the ruling on the court's attempt to curb hardcore "schlock" operators out to make a "fast-buck." Recommended.

*1102 Beaupre, Lee. "Sexploitation Filmmaker Meyer Heeds Court's Obscenity Edict, Turns Attention Elsewhere." *Daily Variety*, 160 (17):2, June 28, 1973.

In the wake of a Supreme Court ruling that permits individual communities to determine what constitutes obscenity, Meyer cancels *Foxy* claiming that he can not risk his investors' potential $400,000 outlay on a film that could be effectively prosecuted in various communities. Besides commenting on film censorship and Hollywood's reaction to it, Meyer also announces the formation of Signal 166, his new production-distribution company that will replace his old Eve Productions. Recommended.

1103 "'Foxy' Undergoes Change in Title." *Hollywood Reporter*, 226 (21):11, May 17, 1973.

Foxy is retitled *Viva Foxy!* to accommodate a script change giving the story a South American background. The production is set to start in June.

1104 Grant, Hank. "Rambling Reporter." *Hollywood Reporter*, 223(18):2, Oct. 6, 1972.

Grant reports on Meyer's search for a "leather lunged hero" capable of making love underwater to wife Edy Williams in *Foxy*.

1105 Grant, Hank. "Rambling Reporter." *Hollywood Reporter*, 223(27):2, Oct. 20, 1972.

Foxy will open with a nude Edy Williams water skiing before the credits.

1106 Grant, Hank. "Rambling Reporter." *Hollywood Reporter*, 224(17):2, Dec. 19, 1972.

Meyer announces that the freezing weather has forced postponement of *Foxy* and wife Edy Williams' nude scenes until January 1973.

1107 Haber, Joyce. "Men into Sex Objects." *Los Angeles Times*, pt. IV, p. 14, Oct. 2, 1972.

Meyer's proposed $500,000 R-rated feature *Foxy*, set to begin shooting in Hollywood on Dec. 1, is described by its star Edy Williams as a "sort of women's lib" that will "turn men into sex objects, instead of women."

1108 Harvey, Steve. "Trouble Ahead for Centerfolds." *Los Angeles Times*, sec. VII, p. 5, July 8, 1973.

The uncertain impact the Supreme Court's community standards definition of obscenity will exert on the film and publishing industries is examined by media representatives who fear the ruling will promote censorship. Reacting to the ruling, Meyer cancelled his $400,000 film *Foxy* to "go fishing."

1109 Ornstein, Bill. "Russ Meyer Plans Production of 'Foxy' with Edy Williams." *Hollywood Reporter*, 222(49):11, Sept. 11, 1972.

A trade paper blurb announcing the proposed early December 1972 start of *Foxy*, Meyer's $300,000 Signal Films sequel to *Vixen*.

1110 "Smut Makers Call Business Viable: Say Supreme Court Ruling Won't Force Them Out." *New York Times*, p. 36, July 1, 1973.

San Francisco–based hardcore erotica producers the Mitchell Brothers *(Behind the Green Door)* and softcore director Meyer comment on the recent Supreme Court ruling on obscenity which empowers each community to ban material deemed offensive by local standards. A worried Meyer cancelled his next feature *Foxy* out of fears that the law would jeopardize his investors' capital since no guarantee now exists that once a film is made it can even be shown in all areas of the country.

Beyond. . .Beyond (1972)

1111 Ornstein, Bill. "Russ Meyer Will Shoot Next Film in Austria or Holland." *Hollywood Reporter,* 222(3):9, July 6, 1972.

Meyer announces that his next independent production to be filmed in either Austria or the Netherlands with an international cast will be *Beyond. . . Beyond,* a non-sequel to his 1970 Fox film which will concentrate more on violence than sex.

Who Killed Bambi? (1977)

1112 Beyda, Kent. "Russ Meyer." *Search & Destroy: Rebel Youth Culture,* 10:11 ff., 1978.

In an October 12, 1978, interview, Meyer discusses in detail the failed Sex Pistols project *Who Killed Bambi?* and suggests that the film was not made due to the financial overcommitments of the band's manager Malcolm McLaren. (2 illus.)

1113 Cromelin, Richard. "Sex Pistols Trigger Punk Rock Invasion." *Los Angeles Times,* pt. IX (Calendar), p. 84, July 31, 1977.

Malcolm McLaren, manager of the Sex Pistols, discusses the anarchistic English punk band's prospects for critical and financial success in the more conservative atmosphere of the United States. In Los Angeles to negotiate the band's U.S. record contract, McLaren also planned to document the group's status

as a "social event" in a full length film to be directed by Meyer. (1 illus.)

1114 Ebert, Roger. "Punk! Sex Pistols Inspire Outrage—and a Film." *Chicago Sun-Times,* sec. Show, pp. 2–3, Sept. 25, 1977.

Ebert, signed by director Meyer to write the screenplay for a film based on and starring the Sex Pistols, discusses the notoriety of England's top punk band and his creative involvement in the proposed film project. (2 illus.)

1115 Grant, Hank. "Rambling Reporter." *Hollywood Reporter,* 248(49):2, Nov. 7, 1977.

Marianne Faithful is reportedly to star in Meyer's *Who Killed Bambi?* in the role of mother to Sex Pistols member Sid Vicious.

1116 Grant, Hank. "Rambling Reporter." *Hollywood Reporter,* 249(2):2, Nov. 10, 1977.

The Sex Pistols sack Meyer as director of their film *Who Killed Bambi?* because they feel he is "leaning too heavily on sex."

1117 McCarthy, Todd. "'Rock 'n' Roll Swindle' Emerges as an Early Success at Filmex." *Daily Variety,* 187(2):6, 12, Mar. 7, 1980.

Julien Temple's Sex Pistols film *The Great Rock 'n' Roll Swindle* is discussed with Meyer's abortive experience with the band *(Who Killed Bambi?)* briefly mentioned. According to Temple, Meyer and the band disagreed over whose film it was to be with the production halted after only three days' shooting when "a camera operator quit when Meyer personally shot a deer with a pistol for a scene." Note: Temple subsequently apologized to Meyer in the British film publication *Screen International* for his slanderous statement and Meyer is currently seeking damages in a British court.

1118 Sperazza, Guy. "Shooting the Sex Pistols: Who Killed the Movie?" *Bomp!,* UNKNOWN, Oct.-Nov. 1978.

A detailed plot synopsis of *Who Killed Bambi?* is offered by Sperazza who quotes liberally from the sixth draft of Ebert's and Meyer's original screenplay. The incidents surrounding Meyer's mid–October 1978 withdrawal from the project are reported with Malcolm McLaren, the manager of the Sex Pistols, stating that band member Johnny Rotten could not get along with the filmmaker. (4 illus.)

1119 Swan, Steve. "British Film Biz Hoping to Cash in on Punk Rock Craze." *Daily Variety*, 176(12):1, June 21, 1977.

Swan reports that one of the three British films set to exploit the punk rock craze will be directed by Meyer from a script by Johnny Speight, writer of the BBC sitcom *'Til Death Do Us Part* that inspired *All in the Family*.

XIII. VIDEOCASSETTES

1120 "The Breast of Russ Meyer." *Video Today,* p. 49, Mar. 1983.

A short article in a British video publication which is significant because in it Meyer states that he was primarily influenced not by going to films, but rather by a childhood gift of a movie camera. The anonymous author theorizes that Meyer's lack of interest in seeing other people's films accounts for his own "completely personal style." *Supervixens* has been released on video in England by Videospace. (2 illus.)

1121 Caen, M. "Russ Meyer: sein thèse." *Video News,* 17:66, 68–69, 78–79, Feb. 1983.

Meyer discusses a myriad number of topics with Caen in a piece written to promote the director's videocassettes in France. Meyer's comments under categories like "Actresses," "Parody," "Fox," and "Feminism" provide interesting insights into the ready-made one-liners he has developed to answer questions already asked him a thousand times before. (Illus.)

1122 Cargin, Peter. "More Meyer!" *Continental Film and Video Review,* 30(4):30, Feb. 1983.

The British video release of *Supervixens* by Videospace through an exclusive agreement with Meyer's company, Lydia U.K. Distribution Ltd., affords Cargin an opportunity to acquaint British readers with historical details of Meyer's career. (4 illus.)

1123 "The Collected Works of Russ Meyer." *Video X,* 2(6):68, Aug. 1981.

A one-page blurb in *Video X,* a monthly magazine featuring interviews with porn stars and announcements of new X-rated videos, heralding the video release of five Meyer films—*Lorna, Mondo Topless, Mudhoney, Up!,* and *Beneath.* (5 illus.)

1124 DiMartino, Dave. "Cat Clip." *Billboard,* 99(37):22, Sept. 12, 1987.

Meyer directs his first music video for the L.A. glamrock band Faster Pussycat! despite fears by Elektra executives who remembered his abortive Sex Pistols project *Who Killed Bambi?* The video single, "Don't Change That Song," incorporates performance shots of the group and footage from the 1966 film *Faster, Pussycat! Kill! Kill!*

1125 "Eve Meyer Sells Films to Optronics Libraries." *Boxoffice,* 98(8):7, Dec. 7, 1970.

Eve Meyer sells the 20-feature film library of Eve Productions to Optronics Libraries, Inc. for home video showings.

1126 Gensler, Howard. "Sultan of Soft-Core: Russ Meyer on Video." *Premiere,* 2(9):100, May 1989.

Meyer's video catalog is featured in an article noting that Meyer personally takes many of the phone orders himself in order to offer "personal service."

Unfortunately, *Beyond the Valley of the Dolls,* once available from CBS/Fox Video, has been withdrawn from circulation by the embarrassed company and Meyer's attempt to purchase the rights have proved financially unfeasible. (1 illus.)

1127 Goldstein, Patrick. "Into the Valley of the Video Vixens." *Los Angeles Times,* sec. Calendar, p. 86, Aug. 23, 1987.

Background details and anecdotes are given on Meyer's debut as a rock video director for Faster Pussycat!, a Los Angeles–based "glam-rock" band, whose name was inspired by the filmmaker's 1966 epic *Faster, Pussycat! Kill! Kill!* A pleased Elektra Records, the group's label, is reportedly sending out 300 Meyer autographed copies of the video ("Don't Change That Song") to various retail and radio executives. (1 illus.)

*1128 Greenfield, Allan. "Direct It: Russ Meyer Tells You How." *Video Review,* 2(6):59–60, Sept. 1981.

Meyer, described by Greenfield as the "consummate do-it-yourselfer," offers photographic and editing tips to home video directors in a fascinating article that provides several key insights into the manner in which he approaches both the creative and technical aspects of filmmaking. Highly recommended. (3 illus.)

1129 Loevy, Diana. "Son of Beyond the Valley of the Dolls." *Home Video,* 2(5):45–47, May 1981.

Meyer, interviewed at the Consumer Electronics Show in Las Vegas in January 1981, discusses his videocassette business and the positive impact home video has had upon his career. (2 illus.)

1130 Mankin, Eric. "Peddling Video Software in Vegas." *Los Angeles Herald Examiner,* sec. B, p. 1, Aug. 29, 1984.

A report on the Video Software Dealers Convention in Las Vegas includes a short discussion with Meyer who

personally mans the "Russ Meyer Productions" table at the show. Such direct contact with the consumer, explains Meyer, allows him to "sample first hand the attitudes and feeling people have toward my films." (1 illus.)

*1131 O'Dair, Barbara. "Tits and Sass." *Village Voice,* 32(48):57, 60, Dec. 1, 1987.

A marathon viewing of eight Meyer videos leads O'Dair to conclude that the filmmaker is "ultimately interesting" because his vision of woman as the sexual aggressor is "not exactly the prototypical male fantasy of the purrrr-fect girl." Terming Meyer's unique brand of softcore porn as "white-trash dynamite," O'Dair offers a perceptive evaluation of the themes in his cinema as well as a list of her top ten Meyer favorites. Recommended. (1 illus.)

1132 Paone, John. "The Adult Film Industry: Waiting and Wondering." *Adult Video News Confidential,* 1(19):8–10, Sept. 1986.

In an informative article about the two main problems facing the adult film industry—product glut and legal pressures—Meyer is briefly questioned concerning the effect the Meese Commission has had on the sales of his softcore videotapes.

1133 "Russ Meyer: Mein Liebe gehört den hervorragen den Dingen." *Video Tip,* pp. 20–21, May 1987.

Four of Meyer's films *(Supervixens, Mudhoney, Up! [Drunter, drüber und drauf], Faster, Pussycat! Kill! Kill! [Die Satansweiber von Tittfield])* are available in Germany through Gloria Video. The "Meyer Touch," pneumatic bosoms and bitingly satirical attacks on U.S. reality, is evident in each. (6 illus.)

1134 "Russ Meyer—the King of the Bosoms on Video at Last!" *Video News,* 3(3):14, Mar. 1983.

Although adult material accounts for only a "relatively small but stable" 5 percent of the total English videocassette market, Videospace expects its exclusive U.K. release of *Supervixens* to do well. While in England to deliver a Guardian lecture at the National Film Theatre retrospective of his films, Meyer resubmitted the uncut version of *Supervixens* to the British censor to receive its official certificate which would protect videocassette dealers from prosecution.

1135   Sherman, Betsy. "Meyer Has a Whole New Audience." *Boston Globe,* p. 11, Sept. 19, 1987.

Sherman notes that the advent of video has made Meyer's films widely accessible to a whole new generation of fans. Interviewed while in Boston to be honored by a 17½-hour marathon of his films at the Boston Film Festival, Meyer also discusses his autobiographical *The Breast of Russ Meyer* and philosophizes that his lasting contribution to posterity will be films instead of progeny.

*1136   Slifkin, I.L. "Softcore Sizzles on Homefront: An Overview." *Adult Video News,* Softcore Supplement, 1(20):1, 3, 6, 9, Dec. 1984.

While primarily an overview of the softcore videocassette market and the revivifying effect cable services and rental have exerted upon it, Slifkin offers a mini-history of the evolution of softcore films which provides an excellent introduction to this long neglected genre. Meyer fondly recollects the filming of *The Immoral Mr. Teas* and enthusiastically reports on the ever burgeoning sales of his "Bosomania" line of videocassettes which currently feature 13 titles. Slifkin includes *Supervixens* in his list of "10 to Own" softcore videotapes. Highly recommended. (16 illus.)

1137   Staten, Vince. "Russ Meyer Reflects on His Pneumatic Career." *Louisville Courier-Journal,* sec. Scene, p. 11, May 6, 1989.

The 13 films Meyer has released on video through his company, RM Films International, are briefly discussed by the filmmaker and a phone number where they can be ordered is given. (1 illus.)

1138   "Wants Russ Meyer." *Adam Film World,* 9(2):7, Dec. 1982.

Responding to a reader who asks that the magazine review Meyer's films recently released on video, *Adam Film World* states their preference is for today's "sophisticated" hardcore films and not for softcore "nostalgia." The magazine also notes that Meyer has not been cooperative in providing them with either stills or interviews, preferring instead "to maintain his image ... in higher-class publications."

1139   Weatherford, Mike. "Cult Director Now Focusing on Himself." *Las Vegas Review-Journal,* sec. E, pp. 1, 3, Jan. 19, 1988.

At the 1985 International Winter Consumer Electronics Show in Las Vegas, Meyer, a frequent exhibitor at such shows, discusses his home video line ("Russ Meyer's Bosomania") and his in-progress print and film autobiographies. (1 illus.)

Censorship

1140   Anderson, Rex. "Meyer—a Cult Fights the Cuts." *Video Business,* 4(33):28, Oct. 8, 1984.

It is hoped that the release of Meyer's work on video will not receive the usual massive cuts which his films have always suffered in the United Kingdom. Such a fate could be avoided under the recently passed Video Recording Act which empowers a censorship board to grant a different type of certificate for video than for film. Meyer, who permitted his films to be heavily censored upon their British release, now flatly refuses to allow any video cuts, preferring instead not to market them. (2 illus.)

1141   Baddeley, Mark. "Thanks for the Mammary." *Video: The Magazine,* pp. 72–73, Mar. 1983.

Meyer, in London to promote the Videospace release of a censored version of *Supervixens* to the British videocassette market, is the subject of a short biographical piece offering little new information on the filmmaker. (3 illus.)

1142 Hocura, Ed. "It's My Bag." *Canadian Film Weekly,* 35(6):3, Feb. 20, 1970.
The implications of whether a commercial videotape theatre is subject to the jurisdiction of the Ontario Board of Censors (as are all Canadian film theatres) is discussed by Hocura in light of the confiscation of videotape copies of the allegedly obscene *Vixen* from Toronto's Cinema 2000, billed as North America's first commercial videotape theatre. Should the court find in favor of Cinema 2000, Hocura predicts a mushrooming of similar operations with an attendant negative financial impact on film theatres subject to strict censorship laws.

1143 Michaels, Eric. "Is Russ Meyer Just a Lot of Hot Air?" *Screw,* 125:16, July 26, 1971.

Marvin Miller of Cinema 2000 in Toronto derides Meyer's international distributor, Foreign Films Cavalcade, for failing to honor its commitment to pick up its percentage of the legal fees ($24,000) engendered by the unsuccessful prosecution of *Vixen* by the Canadian film board. Despite three separate proceedings and $40,000 in legal fees, the Court ruled in favor of Cinema 2000, making it "the first cinema sex censorship case to win in Canada." (1 illus.)

1144 "'Vixen' Videotapes Are Seized by Toronto Police." *Boxoffice,* 96(20):K-1, Mar. 2, 1970.
Four videotape prints of *Vixen* are seized at Toronto's Cinema 2000, "North America's first commercial videotape cinema," by Metro morality police. Although videotapes are not subject to censorship by the Ontario Board of Censors, obscenity charges were filed against the theatre for exhibiting the tapes commercially.

XIV. A CLEAN BREAST (MEMOIR)

1145 Musto, Michael. "Moving Images." *Spin*, 4(10):56, 77, Jan. 1989.

Relaxing in his Hollywood Hills home, Meyer talks about his 600-page plus memoir, *A Clean Breast,* and speaks of his deep affection for Roger Ebert. Meyer notes that the renewed public and critical interest in his films is the most gratifying and important thing in his life. (1 illus.) See entry **3**.

1146 Musto, Michael. "Russ Proof." *Vanity Fair*, 52(4):118, Apr. 1989.

Plugging his massive autobiography, *A Clean Breast,* Meyer declares it to be "the best book ever written" about sexual matters. (3 illus.) See entry **3**.

1147 Poe, Gregory. "Russ Meyer." *Exposure*, pp. 36–37, Mar.-Apr. 1989.

A Clean Breast: The Life and Loves of Russ Meyer, the filmmaker's 800-page autobiography, is discussed as is Meyer's decision to self-publish the tome in order to ensure his complete autonomy over its text and photos. (1 illus.) See entry **3**.

1148 Radakovich, Anka. "Tempest in a D Cup: A Visit with Russ Meyer." *Details*, pp. 122–124, May 1989.

A pleasant piece on Meyer that focuses on his soon-to-be-published autobiography, *A Clean Breast: The Life and Loves of Russ Meyer.* Describing the book as "a movie in a sense," Meyer candidly writes of his sexual liaisons in language that would make "Jackie Collins ... want to crawl under a rock." (4 illus.) See entry **3**.

XV. FILMOGRAPHY

The Immoral Mr. Teas (1959)

63 minutes. Eastmancolor. PAD-RAM Enterprises, Inc. *Director, Cinematographer, Screenplay, Editor:* Russ Meyer. *Editor:* John F. Link (uncredited). *Assistants:* Ken Parker, Eric "Mick" Nathanson (uncredited). *Music, Narration:* Edward J. Lasko. **Cast:** Bill Teas (Mr. Teas), Ann Peters (Waitress), Marilyn Wesly (Dental assistant), Michele Roberts (Secretary), Dawn Danielle (Beach beauty), June Wilkinson (Torso-uncredited), Peter A. DeCenzie (Burlesque announcer); Eric "Mick" Nathanson, Don Cochran, Russ Meyer (Audience — uncredited); G. Ferrus (Narrator — uncredited). **Other titles:** *Steam Heat, Mr. Tease and His Playthings* (Great Britain); *L'Immoral M. Teas* (Canada/Belgium). **Notes:** Shot in five days on a budget of $24,000. Available on videocassette from RM Films International, Inc.

Eve and the Handyman (1960)

65 minutes. Eastmancolor. Eve Productions, Inc. — Distributed by PAD-RAM Enterprises, Inc. *Director, Producer, Cinematographer, Screenplay, Editor:* Russ Meyer. *Art Direction:* Mel Fowler. **Cast:** Eve Meyer (Eve and other female roles), Anthony James Ryan (The Handyman), Frank Bolger (Street sweeper), Florence Moore (Restroom girl), Francesca Leslie (Francesca), Jackie Stephens (Nude model); Mildred Knezevich, Iris Bristol, Gigi Frost, Rita Day (Other girls); Lyle Tolefson, Charles Vaughn, James Evanoff, Ken Parker (Artists). **Other titles:** *Eve et son homme à tout faire* (Canada, Belgium). **Notes:** *Eve and the Handyman* world premiered on May 5, 1961 at the Paris Theatre in Los Angeles, California; Meyer dates film 1960, billed with it was a 10-minute Eastmancolor short written, photographed, and directed by Meyer entitled *The Naked Camera* featuring Mikki France.

Erotica (1961)

65 minutes. Eastmancolor. PAD-RAM Enterprises, Inc. *Director, Producer, Cinematographer, Screenplay, Editor:* Russ Meyer. *Producer:* Peter A. DeCenzie. *Narration:* Jack Moran. *Narrator:* Joe Cranston. *Chief grip:* Peter A. DeCenzie. *Music:* David Chudnow, Tommy Morgan. **Cast:** Sherry Knight (Herself), Werner Otto Kirsch (Himself), Charles G. Schelling (Strongfort), Peter A. DeCenzie (Cave Man), Russ Meyer (Photographer). Others: Althea Currier, Lana Young, Denise Daniels, Elaine Jones, et al. **Notes:** Produced for an estimated $4,000. A series of six vignettes variously subtitled: *Naked Innocence; Beauties, Bubbles and H2O; The Bear and the Bare; Nudists on the High Seas; The Nymphs;* and *The Bikini Busters.*

Wild Gals of the Naked West! (1961)

65 minutes. Eastmancolor. Films Pacifica, Inc. *Director, Producer, Cinematographer, Screenplay, Editor:* Russ Meyer. *Producer:* Peter A. DeCenzie. *Art director:* Mel Fowler. *Chief grip:* Peter A. DeCenzie. **Cast:** Sammy Gilbert (The Stranger), Franklin Bolger (Snake Wolf), Teri Taylor (Goldie Nuggets), Julie Williams (The Bosom). Others: Ken Parker, Jack Moran, James Anthony Ryan, Peter A. DeCenzie, Russ Meyer, Paul Fox, Princess Livingston, Charles G. Schelling, et al. **Other titles:** *The Immoral West—and How It Was Lost, Immoral Girls of the Naked West, The Naked West—and How It Was Lost, Naked Gals of the Golden West* (U.S.). **Notes:** Produced for an estimated $26,000.

Europe in the Raw (1963)

72 minutes. Eastmancolor. Eve Productions, Inc. *Director, Producer, Cinematographer, Screenplay, Editor:* Russ Meyer. **Cast:** Veronique Gabriel, Gigi La Touche, Abundavita, Denise Du Vall, Heide Richter, Greta Thorwald, Yvette Le Grand. Narrators: Vic Perrin, Lynn Held.

Heavenly Bodies! (1963)

62 minutes. Eastmancolor. Eve Productions, Inc. *Director, Producer, Cinematographer, Screenplay, Editor:* Russ Meyer. **Cast:** Rochelle Kennedy, Amber Morgan, Binkie Stewart, Ivana Nolte, Althea Currier, Monica Liljistrand, Yvonne Cortell, Paulette Firestone, Maria Andre, Princess Livingston, F.E. Falconer, Ken Parker, Fred Owens, Donald L. Goodwin, Russ Meyer, Robert J. Ewald, William Knowles, Bill Cummings, Charles G. Schelling, Werner Otto Kirsch, Billy A. Newhouse, Don Cochran, Orville Hallberg. **Other titles:** *Heavenly Assignment* (U.S.). **Notes:** Produced for an estimated $5,000. A ten-minute Eastmancolor short written,

filmed, and directed by Meyer entitled *Skyscrapers and Brassieres* featuring Rochelle played on the same bill with *Heavenly Bodies!*

Lorna (1964)

79 minutes. B&W. Eve Productions, Inc. *Director, Producer, Cinematographer, Editor:* Russ Meyer. *Associate producer:* Eve Meyer. *Screenplay:* James Griffith. *Original story:* Russ Meyer. *Camera operator:* Walter Schenk. *Gaffer:* William Maley. *Sound:* Charles Gilbert Schelling. *Sound editor (uncredited):* Jim Nelson. *Dialogue director:* James Griffith. *Production manager:* Fred Owens. *Assistants to the producer:* Charles Gilbert Schelling, Kenneth H. Parker, W. Brad Kues, Orville S. Hallberg, James Nelson. *Music coordinators:* Hal Hopper, James Griffith (uncredited). *Song:* "Lorna"—by Hal Hopper, sung by Bob Grabeau. **Cast:** Lorna Maitland (Lorna), Hal Hopper (Luther), Mark Bradley (Fugitive), James Rucker (James), Doc Scortt (Jonah), James Griffith (Prophet/Narrator), Althea Currier, F. Rufus Owens, Franklin Bolger, Kenneth H. Parker. **Other titles:** *Lorna, l'incarnation du désir* (France); *Lorna—Zuviel für Einen Mann* (Germany). **Notes:** *Lorna* was produced for an estimated $37,000. Available on videocassette from RM Films International, Inc.

Fanny Hill: Memoirs of a Woman of Pleasure (1964)

104 minutes. B&W. Famous Players Corporation/CCC Filmkunst GMBH. *Director:* Russ Meyer. *Producer:* Albert Zugsmith. *Associate producer:* Billy Frick. *Screenplay:* Robert Hill (Based on the novel *Fanny Hill* by John Cleland). *Film editor:* Alfred Srp. *Director of photography:* Heinz Hölscher. *Director of still photography:* Bruno Bernard. *Assistant director:* Elfie Tillack. *Sound:* Clemens Tutsch. *Art director:* Paul Markwitz. *Unit manager:* Felix Siebenrogg. *Production secretary:* Patricia Houston, Marianne Hennig. *Make-up:*

Freddy Arnold. *Costume design:* Claudie Hahne-Herberg. *Wardrobe:* Vera Mugge. *Decorations design:* Helmut Nentwig. *Research:* Vladek Bijak. *Script girl:* Annemarie Scheu. *Music:* Erwin Halletz. **Cast:** Miriam Hopkins (Mrs. Maude Brown), Letitia Roman (Fanny Hill), Walter Giller (Hemingway), Alex D'Arcy (The Admiral), Helmut Weiss (Mr. Dinklespieler), Chris Howland (Mr. Norbert), Ulli Lommel (Charles), Cara Garnett (Phoebe), Karin Evans (Martha), Syra Marty (Hortense), Albert Zugsmith (Grand Duke), Christiane Schmidtmer (Fiona), Heide Hanson (Fenella), Erica/ Veronica Erickson (Emily), Patricia Houston (Amanda), Marshall Raynor (Johnny), Hilda Sessack (Mrs. Snow), Billy Frick (Percival), Jurgen Nesbach (James), Herbert Knippenberg (Mudge), Susanne Hsiao (Lotus Blossom), Renate Hutte/Rena Horten (Prostitute), Ellen Velero (Prostitute).

Mudhoney (1965)

92 minutes. B&W. Delta Films, Inc. *Director, Producer, Editor (uncredited):* Russ Meyer. *Producer:* George Costello. *Associate producer:* Eve Meyer. *Screenplay:* Raymond Friday Locke, William E. Sprague. (Based on the Raymond Friday Locke novel *Streets Paved with Gold*). *Film editor:* Charles G. Schelling. *Director of photography:* Walter Schenk. *Associate director:* George Costello. *Sound recordist:* Charles G. Schelling. *Gaffer:* William Maley. *Production supervisor:* Fred Owens. *Production assistant/Assistant cameraman (uncredited):* Gil Haimson. *Script supervisor:* William E. Sprague. *Dialogue director:* George Costello. *Hair stylist:* Eddie Crispell. *Music director:* Henri Price. *Coordinators:* Bill Shelton, Don Hansen, Tim Wilson, Tony Enos, Manuel Morais. **Cast:** Hal Hopper (Sidney Brenshaw), Antoinette Cristiani (Hannah Brenshaw), John Furlong (Calif McKinney), Stu Lancaster (Lute Wade), Rena Horten (Eula), Princess Livingston (Maggie Marie), Lorna Maitland (Clara Belle), Frank Bolger (Brother Hanson), Sam Hannah (Injoys), Nick Wolcuff (Sheriff Abel), Lee Ballard (Sister Hanson), Mickey Foxx (Thurmond Pate), F. Rufus Owens (Milton), Gil Haimson (Mourner); William Maley, Russ Meyer (Townspeople); Wilfred Kues, Peter Cunningham, Clarence Lowe, Donald Hansen, Milard Ferla, Bill Gunter (Lynch mob—some uncredited). **Other titles:** *Mudhoney ... Leaves a Taste of Evil!*, *Rope of Flesh* (U.S.); *La Fille du ruisseau*, *Le Désir dans les tripes* (France); *Im Garten der Lust* (Germany); *Esclave de ses passions* (Belgium). **Notes:** *Mudhoney* opened in Boston, Massachusetts on May 25, 1965 at the Symphony Cinema. Produced for $60,000—released in 1965. Available on videocassette from RM Films International, Inc.

Motorpsycho! (1965)

74 minutes. B&W. Eve Productions, Inc. *Director, Producer, Cinematographer, Screenplay, Editor:* Russ Meyer. *Associate producer:* Eve Meyer. *Screenplay:* William E. Sprague. *Original story:* Russ Meyer, James Griffith, Hal Hopper. *Film editor:* Charles Schelling. *Sound:* Carl G. Sheldon (Charles G. Schelling). *Assistant director:* George Costello. *Production manager:* Fred Owens. *Production assistant:* Richard Serly Brummer. *Special photographic effects:* Orville Hallberg. *Music:* Igo Kantor. *Theme song:* Paul Sawtell, Bert Shefter. **Cast:** Haji (Ruby Bonner), Alex Rocco (Cory Maddox), Stephen Oliver (Brahmin), Holle K. Winters (Gail Maddox), Joseph Cellini (Dante), Thomas Scott (Slick), Coleman Francis (Harry Bonner), Sharon Lee (Jessica Fannin), Steve Masters (Frank), Arshalouis Aivazian (Frank's wife), E.E. (Russ) Meyer (Sheriff), George Costello (Doctor), F. Rufus Owens (Rufus), Richard Serly Brummer (Ambulance driver). **Other titles:** *Motor Mods and Rockers* (U.S.); *Les Enragés de la moto* (Canada); *Le Gang Sauvage* (Belgium); *Motor-Psycho—Wie Wilde Hengste* (Germany). **Notes:** Working title: *Rio Vengeance*. Produced for an

estimated $38,000, the film was targeted for the drive-in audience.

Faster, Pussycat! Kill! Kill! (1966)

83 minutes. B&W. Eve Productions, Inc. *Director, Producer, Editor:* Russ Meyer. *Producer:* Eve Meyer. *Associate producers:* Fred Owens, George Costello. *Screenplay:* Jack Moran. *Original story:* Russ Meyer. *Director of photography:* Walter Schenk. *Assistant cameraman (uncredited):* Gil Haimson. *Sound recordist:* Charles Schelling. *Sound editor:* Richard Serly Brummer. *Assistant director:* George Costello. *Production manager:* Fred Owens. *Production assistants:* Gil Haimson, Richard Serly Brummer. *Second unit manager:* William E. Tomko. *Sports car racing consultants:* Harvey Lippert, Vicki Isaacs, Nancy White, Vicki Juday. *Coordinators:* Oliver F. Pesch, Lee Green. *Music director:* Igo Kantor. *Music themes:* Paul Sawtell, Bert Shefter. *Song:* "Faster Pussycat" — music by Paul Sawtell and Bert Shefter, lyrics by Rick Jarrard, sung by The Bostweeds. **Cast (in order of appearance):** Tura Satana (Varla), Haji (Rosie), Lori Williams (Billie), Ray Barlow (Tommy), Susan Bernard (Linda), Mickey Foxx (Gas station attendant), Dennis Busch (The Vegetable), Stuart Lancaster (Old Man), Paul Trinka (Kirk), John Furlong (Narrator). **Other titles:** *Pussycat* (U.S.); *The Mankillers, The Leather Girls* (Great Britain); *Plus vite mes chattes, tuez! tuez!* (Canada), *Die Satansweiber von Tittfield* (Germany). **Notes:** Produced for an estimated $45,000. Available on videocassette from RM Films International, Inc.

Mondo Topless (1966)

61 minutes. Eastmancolor. Eve Productions, Inc. *Director, Producer, Cinematographer, Editor, Music recordist (uncredited):* Russ Meyer. *Associate producer:* Eve Meyer. *Production assistants:* Fred Owen, Bill Newhouse, Richard Serly Brummer. *Sound mixer (uncredited):* Don Minkler. *Music (uncredited):* The

Aladdins. **Cast:** Babette Bardot, Sin Lenee, Donna "X," Diane Young, Pat Barringer, Darla Paris, Darlene Grey, Lorna Maitland; John Furlong (Narrator). **Other titles:** *Mondo Girls, Mondo Top* (U.S.); *La Fête du nu* (Belgium). **Notes:** Produced for an estimated $12,000. Includes footage from Meyer's *Europe in the Raw* (1963) and Lorna Maitland's screen test for *Lorna* (1964). Available on videocassette from RM Films International, Inc.

Common-Law Cabin (1967)

70 minutes. Eastmancolor. Eve Productions, Inc. *Director, Producer, Cinematographer (uncredited), Screenplay (uncredited), Editor:* Russ Meyer. *Producer:* Eve Meyer. *Screenplay:* John E. Moran. *Photography:* Wady C. Medawar, Jack Lucas. *Sound:* Richard Serly Brummer, Irwin Cadden. *Sound mixer (uncredited):* Don Minkler. **Cast:** Jack Moran (Dewey Hoople), Babette Bardot (Babette), Adele Rein (Coral Hoople), Franklin Bolger (Cracker), Alaina Capri (Sheila Ross), John Furlong (Dr. Martin Ross), Ken Swofford (Barney Rickert), Andrew Hagara (Laurence Talbot, III), George Costello (Bartender — uncredited). **Other titles:** *How Much Loving Does a Normal Couple Need?* (U.S.); *Conjugal Cabin* (Great Britain); *Cette soif d'amour* (Canada); *Combien de fois faut-il faire l'amour pour être un couple normal?* (France). **Notes:** Produced for an estimated $50,000. Available on videocassette from RM Films International, Inc.

Good Morning and Goodbye! (1967)

80 minutes. Eastmancolor. Eve Productions, Inc. *Director, Producer, Cinematographer, Editor:* Russ Meyer. *Associate producer:* Eve Meyer. *Screenplay:* John E. Moran. *Editor:* Richard Serly Brummer. *Sound:* Richard Serly Brummer, Jack Moran. *Cameraman:* Fred Owens. *Associate camera operators:* Jack Lucas, Wady Medawar. *Assistant*

director: George Costello. *Production manager (uncredited):* Fred Owens. *Costume designer:* Herberté. *Director of music:* Igo Kantor. **Cast:** Alaina Capri (Angel Boland), Stuart Lancaster (Burt Boland), Patrick Wright (Stone), Haji (The Catalyst), Karen Ciral (Lana Boland), Don Johnson (Ray), Tom Howland (Herb), Megan Timothy (Lottie), Toby Adler (Betty), Sylvia Tedemar (Go-Go Dancer), Carol Peters (Nude); Joe Perrin (Narrator—uncredited). **Other titles:** *The Lust Seekers* (Great Britain); *Bonjour et au revoir* (Belgium); *Bonjour et adieu* (Canada). **Notes:** Produced for an estimated $55,000. Available on videocassette from RM Films International, Inc.

Finders Keepers, Lovers Weepers! (1968)

73 minutes. Eastmancolor by Perfect Photo Laboratories. Eve Productions, Inc. *Director, Producer, Cinematographer, Editor:* Russ Meyer. *Executive producer:* Eve Meyer. *Associate producer:* Anthony James Ryan. *Screenplay:* Richard Zachary. *Original story:* Russ Meyer. *Editor:* Richard Serly Brummer. *Sound mixer:* Richard Serly Brummer. *Assistant sound mixer:* Nikolai Volokhanovich. *Sound re-recording:* Bill Mumford, Don Minkler. *Camera operator:* Wady Medawar. *Assistant director:* George Costello. *Gaffer:* John Furlong. *Assistant gaffer:* Israel Shaked. *Lingerie:* Maria Civetti. *Costumes:* Herberté. *Director of music:* Igo Kantor. *Song:* "Finders Keepers, Lovers Weepers"—sung by Melvin Elling with The Casuals on the Square (uncredited). **Cast:** Anne Chapman (Kelly), Paul Lockwood (Paul), Gordon Wescourt (Ray), Duncan McLeod (Cal), Robert Rudelson (Feeney), Lavelle Roby (Claire), Jan Sinclair (Christiana), Joey Duprez (Joy). Others (some uncredited): Pam Collins, Michael Roberts, Vicki Roberts, Nick Wolcuff, George K. Carll, Barney Caliendo, Louis Innerarity, Robert Pergament, Walter Cummings, Orville Hallberg, Russ Meyer, George Cole,

Robert Massaroli, Harvey Pergament, Robert Mumm, Anthony James Ryan, John Furlong. **Other titles:** *Qui s'y frotte s'y pique* (Canada); *Null Null Sex* (Austria); *Viltar Astridur* (Spain). **Notes:** Produced for an estimated $82,000. The first of Meyer's films to be booked into a first-run, "legitimate" venue, Philadelphia's Randolph Theatre, where it opened in May 1969. Available on videocassette from RM Films International, Inc.

Vixen (1968)

70 minutes. Eastmancolor by Perfect Film Laboratory. Eve Productions, Inc.— Presented by Coldstream Films. *Director, Producer, Cinematographer, Editor:* Russ Meyer. *Associate producers:* Eve Meyer, Anthony James Ryan, Richard Serly Brummer, George Costello. *Screenplay:* Robert Rudelson. *Original story:* Russ Meyer, Anthony James Ryan. *Assistant cameraman:* Anthony James Ryan, John Koester (uncredited). *Film editor:* Richard Serly Brummer. *Art director:* Wilfred Kues. *Sound editor:* Richard Brummer, John Koester. *Sound mixer (uncredited):* Don Minkler. *Music:* Igo Kantor. **Cast:** Erica Gavin (Vixen Palmer), Garth Pillsbury (Tom Palmer), Harrison Page (Niles), Jon Evans (Judd), Vincene Wallace (Janet King), Robert Aiken (Dave King), Michael Donovan O'Donnell (O'Bannion), Peter Carpenter (Mountie), John Furlong (Sam, the gas station attendant), Jackie Illman (Tourist), Russ Meyer (Tourist—uncredited); Vic Perrin (Narrator—uncredited). **Other titles:** *Russ Meyer's Vixen* (U.S.); *Vixen la renarde* (Canada); *Ohne Gnade, Schätzen* (Germany). **Notes:** Produced for an estimated $72,000 and shot on location in Miranda, California. *Vixen* has grossed $15 million worldwide. According to the *American Film Institute Catalog of Motion Pictures,* *Vixen* opened nationally on October 15, 1968. Available on videocassette from RM Films International, Inc.

Cherry, Harry & Raquel (1969)

71 minutes. DeLuxe color. Panamint Films—Eve Productions, Inc. *Director, Producer, Cinematographer, Screenplay, Editor:* Russ Meyer. *Associate producers:* Anthony James Ryan, Thomas J. McGowan, Eve Meyer. *Screenplay:* Tom Wolfe (a.k.a. Thomas J. McGowan). *Original story:* Russ Meyer. *Assistant cinematographer:* John Koester. *Film editor:* Richard Serly Brummer. *Assistant film editor:* Robert Pergament. *Sound editor:* Richard Serly Brummer, Robert Pergament (uncredited). *Production manager:* Anthony James Ryan. *Assistant production manager:* Jacqueline Ryan. *Transportation:* Thomas J. McGowan. *Music:* William Loose. *Music supervisor:* Igo Kantor. *Song:* "Toys of Our Time" by Byron Cole, James East, and Stu Phillips. Performed by The Jacks and Balls. **Cast:** Charles Napier (Harry), Linda Ashton (Cherry), Larissa Ely (Raquel), Bert Santos (Enrique), Franklin H. Bolger (Mr. Franklin), "Astrid Lillimor"/a.k.a. Uschi Digard (Soul), Michele Grand (Millie), John Milo (Apache), Michaelani (Doctor Lee), Robert Aiken (Tom), John Koester (Gas station attendant), Daniel Roberts (Delivery boy). **Other titles:** *Russ Meyer's Cherry, Harry & Raquel* (U.S.); *Three Ways to Love* (Great Britain); *Les Stimulatrices, Ménage à trois* (France). **Notes:** Produced for an estimated $90,000. Available on videocassette from RM Films International, Inc.

Beyond the Valley of the Dolls (1970)

109 minutes. Panavision, DeLuxe color. 20th Century–Fox (MPAA rating X). *Director, Producer, Screenplay, Supervising film editor (uncredited):* Russ Meyer. *Associate producers:* Red Hershon, Eve Meyer. *Screenplay:* Roger Ebert. *Story:* Roger Ebert, Russ Meyer. *Director of photography:* Fred J. Koenekamp. *Film editors:* Dan Cahn,

Dick Wormell. *Art directors:* Jack Martin Smith, Arthur Lonergan. *Set decoration:* Walter M. Scott, Stuart A. Reiss. *Sound:* Richard Overton, Don Minkler. *Assistant directors:* David Hall, C.E. Dismukes. *Assistant to the producer:* Manny Diez. *Special photographic effects:* Jack Harmon. *Unit production manager:* Norman Cook. *Property master:* Syd Greenwood. *Fashions:* De Graff of California by David Hayes. *Makeup supervision:* Dan Striepeke. *Makeup:* Bill Buell. *Hairstyling:* Edith Lindon. *Unit publicist (uncredited):* Jet Fore. *Music:* Stu Phillips. *Music supervision:* Igo Kantor. *Additional music:* William Loose. *Vocal coordination:* Lynn Carey. *Music editor:* Robert Simard. *Songs:* "In the Long Run," "Look Up at the Bottom," "Beyond the Days of Now and Then," "Come with the Gentle People," "Sweet Talkin' Candy Man"—by Bob Stone, Stu Phillips. "Find It," "Once I Had You"—by Lynn Carey, Stu Phillips. "A Girl from the City," "I'm Comin' Home"—by Paul Marshall, sung by the Strawberry Alarm Clock. **Cast:** Dolly Read (Kelly McNamara), Cynthia Myers (Casey Anderson), Marcia McBroom (Petronella Danforth), John LaZar (Ronnie "Z-Man" Barzell), Edy Williams (Ashley St. Ives), Michael Blodgett (Lance Rocke), David Gurian (Harris Allsworth), Phyllis Davis (Susan Lake), Harrison Page (Emerson Thorne), Lavelle Roby (Vanessa), Duncan McLeod (Porter Hall), Charles Napier (Baxter Wolfe), James Iglehart (Randy Black), Henry Rowland (Otto), Veronica Erickson (Lance's blonde date), Haji (Cat woman), Pamela Grier (Black party goer), Garth Pillsbury (Man with newspaper), The Strawberry Alarm Clock (Themselves), The Sandpipers (Themselves). Others: Princess Livingston, Stan Ross, Angel Ray, Karen Smith, Sebastian Brock, Bruce V. McBroom, Ian Sander, Koko Tani, Samantha Scott, Tea Crawford, Heath Jobes, John Logan, Susan Reed, Robin Bach, Ceil Cabot, Mary Carroll, Joseph Cellini, Jackie Cole, Cissy Colpitts, Frank Corsentino, Mibb Curry,

Coleman Francis, Charles Fox, T.J. Halligan, Rick Holmes, Marshall Kent, Michael Kriss, Tim Laurie, Bebe Louie, Lillian Martin, Ashley Phillips, "Big Jack" Provan, Joyce Rees, Chris Riordian, Bert Santos, George Stratton. **Other titles:** *La Vallée des plaisirs, Hollywood Vixens, Orgissimo* (France); *La Vallée des débauches* (Belgium); *Blumen Ohne Duft* (Germany); *Lungo la valle delle bambole* (Italy). **Notes:** *Beyond the Valley of the Dolls* had its world premiere at the Pantages Theatre in Hollywood on June 17, 1970.

The Seven Minutes (1971)

115 minutes. DeLuxe color. 20th Century–Fox (MPAA rating R). *Director, Producer:* Russ Meyer. *Associate producers:* Red Hershon, Eve Meyer. *Screenplay:* Richard Warren Lewis. (Based on the Irving Wallace novel *The Seven Minutes.*) *Director of photography:* Fred Mandl. *Camera operator:* Orville Hallburg. *Film editor:* Dick Wormell. *Art director:* Rodger Maus. *Set directors:* Walter M. Scott, Raphael Bretton. *Sound:* Don J. Bassman, Theodore Soderberg. *Assistant director:* David Hall. *Special photographic effects:* Howard A. Anderson Company. *Unit production manager:* William Eckhardt. *Property master:* Robert Steffensen. *Costumes:* Bill Thomas. *Makeup supervision:* Dan Striepeke. *Makeup artists:* Del Acevedo, Lynn Reynolds. *Hairstyling:* Mary Keats. *Dialogue director:* Manny Diez. *Legal technical advisor:* Burton Katz. *Unit publicist (uncredited):* John Campbell. *Music:* Stu Phillips. *Songs:* "Seven Minutes" — by Stu Phillips and Bob Stone, sung by B.B. King. "Love Train" — by Stu Phillips and Bob Stone, sung by Don Reed. "Midnight Tricks" — by Stu Phillips and Bob Stone, sung by Merryweather & Carey. **Cast:** Wayne Maunder (Mike Barrett), Marianne McAndrew (Maggie Russell), Philip Carey (Elmo Duncan), Jay C. Flippen (Luther Yerkes), Edy Williams (Faye Osborn), Yvonne De Carlo (Constance Cumberland), Lyle Bettger (Frank Griffith), Jackie Gayle (Norman Quandt), Ron Randell (Merle Reid), Charles Drake (Sgt. Kellog), John Carradine (Sean O'Flanagan), Harold J. Stone (Judge Upshaw), Tom Selleck (Phil Sanford), James Iglehart (Clay Rutherford), John Sarno (Jerry Griffith), Stanley Adams (Irwin Blair), Billy Durkin (George Perkins), Yvonne D'Angers (Sheri Moore), Robert Moloney (Ben Fremont), Olan Soulé (Harvey Underwood), Jan Shutan (Anna Lou White), Alex D'arcy (Christian Leroux), David Brian (Cardinal McManus), Berry Kroeger (Paul Van Fleet), Ralph Story (TV Commentator), Charles Napier (Officer Iverson), Kay Peters (Olivia St. Clair), Richard Angarola (Father Sarfatti), "Baby Doll" Shawn Devereaux (Yerkes' girlfriend), Regis J. Cordic (Louis Polk), John Lawrence (Howard Moore), Mora Gray (Donna Novick), Stuart Lancaster (Dr. Roger Trimble), Henry Rowland (Yerkes' butler). **Others:** Barry Coe, Calvin Bartlett, Wolfman Jack, Ken Jones, Bill Baldwin, Vince Williams, Robin Hughes, Jim Bacon, John Gruber, Chris Marks, Peter Shrayder, Lynn Hamilton, Patrick Wright, Lillian Lehman, Judy Baldwin, Paul Stader, George De Normand, Jeffrey Sayre, Barry Coe. **Other titles:** *I 7 Minuti che Contano* (Italy).

Blacksnake! (1973)

85 minutes. Movielab color. Trident Films, Ltd. — Signal 166, Inc. Release (MPAA rating R). *Director, Producer, Second unit photography, Screenplay:* Russ Meyer. *Associate producer:* Anthony James Ryan. *Screenplay:* Len Neubauer. *Original story:* Russ Meyer, Anthony James Ryan. *Director of photography:* Arthur Ornitz. *Film editor:* Fred Baratta. *Sound:* Richard Serly Brummer. *Sound effects:* Paul Laune, Sam Shaw. *Art director:* Rick Heatherly. *Assistant to producer:* Don Dorsey. *Production manager:* Fred Owens. *Production assistant, U.S.A.:* Jacqueline Ryan. *Assistant cameraman:* Arthur Browne.

Key grip: Carl Corbin. *Assistant grip:* Mario Harris. *Head gaffer:* Victor Houston. *Best boy:* Anthony Ellie. *Wardrobe:* Elsie Gittins. *Makeup artist:* Bud Miller. *Script supervisor:* Margaret Dowding. *Coordinator:* Alfred Pragnell. *Assistant coordinators:* Pearson Grazette, Tony Murrell, Mark Williams. *Security:* Cpl. Baptiste. *Publicity:* Julian A. Marryshow. *Stunt coordinator:* Bob Minor. *Rerecording:* Producers' Sound Service. *Titles & opticals:* Jack Harmon, Paul Cappel. *Casting director:* Maggie Cartier. *Music:* Bill Loose, Al Teeter. **Cast:** Anouska Hempel (Lady Susan Walker), David Warbeck (Sir Charles Walker & Ronald Sopwith), Percy Herbert (Joxer Tierney), Milton McCollin (Joshua), Thomas Baptiste (Isiah), Bernard Boston (Capt. Raymond Daladier), Vikki Richards (Cleone), Jean Duran (Sgt. Pompidoo), Dave Prowse (Jonathan, the Duppie), Bob Minor (Barnaby), Bloke Modisane (Bottoms), Anthony Sharpe (Lord Clive), Robert Lee (The Informer), Carl Corbin (Stalwart), Eggie Clark (Cart Driver), Sydney A. Harris (Village Elder), Donna Young (First Running Girl), Lawanda Moore (Second Running Girl), Wendell Williams (Ton-Ton Soldier), Bruce Richard (First Running Boy), Don Dandridge (Second Running Boy). **Other titles:** *Sweet Suzy, Dutchess of Doom* (U.S.); *Slaves* (Great Britain); *Le Serpent noir* (France); *Carne Cruda* (Italy). **Notes:** Produced for an estimated $300,000. The first feature length movie filmed entirely in Barbados, *Blacksnake!* premiered in Bridgetown, Barbados on March 14, 1973 at the Empire Theatre and Roodal's Drive-In. The U.S. premiere was held at the UA Capitol Theatre in Little Rock, Arkansas on March 28, 1973.

Supervixens (1975)

106 minutes. DeLuxe color. RM Films International, Inc.—A September 19 Production. *Director, Producer, Cinematographer, Screenplay, Editor:* Russ Meyer. *Associate producers:* Wilfred Kues, Charles Napier, Fred Owens, James Parsons. *Executive producer:* Anthony James Ryan. *Camera operator:* Douglas Knapp. *Assistant cameraman:* Tom Neuwirth. *Recordist & Sound effects editor:* Richard Serly Brummer. *Rerecording:* Producers' Sound Service. *Art director:* Michael Levesque. *Production manager:* Fred Owens. *Assistant production manager:* Jacqueline Ryan. *Grip:* Stanley Berkowitz. *Makeup:* Barbarella Catton (Haji). *Costumes:* Maureen of Hollywood, Paulette, Yves Meyer. *Music:* William Loose. *Original song:* "Scottsville Express"—by Daniel Dean Darst. **Cast:** Shari Eubank (SuperAngel/SuperVixen), Charles Napier (Harry Sledge), Uschi Digard (SuperSoul), Charles Pitts (Clint Ramsey), Henry Rowland (Martin Bormann), Christy Hartburg (SuperLorna), Sharon Kelly (SuperCherry), John LaZar (Cal MacKinney), Stuart Lancaster (Lute), Deborah McGuire (SuperEula), Glenn Dixon (Luther), Haji (SuperHaji), "Big Jack" Provan (Sheriff), Garth Pillsbury (Fisherman), Ann Marie (Fisherman's wife), Ron Sheridan (Policeman), John Lawrence (Dr. Scholl), Paul Fox (Tire thief), F. Rufus Owens (Rufus), John Furlong (CB commentator), Russ Meyer (Motel manager). **Other titles:** *Vixens, Les superbes renardes* (Canada); *SuperVixens Eruption* (Germany). **Notes:** *Supervixens* world premiered in Dallas, Texas on April 2, 1975. Produced for $221,000, the film has grossed over $17 million worldwide. Available on videocassette from RM Films International, Inc.

Up! (1976)

80 minutes. Eastmancolor. RM Films International, Inc. *Director, Producer, Cinematographer, Editor:* Russ Meyer. *Associate producers:* Fred Owens, Uschi Digard, George K. Carll. *Screenplay:* B. Callum (Russ Meyer). *Original story:* Russ Meyer, Jim Ryan, Reinhold Timme (Roger Ebert). *Camera operators:* Pat Lennef, Russ Meyer. *Second unit cameraman:* Fred "Fritz" Mandl. *Camera*

assistant: Tom Hammel. *Art direction:* Michele Levesque. *Location sound mixer:* Dan Holland. *Looping sound mixer:* Fred Owens. *Stunt coordinator:* Kim Kehana. *Dialogue and Sound effects editor:* Richard Anderson. *Rerecording:* Producers' Sound Service. *Production coordinator:* Wilburn Cluck. *Locations:* Wilfred Kues. *Ichthyologist:* Charles E. Sumners. *Casting:* Eddie Foy III, Samantha Mansour. *Assistants to the producer:* Ken Kerr, Ann Barton, Bill Barton, Robbie McClure, John English, Nick Scott. *Costumes:* Maureen of Hollywood. *Accoutrement:* Roschu. *Music:* William Loose, Paul Ruhland. *Conductor:* Syd Dale. **Cast (in order of appearance):** Francesca "Kitten" Natividad (Greek Chorus), Robert McLane (Paul), Edward Schaaf (Adolph Schwartz), Candy Samples/pseud. Mary Gavin (The Headsperson), Elaine Collins (The Ethiopian Chef), Su Ling (Limehouse), Janet Wood (Sweet L'il Alice), Linda Sue Ragsdale (Gwendolyn), Harry (The Nimrod), Raven De La Croix (Margo Winchester), Monte Bane (Homer Johnson), Marianne Marks (Chesty Young Thing), Larry Dean (Leonard Box), Bob Schott (Rafe), Foxy Lae (Pocohontas), Ray Reinhardt (The Commissioner), Russ Meyer ("Hitchcock" — uncredited). **Other titles:** *Russ Meyer's Up!, Up! Smokey, Over, Under and Up!* (U.S.); *Megavixens* (France); *Drunter, drüber und drauf* (Germany). **Notes:** Available on videocassette from RM Films International, Inc.

Beneath the Valley of the Ultravixens (1979)

93 minutes. Eastmancolor. RM Films International, Inc. *Director, Producer, Cinematographer, Editor:* Russ Meyer. *Associate producers:* Fred Owens, Richard Serly Brummer, Uschi Digard (uncredited). *Screenplay:* R. Hyde (Roger Ebert), B. Callum (Russ Meyer). *Original story:* Russ Meyer. *Sound:* Fred Owens. *Sound effects editor:* Richard Serly Brummer. *Art director:* Michele Levesque. *Assistant to the producer:* Les Barnum. *The Crew:* Uschi Digard, Don Oulette, Bruce Pastarnack, Mitch Browne, Frank Scarpitto. *Music:* William Tasker. **Cast:** Francesca "Kitten" Natividad (Lavonia & Lola Langusta), Ann Marie (Eufaula Roop), Ken Kerr (Lamar Shedd), June Mack (Junk Yard Sal), Pat Wright (Mr. Peterbuilt), Henry Rowland (Martin Bormann), Robert Pearson (Asa Lavender), Michael Finn (Semper Fidelis), Sharon Hill (Nurse Flovilla Thatch), Don Scarbrough (Beau Badger), Aram Katcher (Tyrone), De Forest Covan (Zebulon), Steve Tracy (Rhett), Uschi Digard (Supersoul), Candy Samples/pseud. Mary Gavin (The Very Big Blonde), Stuart Lancaster (The Man from Small Town U.S.A.), Russ Meyer (Director). **Other titles:** *Russ Meyer's Beneath the Valley of the Ultravixens* (U.S.); *Im tiefen Tal der Superhexen* (Austria). **Notes:** Produced for $239,000. Available on videocassette from RM Films International, Inc.

Russ Meyer,
American *auteur*
(circa 1979)

AUTHOR INDEX

References are to entry numbers rather than pages.

SOURCE INDEX

References are to entry numbers rather than pages.
Monograph titles are in italics; others are periodicals.

SUBJECT INDEX

References are to entry numbers; film and monograph titles are italicized.